FROM NAPOLEON TO STALIN
AND OTHER ESSAYS

FROM NAPOLEON TO STALIN AND OTHER ESSAYS

by

E. H. Carr

St. Martin's Press   New York

Library of Congress Cataloging in Publication Data

Carr, Edward Hallett, 1892–
From Napoleon to Stalin, and other essays.

Includes index.
1. Europe–History–1789–1900–Addresses, essays,
lectures. 2. Europe–History–20th century–Addresses,
essays, lectures. 3. Russia–History–20th century–
Addresses, essays, lectures. 4. Intellectuals–
Addresses, essays, lectures. 5. Socialism–Addresses,
essays, lectures. I. Title.
D359.C37   1980   940   80-18439
ISBN 0-312-30774-8

Contents

v

Introduction

If any unity can be claimed for this collection of essays and reviews written on particular occasions over the past thirty years, the clue must be sought in the title which I have given to the first section, "Historical Perspectives". A certain advantage perhaps accrues to the historian who grew up, and formed his first impressions, in a society which had no premonition of the catastrophe of 1914. The doctrines of liberalism and individualism held virtually unchallenged sway. In Britain, progress towards their realization was the core of the now derided "Whig interpretation of history". Even "the nations not so blessed as thee" were travelling along the same path. The standard of living of the "workers", of the depressed classes, was slowly rising. Beyond the civilized pale, primitive peoples benefited from the benevolent and nurturing supremacy of the white race. By the turn of the century some cracks had begun to appear in the seemingly solid structure. But these did not matter too much. Admitted imperfections could and would be dealt with. The world was on the whole a good place; and it was getting better.

Remembrance of these things sixty or seventy years later must, I feel, sharpen one's consciousness of the deep cleft which divides that remote age from the present, and of the historical process that brought it about. A civilization perished in 1914. The Second World War demolished even the ruins which the first had left standing. Technological advances have both softened and intensified the impact of change. But nobody who lived in that past, and is conscious of the magnitude of the gulf which separates the then from the now, can believe that the option of a return to it is open. The historical process cannot be reversed.

Indeed, if we sought to enumerate the reasons why Britain, which in the last century led the world economically and politically, now lags behind almost all the other Western nations, we should have to accord a high place on the list to the nostalgia for past glories which dominates—unconsciously, but none the less profoundly—our national thought and attitudes. If Britannia ruled the waves in

vii

virtue of the elusive values of liberalism and individualism, of "free" enterprise, "free" trade, "free" market prices, "free" wage bargaining, "free" floating interest rates, it seems natural to attribute our decline to the abandonment of these principles and practices, and to assume that a revival of them would ensure our return to former greatness. Other nations, not burdened with this memory of nineteenth-century supremacy, find it less difficult to face the problems of the present and the future. We face only the past. The remedies we seek to apply belong to the past, and are irrelevant to the present or the future. The forward-looking utopias of the New Left are out of fashion, and have been replaced by the backward-looking utopias of the New Right. It is no improvement.

Only a few of the essays in this volume deal with the subject which has been the main theme of my work since 1945, and about which I have written amply elsewhere—the history of the Russian revolution. But this has never been far from my thoughts. Most modern historians would agree in regarding the First World War and the Russian revolution as two facets of the same turning-point in history. But this does not take us far. Several of these essays relate to nineteenth-century Russian history, and are designed to illustrate the incompatibilities existing before the revolution between the Russian and Western traditions. The Russian revolution reflected these incompatibilities. It was an event in Russian history, but it was also an event of worldwide significance. The balance is important. If we overemphasize its Russian aspect, we treat it as an event in a far-away country with no lessons, or no positive lessons, for the West. If we underemphasize its Russian characteristics, we assume that a Western revolution pursuing aims akin to those of the Russian revolution would necessarily have taken the same course and incorporated the same elements of a specifically Russian background. Both these·views seem to me fallacious.

None of the essays were, however, written with any direct political purpose. I have strayed at random along some by-paths which proved agreeable and rewarding—at any rate, to myself. But all of them are imbued with a sense of the gulf which separates the world of today from the world in which I first began to observe and reflect. In so far as they have any unity, they were inspired by my constant preoccupation with the pace and direction of the historical process, and represent a protest against the profoundly unhistorical view which elevates the values of a comparatively recent Western European past into an absolute standard, a touchstone by which the values of the present and the future—not to mention those of a remoter past—are to be assessed and judged. Even in writing the personal sketches which I have grouped together under the heading "Profiles", I have been concerned to depict my subjects—five of them historical figures, five of them friends with whom I was more or less closely associated at different periods of my life—against the social and political background of their careers. But I hope that these profiles, as well as some of the other essays, will suffice to show that I am in no way committed to an impersonal view of history.

All but two of these articles were originally published in the *Times Literary Supplement*, one (No. 11) in the *New York Review of Books* and the last (No. 32) as an interview in the *New Left Review* in the autumn of 1978; and I am indebted to the editors of these journals for kind permission to reprint them here. A few of them may show here and there traces of their date of composition. But any attempt to rewrite them would have been misleading as well as laborious; and I submit them to the critical reader in the form in which they appeared. For the title of the volume I owe a debt of acknowledgement to A. J. P. Taylor, since the first item in it is a review of a book of his published under that title just thirty years ago.

1979   E. H. CARR

Part I Historical Perspectives

1 From Napoleon to Stalin

Contemporary Europe—and Europe is still the passive, if not the active, centre of the world—is the product of the span of history which runs from the French to the Russian revolution: "from Napoleon to Stalin", in the words of the title of Mr. A. J. P. Taylor's latest collection of articles and essays.[1] It was a period of immense achievement and immense fertility in ideas, whose general shape is only just beginning to emerge. All that we can yet clearly discern in retrospect is that a period of history has come to an end, in so far as anything in history ever ends, and that, like every other period of great historical achievement, it bore the seeds of its destruction within it. "The history of modern Europe", to quote Mr. Taylor again, "can be written in terms of three Titans: Napoleon, Bismarck and Lenin. Of these three men of superlative political genius, Bismarck probably did least harm." Setting aside for a moment the intrusive moral judgment, it may be admitted that Bismarck stood on a lower level of universal, or European, significance. The real middle term between the French and Russian revolutions is constituted not by any great man but by the abortive European revolution of 1848, to which Mr. Taylor's longest essay is devoted.

The essential result of the French revolution was to establish the doctrine of popular sovereignty as the foundation of modern Europe, though with no more precise. definition of that elusive category "the people" than that popular sovereignty was the antithesis of the personal authority of the monarch. In France Napoleon tamed the revolution and put it into the imperial strait-jacket (and, in so doing, perhaps did more than the revolution itself to make a Bourbon restoration permanently impossible); beyond the borders of France he was the missionary and disseminator of the ideas of the revolution. Hence, as the Napoleonic legend grew through the succeeding century, the literary champions of

[1] A. J. P. Taylor, *From Napoleon to Stalin* (London: Hamish Hamilton).

3

Napoleon in France tended to be men of the Right, whereas outside France it was generally the Left which made him its idol—a perfectly natural phenomenon which Mr. Taylor needlessly attributes to the perversity of the English Left. This ambiguous role is the common destiny of heirs of revolutions, whose business it is to consolidate and stabilize the achievements of the revolution at home and capitalize them abroad.

The French revolution of 1848 was the most significant fiasco in modern history. Its two most percipient observers, Marx and Tocqueville, both seized on its bogus character. "Hegel says somewhere," runs the famous opening passage of Marx's *Eighteenth Brumaire of Louis Bonaparte,* "that all great historic events and personages recur twice; he forgot to add, 'Once as tragedy, the second time as farce.' " And Tocqueville, who describes the makers of 1848 as "endeavouring to warm themselves at the fire of our fathers' passions", compared it with "a bad tragedy performed by provincial actors". Mr. Taylor rather gratuitously seeks to do justice to Tocqueville at the expense of Marx who should, however, not be accused of having overlooked the conservatism of the French peasantry. But in truth both men in their different styles pronounced a strikingly similar verdict. It was Tocqueville in his Memoirs who declared that "socialism will always remain the essential characteristic and the most redoubtable remembrance of the revolution of February", and penned this cautiously worded but profound diagnosis:

> How should the poor and humble and yet powerful classes not have dreamed of issuing from their poverty and inferiority by means of their power, especially in an epoch when our view into another world has become dimmer and the miseries of this world become more visible and seem more intolerable? They had been working to this end for the last 60 years. . . . And to speak more specially of property, which is, as it were, the foundation of our social order—all the privileges which covered it and, so to speak, concealed the privilege of property having been destroyed, and property remaining the principal obstacle to equality among men, and appearing to be the only sign of inequality—was it not necessary, I will not say that it should be abolished in its turn, but that the thought of abolishing it should occur to the minds of those who did not enjoy it?

In short, with the triumph of the industrial revolution and its inevitable consequence, the rise of the class-conscious proletariat, nothing could ever be the same again—not even political revolutions. In the Europe of 1848 no revolution could be other than a sham if it burked the new issue of socialism, in the sense of the demand for social and economic equality and the challenge to the rights of property. In England the industrial and commercial class, thanks to English leadership and predominance in the industrial revolution, had got what it wanted in the 1830s, and in the next decade successfully faced and nipped in the bud the Chartist rebellion; England had no 1848. In France 1830 had failed to satisfy the ambitions of the French bourgeoisie. The blame fell on Louis Philippe; and for the French middle class the revolution of February, 1848, was a move to consolidate its position and complete the achievement of the great revolution. This was a grave miscalculation. A repeat performance more than 50 years after is always a hazardous enterprise. When the good bourgeois revolutionaries of February 1848, perceived that the driving force of the revolution had passed into the hands of the new proletariat, and that what was being assailed was not monarchy but property, they hastily changed over to the other side of the barricades. The June days bloodily and dramatically drove home the lesson already inherent in the undramatic and bloodless defeat of the Chartists: the rift between bourgeois democracy and socialism.

In central Europe the fiasco of 1848 was gravest of all. For here the bourgeoisie had not merely failed, as in France, to consolidate its achievements, but had failed altogether to attain political power; the counterpart of the English and French revolutions had not occurred at all. In the German-speaking lands, where the industrial revolution had already made progress second only to that made in England, the revolution of 1848 was an attempt by the German bourgeoisie to carry to victory the principles of the English and French revolutions at a time when the socialist revolution had already begun to knock at the door. This attempt, which was to be repeated more than 50 years later in the Russian revolution of 1905, could not succeed. The futilities and inconsistencies of the German democrats of 1848 have often been exposed. But their position between the still undefeated strongholds of monarchy and the rising proletarian tide left them without any secure foothold; they could only throw themselves, as did the Frankfurt Assembly, on the dubious good faith and none too tender mercies of the King of Prussia. For Germany, 1848 came too early or too late—too late for a victorious democratic revolution, too early for socialism to seem anything but a vague and sinister menace to the established order.

Ultimately perhaps no less significant than the rise of the new proletarian socialism, and more immediately spectacular, was the rise of the new nationalism. Here, too, 1848 proved an important turning-point. The doctrine of popular sovereignty consecrated by the French revolution carried with it by implication the doctrine of national self-determination, which seemed an inescapable corollary of democracy. If it was a right of man to have his voice in the affairs of the nation, it was an even more elementary right to have a voice in choosing to what nation he should belong. In practice national self-determination appeared at this time to operate as a uniting, not as a dividing, force. In France one of the consequences of the revolution had been to make an end of traditional Breton, Norman, and Provençal separatism and weld the nation together as an indissoluble whole. The first great national movements in Europe— the only ones of which anything had been heard before 1848—were movements for the national unity of Germans, Italians, and Poles. In so far as these movements were movements of disintegration, they were at the expense of the Habsburg and Russian empires, the bugbears of all nineteenth-century radicals and progressives. Thus, both in theory and in practice, democracy and nationalism could advance triumphantly hand-in-hand.

It was 1848 which shattered this comfortable dream. The dynastic principle, finally destroyed in France, was called in question and discredited all over central Europe; and, with popular sovereignty being now everywhere invoked as the basis of political authority, new nations began to make their voice heard. It was no longer the disreputable autocrats in Vienna and St. Petersburg whose dominions were threatened with disruption in the name of the new national principle. German unity was subject to challenge by Danes and Czechs, Polish unity by Ruthenians, Magyar unity by Slovaks and Croats, Italian unity by Slovenes—and British unity by the Irish. The new phenomenon found dramatic expression at the Slav congress in Prague in June, 1848, which Mr. Taylor calls "the least expected event in the year of revolutions". Just as Woodrow Wilson, arriving 70 years later in Paris, was shocked and embarrassed by claims to self-determination from nations of which he had never heard or dreamed, so the democrats of 1848 stood aghast at these new entities springing unwanted and unheralded from the soil of central and eastern Europe. The Germans tried to spirit them away by throwing doubt on their national credentials and calling them contemptuously *Nationalitäten*; later on somebody, in the familiar and futile attempt to avert the future by invoking the past, dubbed them "unhistorical nations". All this did not help. The Slav congress did nothing constructive; it certainly did not demonstrate the solidarity of the Slavs. But it did demonstrate "beyond a peradventure" (in the Wilsonian phrase) that national self-determination was a principle with awkward implications both for bourgeois democracy and for international concord.

As the century went on, the new socialism and the new nationalism which had first reared their heads in 1848 began to exhibit some common symptoms. Both took on the colour of the mass civilization which emerged from the industrial revolution. Middle-class democracy had been essentially the creation of a society of independent *entrepreneurs*, producers and traders, of the world of individual enterprise, individual competition and economic *laissez-faire*, of men of property and substance who had a stake in the country. There was no single point which could be said to mark the transition from the world of small business to the world of nation-wide trusts and international cartels, from the world of independent artisans to the world of giant trade unions and the closed shop: the change came by a process of gradual and almost undetected evolution. In politics it is equally difficult to mark the line which divided the bourgeois democracy of the mid-nineteenth century from the mass democracy of the twentieth; in Britain, where the process was signalized by the gradual transformation of a property franchise into universal suffrage, a transformation not formally completed till well on into the present century, the evolution seemed particularly smooth and natural. It may also be said that all the implications of modern mass democracy were already present in Rousseau's "general will", so that even in theory the germs of the new could be traced in the old. Nevertheless, while it may be more accurate to speak of evolution than of revolution, society in our time has passed over with extraordinary rapidity from predominantly individual to predominantly collective forms of organization; and, while many institutions continue to be called by their old names, hardly one of them has escaped vital and fundamental change.

The change was particularly apparent in its application to the phenomenon of nationalism. In the early democratic conception the nation was simply the national expression of the wills and preferences of its individual members; it was, in a phrase coined by Renan when it had already ceased to be appropriate, *un plébiscite de tous les jours*—or, in a more flippant formula, the result of a choice made "in spite of all temptations to belong to other nations". But long before the nineteenth century was out this individualist view of the nation had become obsolete. As early as 1848 the Slav congress in Prague had celebrated the "liberty, equality and fraternity of nations". The rights which the French revolution had accorded to man were transferred to the nation. The nation was the new entity enjoying and asserting its rights in the world. The man, who had rights, was slowly and imperceptibly transformed into the citizen, who had obligations. The man had been the maker and the *raison d'être* of the nation; the citizen was its loyal and humble servant. Much has been written of the aura of mysticism which came to surround the nation. But what happened here was not substantially different from what happened elsewhere. In all significant fields of organized activity the individual has been superseded by the collective group. Nor is it, generally speaking, true that the individual has been collectivized against his will. Far more often he has deliberately sought the support and protection of the collective group because, in the highly organized mass society of the modern world, he could not stand or work effectively in isolation. This is the problem which the nineteenth century bequeathed to its successor, and which that successor has scarcely yet fully diagnosed—much less solved.

The main casualty of this transformation in the foundations of society has been the theory and practice of liberalism, of the old liberal democracy and the old liberal nationalism. The fundamental tenet of a liberal creed was the belief in the power of individual reason and in the reasonableness of man. Rational discussion and argument, the interchange of individual opinions, was the sure way to find the answer to any problem; and, since men were reasonable, difficulties could always be solved by compromise, not by fighting it out. Nationalism, in the liberal creed, meant the rational desire of men of the same race and kind for freedom to live together and run their affairs in common; those who enjoyed this freedom themselves would naturally respect it in others. Modern collective man shares none of these beliefs. The problems of our highly complicated and highly organized modern societies no longer seem of the kind which lend themselves to solution through a process of discussion and argument by rational individuals; they are referred to experts in the particular subject at issue. It is no longer a question of either arguing it out or counting heads, but of finding the right expert. Nor does it appear that major political conflicts are commonly resolved by compromise; power often plays as large a role as reason in the settlement. It is this sense of helplessness, or this desire for power, which has welded the individual into the collective group. It is not, as is sometimes said, that he barters freedom for efficiency. Standing alone, he feels himself neither free nor efficient.

In the most brilliant of the articles in this volume, "Munich Ten Years After", Mr. Taylor diagnoses Munich as the final downfall of liberalism. If the liberal doctrine of national self-determination was right, then the Versailles Treaty was an abomination and Hitler's claim was justified—which was what many, perhaps most, thinking Englishmen, bred in the liberal tradition, had believed after 1919; some had abandoned this belief (and, by implication, their liberalism) before 1938, others more consistently stuck to it. Moreover, if discussion and compromise, rather than fighting it out, were the right methods of settling a dispute, then Munich was the expression of sound liberal principles; it is difficult to contest that this was the angle, or one of the angles, from which Neville Chamberlain regarded it. Even the Czechs, as Mr. Taylor points out, were steeped in the liberal tradition.

> The Czech leaders, Beneš most of all, were liberals by historical background and social origin—men of bargaining and discussion. They could manoeuvre and evade; they could not defy and perish.

It was thus not the Czechs but the Polish leaders, men of the eighteenth century and among the most illiberal politicians in Europe, who found the answer. It was not Beneš but Beck, "a man of infinitely lower moral calibre", who "gave the signal for Hitler's fall". By the same token liberal Britain fought Hitler not for democratic Czechoslovakia, but for retrograde Poland.

Mr. Taylor's volume is valuable for such intermittent flashes of insight lighting up a whole period rather than for any systematic presentation, which could indeed not be attempted in a somewhat random collection of essays. The items are of varying length, calibre, and merit. Mr. Taylor's tastes are catholic enough to appreciate two such very different figures in the roll of English Prime Ministers as Lord John Russell and Salisbury; and even about figures for whom in general he shows little sympathy or understanding, notably Bismarck, he often has acute observations. While it would probably be fair to sum up the volume, in the impression it leaves on the reader's mind, as an obituary of liberalism, Mr. Taylor's own deepest roots are in the liberal tradition. His inherent tendency to believe that God is on the side of the small battalions is well illustrated in two items at the end of the book. One is a brief note on the Wroclaw congress of intellectuals in 1948, where he helped to organize a cave against the unanimous resolution which the Russian and other communist delegates hoped to produce. The other is a sympathetic portrait of Marshal Tito originally broadcast in the same year after the Stalin–Tito quarrel. Not only is it far more desirable, in Mr. Taylor's view, that Tito shall remain a dissentient minority in the eastern group than that he should be seduced into giving his allegiance to the West, but there is also a lesson to be drawn on the other side of the curtain: "The best thing for us and for the world in general is that we should be America's Tito."

2 Rights and Obligations

The renewed interest of the past two decades in "the rights of man", itself the product of notorious historical events, shows that mankind is at another of the great turning-points of history. Throughout the nineteenth century the issue seemed to what called itself progressive thought to have been settled and decided once for all in the sense of the declarations of the French and American revolutions. "The natural and imprescriptible rights of man . . . are liberty, property, security and resistance of oppression . . . the unrestrained communication of thoughts and opinions." Roman Catholic thinkers contested, though with less emphasis as the century went on, the appositeness and adequacy of some of these definitions; in Orthodox Russia, apologists for autocracy like Dostoevsky dismissed them as superficial and incompatible with the true nature of man; the non-European world, other than those parts of it which had inherited the European tradition, remained unmoved and inscrutable. These exceptions did not, however, seem very important to those who felt themselves in the van of civilization's forward march. No doubt man was still, especially in backward countries, often deprived of the enjoyment, and even of the knowledge, of his rights. To spread the recognition and exercise of these rights was the ardent wish and missionary task of liberal-minded men and women. But to question what the rights of man were was surely perverse or cynical.

The last few years have thrown back into the arena of heated discussion the whole nature of human rights. The charter of the United Nations required the Social and Economic Council of the new organization (the choice of this particular organ was perhaps significant) to draw up recommendations for the better observance of "human rights and fundamental freedoms". A commission was set up; and the product of its labours was a Declaration of Human Rights adopted by the General Assembly of the United Nations in December, 1948. The discussions of the commission remained on the political level; they professed to concern themselves with questions of application rather than with the fundamental nature of human rights, and the document finally agreed on was pale, eclectic and unconvincing. But the fact that human rights had become a matter, not of assumed common agreement among men of good will, but of a political sparring-match between two groups of nations, showed that the classic issue of the relation of man to society had once more been reopened.

To examine the questions of political philosophy which lay behind the political manoeuvres at Lake Success was a suitable task for Unesco. The Unesco inquiry was set on foot in 1947, was carried on simultaneously with the debates of the United Nations Commission, and was completed long before the United Nations Declaration of Rights was drafted in its final form. The volume now published[1] contains the original *questionnaire* issued by Unesco, a selection from the comments and essays written by a large number of scholars throughout the world to whom the *questionnaire* was sent, and a report by the Unesco committee which examined and edited these contributions. The result is one of the most interesting and fruitful examples of Unesco's work. Immune from political preoccupations and inhibitions, the collaborators of Unesco have for the most part made a serious attempt to delve into the fundamental issues which were slurred over or by-passed in the United Nations Commission. The interest of the volume resides not so much in the amount of agreement recorded in the final report (as M. Jacques Maritain says in his introduction, it is sometimes possible to reach agreed practical conclusions from different theoretical premises), but in the diversity of opinions expressed in the body of the book. The much abused word "symposium" is for once not wholly out of place.

M. Maritain suggests that the touchstone of the approach to the rights of man resides in the attitude to natural law, and that the difference is between those who regard them as "fundamental and inalienable rights antecedent in nature, and superior, to society", and those who believe that "man's rights are relative to the historical development of society, and . . . are a product of society itself as it advances with the forward march of history". But he himself agrees that the distinction is less absolute in practice than it appears in theory; for though natural law may be conceived as an

---

[1] *Human Rights. Comments and Interpretations.* A symposium edited by Unesco, with an introduction by Jacques Maritain (London: Allan Wingate).

absolute enjoying divine sanction, current human interpretations of the content of that law are always "relative to the historical development of society" at a given moment. The present symposium seems rather to justify a tripartite classification into Roman Catholics, represented by Father Teilhard de Chardin and M. Maritain (in his personal contribution), Marxists, represented by Mr. John Lewis and M. Tchechko (whose contribution, incidentally, contains a useful collection of Soviet texts), and "Liberals", represented by Professor McKeon, Don Salvador de Madariaga and Signor Croce (though this collocation of names already shows the difficulty of any classification); and in this tripartite grouping, it is noteworthy how often the Catholic, who believes in natural law, and the Marxist, who presumably rejects it, find common ground against the Liberal, whose attitude towards it is fluctuating.

A more fruitful practical approach may perhaps be found by asking how far the conception of human rights propounded at the end of the eighteenth century is still valid to-day, and how far, and for what reasons, it needs to be corrected or supplemented. This is the question to which most contributors to this volume have directly or indirectly addressed themselves. The unqualified upholders of the eighteenth-century bill of rights are surprisingly few—perhaps rarer among the intellectuals than among the politicians who directed the proceedings of the United Nations. But it is both fair and convenient to quote one contribution from an American scholar—not, it may be said, of American birth—from what may be called the extreme "conservative" camp:

> Any bill of rights that makes the rights conditional on duties towards society or the State, however strong its emphasis on human dignity, freedom, God or whatever else, can be accepted by any kind of totalitarian leader. He will enforce the duties while disregarding the rights.
>
> Hence a bill of rights would better be restricted to rights, *i.e.*, to those rights which as minimum conditions, however insufficient, of human freedom, any State or society can respect and protect— these are the old civil liberties. Any addition, be it of economic rights, be it of duties, means in practice weakening the old civil rights and their hold on the human mind.

This quotation makes a good starting-point, since it is precisely on these two points—the need to add economic to political rights and the need to consider the duties as well as the rights of man—that most thinkers to-day are conscious of a certain inadequacy in the old eighteenth-century formulas.

It will seem clear to many that the addition of social and economic rights to the political rights which appeared all-important to the revolutionaries of the eighteenth century has been the most signal and unmistakable advance in the conception of the rights of man registered in recent times. This has been the natural and necessary corollary of the extension of the functions of the State from the narrowly defined sphere of classical liberal democracy to those social and economic preoccupations which have become the primary concern of the modern legislator and administrator. The scope of human rights has widened with the scope of government; it is no more possible to return to the purely political eighteenth-century conception than to restore the *laissez-faire* State. The assertion of social and economic rights was a distinctive characteristic of the Russian revolution thirty years ago: The Declaration of Rights of the Toiling and Exploited People, which dates from January, 1918, proclaimed its fundamental purpose as being "to suppress all exploitation of man by man, to abolish for ever the division of society into classes, and to bring about the socialist organization of society in all countries". Lenin, and other Bolshevik writers after him, have continually insisted on the hollow and "formal" character of political rights isolated from social and economic rights. The millionaire landlord or factory-owner who counts for one and no more than one in a political democracy is notoriously a mythical figure.

Recognition of the truth behind the over-statements of revolutionary propaganda has long penetrated to circles which cannot be brought by any stretch of imagination within the orbit of socialism. The essence of Franklin Roosevelt's "four freedoms" was the linking of the newer economic with the older political interpretation of the rights of man. The main anxieties of human beings at the present time in almost all countries are clearly quite as much social and economic as political. No political party would venture to appeal to the electorate of the most orthodox democracy to-day without inscribing in its programme the right to work, the right to a living wage, and the right to care and maintenance in infancy, old age, ill-health or unemployment. These rights today—far more than the right to vote or freedom of speech and assembly—make up the popular conception of the rights of man. We have moved on from the age of bourgeois individualism to the age of mass industrial civilization. The rights of man, the things which he most wants from society, have changed with the times.

But does this mean that the new social and political rights can simply be added to the old political rights, so that we have merely broadened our conception of the rights of man in general? Things are not quite so easy as this. The fact of juxtaposition produces a process of interaction between different rights which must end by altering their character. The dilemma of reconciling political equality with political liberty was always resolved, down to the time of J. S. Mill, by defining liberty as freedom to do everything that did not restrict the liberty of others. But when equality comes to mean economic equality—or at any rate some enforced mitigation of economic inequality—and when liberty comes to mean something like liberty of opportunity, or free and equal access to the good things which society has to offer, the relation between equality and liberty takes on a new and much more baffling complexion. To claim that "freedom from want" is merely an extension of the older conceptions of freedom, without freedom from want no other freedom can be real, is plausible enough. But the fact remains that "freedom from want" is not only not an emanation from the older freedoms but is incompatible with some of them: it is, for example, incompatible with the freedom of a *laissez-faire* society. The present conflict about human rights does represent to some extent the difficult choice between incompatible alternatives. Both sides are to this extent insincere when they pretend to offer a formula that makes the best of all worlds.

This is the first profound problem which dogs those who embark on the discussion of human rights in our time; and, if the contributors to the present book have done no more than scratch its surface, they have performed a useful function. The second problem is older and more familiar; for at no period of history has the correlation between rights and obligations been denied. Any definition of the rights of man is a definition of the relation between the individual and society; and this relation necessarily involves rights and obligations on both sides. It is, however, no accident that the emphasis should have shifted since the last great debate on human rights in the latter part of the eighteenth century. Europe was at that time at the end of a long historical epoch in which the duties of the individual to society had been heavily emphasized; the hierarchy of the feudal order had not yet been broken down. The revolution, which represented the revolt of the individual against a rigid and cramping social system, insisted on the rights of the individual against society. The modern revolution comes at the end of a long period of buoyant and almost unrestrained individual enterprise, when the individual has tended more and more to claim his rights against society and to forget the corresponding weight of his social obligations. The wheel has come round; the leaders of liberal democracies, no less than of totalitarian States, are finding it to-day increasingly necessary to dwell on what the citizen owes to the community of which he forms a part.

The truth that rights cannot be divorced from obligations would seem trite if it had not been so often overlooked in recent years. It applies to political rights. M. Sergius Hessen, a Polish scholar of Russian origin, who contributes a thoughtful and balanced paper to the Unesco volume, aptly quotes one of the fathers of nineteenth-century Liberalism, Benjamin Constant, to the effect that "liberty in the sense of negative freedom was a modern idea unknown to the ancients"; the classical conception of liberty was "the participation of every free man in the exercise of State sovereignty and by no means freedom from the interference of the State in the private life of man". One of the writers in this volume describes the political obligation which is the correlative of political rights as "mainly passive", being confined to loyalty to the political order. This is not wholly correct. Liberal democracy worked because a sufficient number of those who profited by its privileges recognized the positive obligation to play their part in making it work. The tradition of public service—and even of unpaid public service—was one of its essential attributes. It is doubtful whether western democracy has given sufficient attention to the problem of transferring this conception of individual public service to the conditions of mass civilization. Decay of belief in the importance of political rights—which is apparent to all save those who do not wish to see— has gone hand in hand with decay of the sense of political obligations. The stumbling-block has been the difficulty of transplanting them both from the context of a bourgeois civilization to the context of a mass civilization.

What is true of political rights is still more plainly true of economic rights. It is not always recognized how far the most advanced modern democracies, with their policies of a "national minimum" of cheap basic foodstuffs, of free milk for children, free health services and free education, have moved, not merely towards Socialism, but towards the ultimate Communist goal of "to each according to his needs". But even Communists have always argued that this goal can be reached only under a regime of economic abundance, when, in Marx's famous words, "the springs of wealth will flow more abundantly". This is only another way of expressing the truism—or what should be a truism—that a community claiming a high standard of social and economic rights is by necessity a community maintaining a high standard of productivity. In any modern declaration of rights which recognizes the right of the citizen to "freedom from want" in all its implications, it would seem not merely legitimate but imperative to include some declaration of the obligation of the citizen to make available those productive forces without which "freedom from want" must necessarily remain on illusion.

The question of the social and economic rights of man is thus closely bound with that other vexed question of contemporary civilization—the question of incentives to work. To neglect or ignore the link between them is to make it appear that these rights are the inherent property of the man or the citizen—something which society or the State owes to him irrespective of any action or effort by himself. Members of the British Government are now busy trying to make plain what has so long—and partly through their own fault—been obscured by loose talking and thinking about human rights. All that a declaration of rights in this field can register is a determination by a given community to distribute its available resources in a certain way and to recognize certain priorities—say, to reserve scarce milk supplies for the children or the hospitals, or scarce building resources for the construction of houses and factories rather than of offices or cinemas. It cannot by itself create new resources, or make rights effective which presuppose the availability of non-existent resources. This can only be done by the recognition and enforcement of the corresponding obligation of the individual to produce by his work the minimum resources that are required.

Human rights, though in principle rights recognized as valid for mankind as a whole, are generally discussed in the framework of the particular society to which the individual belongs. In other words, what are in question are not so much the rights of man as the rights of the citizen. Attention should therefore be drawn to two contributions to the Unesco symposium which stand a little apart from the rest in that they deal with the rights of "outcasts". One, by Miss Margery Fry, long known for her devoted work in the cause of penal reform, is concerned with the rights of the "law-breaker" subjected to penal discipline—an issue which leads far away from the ordinary problems of human rights into those of the philosophy and purposes of punishment. The other is a study by Mr. A. P. Elkin on the rights of primitive peoples, with special reference to the case of the Australian aborigines, in which he is an expert. This is a thought-provoking essay, and shows how difficult it is to bring the destinies of some at least of the primitive peoples within the limits of the problem of racial discrimination, which has been one of the favourite weapons in the debate between the two groups of Powers on human rights. To remove racial discrimination is here the beginning, but certainly not the end, of wisdom.

Had the promoters of the Unesco inquiry into human rights desired to provide a justification for their work, they could hardly have done so more eloquently than by printing without comment in an appendix the text of the declaration adopted by the United Nations last December. In the light of the preceding pages its emptiness becomes all the more striking; and, since its authors were certainly not ignorant of the real issues, it can only be supposed that political expediency made it necessary to keep them decently out of sight. In other words, this is a subject which is ripe for anxious and searching inquiry by students of political philosophy and of the discontents of our present civilization, but not for legislation by international lawyers and politicians. The present volume professes to do no more than stimulate thought; and this it is well qualified to do. It only remains to add that the translations have been superlatively done, so that it is rarely possible to discern from internal evidence whether any particular contribution was originally written in French or in English; but there are a number of errors in the spelling of the proper names.

3 The League of Nations

It is now more than 30 years since the league of Nations was born, 15 years since it played any active role in international politics, and almost six since its last formal Assembly met to conduct its obsequies and transfer its assets to the expectant and eager heir, the United Nations. The league with all its hopes and disappointments, its achievements and its failures, has passed into history, and the time has come to draw up the balance-sheet. The moment is indeed perhaps more propitious to the memory of the League than could well have been expected. Those who prepared the Charter of the United Nations naturally hoped, by building on the experience of the League of Nations and learning the lessons of its shortcomings, to improve on the old model. The last six years have done little to flatter their reputation for perspicacity. The fault certainly does not lie with them. But the record of the United Nations, far from eclipsing that of its predecessor, has tended to mitigate the severity of the judgments formerly current on the League and to increase appreciation of its achievement. It is even possible that some who have known both the old and the new—both delegates and officials—may from time to time have sat down by Lake Success and wept for the more limpid and more fragrant waters of Lake Leman.

Nobody could have been better fitted to write the story of the League of Nations than Mr. Walters, who was on Lord Cecil's staff in Paris when the League Covenant was drafted, became principal private secretary to the first Secretary-General of the League, and ended as its senior British official. Few were so intimately associated—and none in such a high capacity—with the work of the League from the first day to the last. The qualities which made Mr. Walters a first-rate official have gone to the making of the historian. They include patience, thoroughness, meticulous accuracy and an almost excessive personal modesty. Historical detachment and long-term perspectives were scarcely to be expected at this stage, especially from one who is not a historian by habit or training. *A*

History of the League of Nations[1] has some of the characteristics of a two-volume Victorian official biography of a great man, devoted to the pious celebration of its subject's memory rather than to a critical appraisal of his virtues and vices, or to an assessment of his place in history. It would not be fair to say that Mr. Walters ignores the warts. But he treats them as extraneous accidents, and generally blames someone else for them. This is, however, a sound start. There will be plenty of time later for attempts at a more critical and perhaps more profound approach.

The League of Nations was a product of the burst of idealism generated in the English-speaking countries by the First World War. For the United States, and in almost equal measure for Great Britain and the British Dominions, large-scale war, war between "civilized" nations, had before 1914 become an unthinkable monstrosity. It occurred. And the reaction was an immensely powerful demand for something which would ensure that this monstrosity should never appear again. Moreover, it was clear both to the British and to the Americans what shape this "something" must take. It must be an institution which would universalize the principles of liberal democracy, the form of government of the English-speaking peoples, the highest form of government the world had yet known. Unfortunately, two incompatible strands were closely interwoven in the liberal democratic ideology. Respect for the rule of law, which implied enforcement of the law in cases of infringement or threatened infringement, went hand in hand with a profound hatred of war, which was the use of force in international relations: an exaltation of peace above all other values in international affairs made the problem of "sanctions" insoluble. The League never really escaped from this dilemma.

The two strands could be reconciled only for so long as the League could proceed by methods of persuasion and rely on that somewhat dubious entity, world public opinion, for the carrying out of its decisions. The reader of Mr. Walters's book may be surprised to discover how much was in fact achieved by these methods. The whole of the economic, social and health aspects of the work of the League rested on this basis of voluntary cooperation; and, though it

---

[1] F. P. Walters, *A History of the League of Nations*. Two volumes. Published under the auspices of the Royal Institute of International Affairs (London: Oxford University Press; Cumberlege).

is true that much of this continued work previously undertaken by other international agencies, tribute may be paid to the largely increased drive and efficiency imparted to it by its concentration under the single authority of Geneva.

But what is more significant is that such success as the League achieved in the political field in the settlement of disputes between nations was also virtually all achieved through the machinery for negotiation and consent. The famous Article 11 of the League Covenant, under which decisions could be taken only by a unanimous vote of all members of the Council, including the parties to the issue in dispute who would be invited *ad hoc*, if not already members, to sit with the Council, was the stand-by which enabled the League to win its only political victories. Once disputes proved intractable to this method, once the League was forced on to the ground of sanctions and enforcement, it broke down. The virtue of Article 11 and of the unanimity rule was one of the lessons which the framers of the Charter of the United Nations failed to learn.

Mr. Walters's account distinguishes clearly enough the different phases through which the League passed. In the first period, which lasted till 1923 or 1924, it was still under the weight of its initial difficulties of organization and, above all, of the defection of the United States, which seemed at first a crushing blow. This was, politically speaking, a period of retreat, when the general mood sought to whittle down the obligations of the Covenant on the solid and reasonable plea that many of these could scarcely be fulfilled without the cooperation of the United States. It is not surprising to find Canada playing an important part in this movement.

Then followed the great boom period of inter-war Europe, a period of reconstruction, pacification and large-scale American investment, inaugurated by the Dawes plan and carried over into the political sphere by the Locarno treaties. The League of Nations rode high on the crest of this wave. Its rise was heralded by the appearance of the first Labour Government of Ramsay MacDonald in Great Britain, followed by the Radical victory and the Herriot Government in France. The appearance of Ramsay MacDonald and Herriot in person at the fifth Assembly of the League in September, 1924, made it, in Mr. Walters's words, "such an occasion as had long been hoped for, but never yet realized". Hitherto the example of Lloyd George and Curzon—at one, if in nothing else, in their low estimate of the League—had proved decisive. No leading statesman—for Balfour was now a dignified but secondary figure—had ever appeared on the tribune at Geneva. From 1924 onwards, the Assembly and Council of the League became a recognized meeting place for the Foreign Ministers of Europe, of great and small Powers alike. It is significant of the spirit of the time that even so lukewarm an admirer of the League as Austen Chamberlain did much, by his regular personal attendance, to establish the tradition. It really began to seem as if Geneva was the hub of the universe, and the leading-strings of international politics were really being manipulated in its debating halls, corridors and hotel bedrooms.

This illusion bred the hubris which was the ultimate undoing of the League. The decisions that moulded the future of the world were being taken—not necessarily even by Governments—in Washington and New York, in London, in Berlin, even in Moscow. What was current in Geneva was the small change of diplomatic intercourse. Minor disputes were successfully settled, and turbulent minor Powers kept in order. All this was to the good. But the machinery of the League sometimes performed the more dubious service of providing discreet "formulae" to plaster over real cracks, thereby concealing both the seriousness and the character of the issues at stake. Disarmament was an excellent illustration of this. Repeated pious resolutions at Geneva about the desirability of disarmament, and a proliferation of commissions working out "technical" schemes, encouraged the world to forget that one, and only one, real question mattered in this field: the rearmament of Germany.

It was in this mood of high-minded but presumptuous idealism that League enthusiasts set out to retrieve the retreat of the first years, to provide impregnable bulwarks for peace, to "annihilate" war, as Beneš once put it. When the League Covenant was drafted in Paris in 1919, memories of war were still very real and ever-present; and many of those who helped to shape its clauses had had practical experience of the conduct of international relations. Its aims and pretensions, though they can scarcely be called modest, were at any rate limited; the League was not marked from birth with the illusion of omnipotence. It did not set out to prohibit or exorcise entirely so ancient and ingrained an abuse in human affairs as war. It was content to make provisions which, if observed, would render resort to war more difficult, would provide a "cooling-off period" for reflection before the dire decision was actually taken, and would mobilize the rest of the world against the rash offender who plunged into war without sufficient cause. Even the ultimate provisions for "sanctions" were enveloped in a certain discreet vagueness.

In the later 1920s all this came to seem shockingly pussillanimous. Bold men stood up at Geneva to multiply the number of protocols and conventions designed to prohibit recourse to war, to close the "gaps" in the Covenant, to make certain and "automatic" the application of sanctions to the aggressor. It is one of the odd paradoxes of the history of the League that this movement received a strong impetus from the other side of the Atlantic. By this time the initial boycott was more or less over, and the American official attitude had settled down to one of cooperation with many of the social and technical activities of the League (there had been an American representative on its health committee as early as 1922) and of polite indifference to its political machinery. But in the middle 1920s an influential group of American intellectuals, disappointed in their ambition of bringing their own country into the League, embarked on the apparently less unpromising mission of going one better than the League. At Geneva they lent the prestige of unofficial American backing to every project for "strengthening" the Covenant. In the United States they inspired the extraordinary interlude of the "Kellogg Pact", by which in 1928 virtually every nation in the world, including the United States and the Soviet Union, bound itself to renounce war as an instrument of national policy. Not content with this pious and impressive declaration, League enthusiasts at once promoted a proposal to "write the Kellogg Pact into the Convenant", which would thus be converted into an absolute prohibition on resort to war. This scheme was still under discussion when the curtain fell on the halcyon period of League history.

The last two sections of Mr. Walters's book, which occupy his second volume, are entitled respectively "The Years of Conflict" and "The Years of Defeat". They start with the Japanese action in Manchuria in 1931, and tell a tale whose tragic course is still familiar to all but the post-war generation of to-day. As the well-remembered milestones are passed one by one—the Japanese crisis, the fiasco of the Disarmament Conference, Abyssinia, the

Rhineland, the Spanish Civil War, Austria, Czechoslovakia—the League recedes further and further into the background of the international scene. At the assembly of September, 1938, the month of Munich, the only Foreign Minister present from any major country was Litvinov; only the latest recruit to the League from among the great Powers still paid it honour—and for the last time. The hopes and ambitions and illusions of the 1920s, the pacts and the protocols, the clauses of the Covenant itself, lay in ruins.

This was the real end of the history of the League of Nations. The epilogue had its garish episodes, notably the expulsion of the Soviet Union after the Finnish war in December, 1939, the only practical consequence of which was that a revival of the league of Nations after the Second World War, and even a physical return to Geneva, were ruled out of court by Soviet antipathies. But Mr. Walters has found ample room for the whole period from 1938 to the final winding-up ceremony in April, 1946, in three short chapters. The machinery of the League was kept more or less intact in Geneva till the collapse of June, 1940. Then everything fell to pieces. The economic and social activities of the League were transferred across the Atlantic, where a handful of League officials enjoyed the hospitality of American universities or public bodies. The French Secretary-General, after some embarrassing episodes into which Mr. Walters does not enter, resigned and transferred his personal allegiance to the Vichy Government. A skeleton staff continued to occupy a corner of the vast palace of the League of Nations in Geneva throughout the war. This sufficed to maintain continuity, and to hand over the material assets of the League to its successor. "The League of Nations is dead, long live the United Nations."

Mr. Walters deserves whole-hearted congratulations on having written a book which will never be superseded, and is final within the limits set. In one sense the task was technically easy for anyone sitting in Geneva. The book has been written entirely from the published records and unpublished archives of the League; neither in collecting his material nor in writing his history has Mr. Walters suffered any of the difficulties or embarrassments, known to most contemporary historians, of access to sources or of doubt about what sources are available. It may perhaps be regretted that he does not seem anywhere to have quoted any of the unpublished material on which he evidently relies, and which was apparently placed at his unfettered disposition. Presumably the scruples which have excluded departmental minutes from the official collection of *Documents on British Foreign Policy* have been operative in this case as well. But, in spite of this omission, nobody will doubt that this is as fair and complete a record of the League, from the standpoint of one of its leading officials, as could have been expected or desired.

It is not therefore in any grudging spirit, or in any desire to belittle what has been done, that the critic will exercise his function of indicating some of the book's deficiencies and limitations as a contribution to contemporary history. The reader who, unlike the author, has not spent a large part of his active life immersed in the affairs of the League, will be likely, as he makes his way through these closely packed pages, to experience a sense of what may perhaps be called "other-worldliness"—an impression that he has entered a territory set apart and isolated from the everyday political world, subject to laws of its own, immune from the standards of judgment that are commonly applied to ordinary political institutions, though itself entitled to apply its own standards of judgment to the world outside. This esoteric quality, which in its day tinged the outlook of League officials, enthusiastic League supporters, and even many delegates to the League, comes out very strongly in Mr. Walters's book, and accounts in one way or another for most of the criticisms which can be justly made of it.

The least damaging, and most agreeable, of the symptoms of this esoteric outlook is the hyperbolic language in which the progress and achievements of the League are celebrated. At the first Assembly, we are told, "the League had rediscovered its links with the past and had begun to establish a steady foundation for its future expansion". When the Locarno treaty was concluded, "the new situation could never have been brought about but for the past efforts of the Council and the Assembly, nor could it be maintained in the future without their help"; and a year later the Dutch Foreign Minister is quoted as hymning, in a reference to the Covenant, "the infinite riches of that marvellous instrument". No doubt ancient political institutions do acquire a tradition and a strength which makes it seem at times as if they functioned by their own momentum and independently of those who are carrying them on. But the league of Nations was a very young institution. It was unique among political institutions in being an emanation, not of one Government, but of many; and of these many, some—perhaps a majority—were in a greater or less degree mistrustful of it. These were sources of weakness in an institution still scarcely out of the swaddling-clothes. To speak of the League—as was often done in the 1920s, and as Mr. Walters still does—as if it were an entity acting independently of the Governments which composed it, and at times even in opposition to them, is to fly in the face of reality.

If, however, the successes of international politics in the period between the two wars are to be credited to the League, the failures were, in Mr. Walters's diagnosis, no less clearly due to failure to apply principles and precepts. The great economic depression resulted from the supineness of Governments which "ignored" the advice of the League experts, including the advice of the Financial Committee to spend less on armaments; and the implication lies heavily on all the later sections of the book that the disasters of the 1930s were due to failure to invoke the terms of the Covenant in their full rigour against Japan, Italy and Germany. The historian of the League is not required to present a profound analysis of the underlying causes of the economic and political calamities of the 1930s; and no historian will be blamed for having failed to plumb the depths of causes which will continue to be debated for years to come. But to pretend that these calamities occurred because the Governments rejected the precepts of current economic orthodoxy (which was all that the economic recommendations of the League amounted to), or because the "satisfied" Powers failed to combine in time to resist the challenge of Japan, Italy and Germany (which is what the rigorous application of the League Covenant would have meant), is little more than a tautology, and does nothing to explain why Governments in fact acted, or failed to act, as they did. The League was and remained an instrument of the policies of the Governments which created it and lent it its authority: only superficial judgments can result from treating it as an independent entity standing above and beyond the Governments.

It is above all in his judgments of individuals that the limitations of Mr. Walters's perspective become most apparent. A large number of the leading European statesmen of the 1920s and 1930s step across his pages, but their figures are curiously foreshortened; they are seen and judged as they appeared on the Geneva stage, shadowy figures who seem to have no existence off that stage, so that they scarcely belong to real life. This comes out most strongly in Mr. Walters's treatment of the Germans. Statesmen before (and, no doubt, since) Stresemann have often recognized the obligation to lie abroad for their countries. But no statesman who appeared at

Geneva was so deeply involved as Stresemann in the duplicity of playing up to the Western Powers through professions of fidelity to the league while at same time keeping up a working collaboration with Soviet Russia, at that moment the declared enemy of everything the League stood for. It is notorious that, at the moment when Stresemann was proclaiming at Geneva the fidelity of Germany to her disarmament obligations, this Government had for several years past been carrying out a policy of secret rearmament in agreement with Russia. Yet Stresemann, because his utterances at Geneva were always correct and conciliatory in terms of League rules and of the clauses of the Covenant, remains one of Mr. Walters's heroes (among delegates, only Lord Cecil and Litvinov score higher marks in his examination), while the German National Party, which crudely and clumsily proclaimed its hostility to the League, is accused of behaving with its "habitual perfidy", and Nadolny, the German delegate who protested with patience and courtesy against the procrastinations of the Disarmament Conference and made no secret of his belief in a German-Russian alliance as the only salvation for Germany, was a "dull and disagreeable diplomatist". In reading such judgments one cannot help being conscious of something a little parochial in the Geneva air.

These criticisms, however cogent, relate not to what Mr. Walters has done, but to what he has neither done nor attempted; and it would be unfair to end on this note. Mr. Walters has discharged the task which he set himself with complete mastery, and with a high measure of literary skill. Considering the vast mass of detailed material embodied in it, the book is strikingly readable; and there should be no qualification in the praise given to this achievement. Nor can one say, in spite of some exaggerated eulogies, that the League of Nations as an institution emerges with any thing but credit from these pages. While it did not perform all the functions which those who established it had hoped from it, it rendered signal service in a large number of fields—including some which had not been thought of when it was founded. If it did little to settle major disputes or solve major problems, it at least did nothing to aggravate them or render them more difficult of solution. Most of what it did was sensible and useful. Its worst enemies were those who put forward extravagant pretensions on its behalf, and expected it to perform miracles that lay far beyond its scope or its powers.

4 Lloyd George, Churchill, and the Russian Revolution

I

When Mr. Ullman's first volume on the British involvement in revolutionary Russia, *Intervention and the War*, appeared in 1962, it was natural to lament that, while the author had access to personal papers of participants and other unpublished material, the official records were still closed to him. No such complaint can be made about the second volume, *Britain and the Russian Civil War*, which carries on the ill-fated story from the German armistice of November, 1918, to February, 1920, when intervention was virtually at an end.[1] The author has now been able to make full use, not only of a further release of memoirs and private papers, but of the Cabinet records and the Foreign Office and War Office files in the Public Record Office. It is unlikely that any further large body of documents still remains undisclosed in this country.

It is in a sense, however, true that, the more information we have, the more difficult does it become to explain what happened. It might have been assumed that there would, somewhere in the archives, be some record of a decision by which the intervention in Russia, ostensibly undertaken as a part of the German war to counter threatened German encroachments, was transformed into an operation designed to bring about the overthrow of the Bolsheviks. It is clear that no such decision was ever taken. The operation continued under its own momentum: in mid-winter, 1918, it would have been impossible to withdraw the British troops from the Archangel front where most of them were engaged. Only the reasons, or pretexts, for the operation were gradually, and almost insensibly, modified; and the ease of the change-over throws

---

[1] Richard H. Ullman, *Britain and the Russian Civil War, November, 1918–February, 1920* (Princeton: Princeton University Press; London: Oxford University Press).

some retrospective doubts on the sincerity of the reasons given for the original intervention in 1918. One has the impression that hostility to the Bolsheviks, explicable both by their revolutionary policies and by their abandonment of the Allied cause, had been the most powerful motive force behind it from the start, and that there was in fact little to change in mood or motive after the November armistice.

When the delegations assembled in Paris in January, 1919, for the Peace Conference, the magnitude of the Russian dilemma quickly became apparent. The Prinkipo proposals revealed the depth of the fear and animosity which the Bolsheviks inspired in French, and rather less widely in British, official circles, and how easily popular indignation, raised to fever-pitch by the experiences of the war, could be transferred to this new target. Lloyd George and Woodrow Wilson continued, at least as late as March (the month of the Bullitt mission), to want negotiations with the Bolsheviks. But any such proposal, once it came into the open, seemed doomed to be shot down by the mass of opinion in the delegations and the greater mass of public opinion at home.

On the other hand, Lloyd George plainly recognized from the first that British soldiers were no longer prepared, after the armistice, to fight another war on foreign soil for purposes which they did not understand, and which some of them found highly suspect. Above all, they wanted to go home. The peace congress opened to rumblings of discontent and incipient mutiny among military units, both in France and on the north Russian front. By February both Foch and Churchill accepted that the war against Russia could not be fought by French or British conscripts, though Churchill continued to talk optimistically from time to time of raising volunteers. But military supplies were another matter. The war had left on the hands of the Allies enormous dumps of munitions and military equipment of all kinds. Why not send some of these to the White forces now mustering under various Russian generals on the peripheries of Soviet territory, and enable these forces to destroy the Bolsheviks with Allied weapons? The compromise imposed itself, almost without argument. Lloyd George was pacified by the withdrawal of the demand for troops. Churchill threw himself with gusto into the work of encouraging and arming the Whites.

Equipped with his abundant sources, Mr. Ullman is able to give a day-to-day picture of the changing and sometimes tortuous attitudes of the Allied governments and of their plenipotentiaries in

Paris throughout the dramatic year 1919. While rarely displaying any sympathy for the dilemmas or the desperate plight of the Bolsheviks, he also does not spare the tergiversations of the Allies or the hysteria of parliamentary and public opinion, often deliberately whipped up by official propaganda. The author must have ploughed through a formidable mass of official paper; he has reduced it to order, and presented a coherent and convincing account of what the Allied statesmen did, or thought they were doing, about the Russian question. The picture is clear, even if its theme often seems an almost total muddle. Mr. Ullman has produced a model piece of research, and all who seek in the future to investigate this thorny subject will profit by it.

The reservations which suggest themselves are for the most part not peculiar to Mr. Ullman, but are inherent in the nature of the work; and, since the opening of the archives is likely to provoke in the near future a spate of books based on a similarly detailed examination of similar official documents, it may be timely to take a look—using *Britain and the Russian Civil War* not merely as the first but as an outstanding example of its kind—at the sort of history which research into such documents is likely to produce. Off-the-cuff remarks of statesmen in close argument with their colleagues, without thought of publicity then or later, are often revealing and valuable to the historian. But they are also—since statesmen are human—often silly and ill-judged, and can easily mislead if taken too seriously. Impromptu remarks are not always wiser, or even more sincere, than considered statements. History which uses them extensively has its pitfalls as well as its advantages.

Both are traceable in Mr. Ullmann's book. One of its most fascinating features is the clarity with which the differing tempera-ments and points of view of the British *dramatis personae* emerge from his skilful treatment. Lloyd George was incomparably the quickest-witted and most perceptive of the group. About the essentials of the Russian problem he was far more often right than wrong—which is more than can be said of almost any other of the statesmen in Paris. But he knew and cared little about foreign affairs, except in so far as they impinged on the domestic political scene. His power was limited—his personal authority was probably never so great or so uncontested as Churchill's towards the end of the Second World War; and, when he had to compromise, he would always yield a point of foreign policy in order to secure what he judged essential on the home front. Hence his influence on policy towards Russia was spasmodic, and he sometimes accepted or sponsored decisions in which he did not believe. This made his attitude, as Mr. Ullmann says at one point, seem "less than straightforward".

Churchill remained wholly committed to the traditional past. Alone among the British delegates, he would have liked to see the old Russian empire reconstituted, and had little or no sympathy for the breakaway aspirations of the national minorities. He listened with a sympathy and patience felt by few to the numerous groups of Russian émigrés thronging the Allied capitals; he even fell for the ex-Social Revolutionary terrorist, Savinkov. Curzon, who was not in Paris but reigned *pro tem* in the Foreign Office in London, was fundamentally more at odds with Churchill than with Lloyd George. He detested and distrusted all Russians, Red or White, and had no use for Churchillian schemes of campaigns in Europe. But he wanted a screen of British troops in Transcaucasia or Central Asia as a safeguard against Russian incursions into the British imperial preserves of Persia and Afghanistan. Balfour remained aloof, and used his wit, his charm, and his outstanding intelligence to pick holes impartially both in the arguments in favour of action and in the arguments against it, so that his ideal goal was usually to reach no conclusion at all.

History seen, thanks to the documents, through the eyes of these and of a number of minor figures, tends to become personalized in a way we had begun to think of as old-fashioned. We are tempted, almost invited, to think of decisions taken in Paris about Russia as the product of a personal duel between Lloyd George and Churchill; and this impression may well be enhanced when we are allowed to see the still unpublished correspondence between the two statesmen. The documents, these documents at any rate, not only give no indication of the deeper forces at work which produced these confusions and these compromises, they positively obscure them: and these are the factors with which the historian is ultimately most concerned—the clash between the illusion of omnipotence commonly nourished by the victors in a great war and the reluctance of war-weary populations to engage in fresh exertions, the clash between traditional British views of European monarchy or the British Empire and a new social outlook which Lloyd George, alone of the British delegates, dimly apprehended, the clash between underlying reactions to the Russian Revolution.

A minor pitfall for users of these documents is revealed by Mr. Ullman's book, and is likely to become more apparent as the documents are more widely, and perhaps less discriminately, used. It is well known that the documents contain not only letters, notes and memoranda in finished, and sometimes also in draft, form, but "minutes" written by junior and senior departmental officials. Some of these were merely brief indications of the action required on a particular paper; but many raised, implicitly or explicitly, major issues of policy. Most of them were written within hours, if not minutes, of the paper reaching the official's desk, and could at best be regarded as first impressions, not as considered pronouncements. Foreign office officials were especially prolific in the output of such "minutes", whether because they were more articulate than members of other departments, or because the elaborate Foreign Office filing system provided for every paper received a separate "jacket" which offered ample space, and set the tradition, for copious "minutes".

Mr. Ullman quotes many of these F. O. minutes, often by quite junior officials. But, among the mass of War Office documents which he uses, no corresponding minutes appear to have been found; and there were, of course, no junior officials to write minutes on Cabinet papers. The very nature of the documentation means, therefore, that Foreign Office opinion is heavily over-represented; and this, while it might be less detrimental in other contexts, is particularly unfortunate for Mr. Ullman's purposes. For, while the Staff Officers, senior and Junior, in the War Office and in the military delegation at the Paris conference were in the main sympathetic to Churchill's views on the Russian question and may have helped to frame them—a point about which no information is given—the Foreign office delegation in Paris remained, so far as the Russian question was concerned, entirely on the side-lines and played no part at all in decision-taking.

It was perhaps nobody's fault. The Foreign Office delegation was headed, naturally enough, by the Permanent Under-Secretary, Hardinge. But an ex-Viceroy of India and protégé of Edward VII was hardly the right person to engage in the rough-and-tumble of policy-making under a dynamic Prime Minister. Hardinge lacked altogether the adaptability, the technical competence, the patience and the devotion which Hankey so abundantly displayed; and, for anything that he did, he might just as well not have come to Paris. The other leading members of the Foreign Office delegation frankly distrusted and detested Lloyd George, and he despised or ignored them. In matters in which specialist knowledge was required, and in which Lloyd George took no personal interest—and this covered most of the territorial settlements all over Europe—the Foreign Office delegation played an active and effective part. But, when major decisions of policy were taken, as for instance in the Russian question, it was seldom consulted and not always even informed. Foreign Office correspondence of July, 1919, shows that in that month there was no record of the Bullitt mission of March, 1919, in the F. O. files, either in Paris or in London. In the near future, more and more research workers will decipher more and more minutes in official files. The circumstances in which they were written and the authority behind them should be carefully weighed. All documents are important for the historian: but not all documents are equal.

Britain and the Russian Civil War naturally challenges comparison with Professor Arno J. Mayer's *Politics and Diplomacy of Peacemaking*, which was published last year and indeed appears to confirm the view recorded there of the overwhelming importance of the Russian question in the deliberations of the Paris conference. Rather oddly, Mr. Ullman takes issue with this view and finds it "ultimately misleading", since the problem of French security against Germany "cannot be satisfactorily explained in these terms" and was "at least as important as that of Russia and Bolshevism".

It may be suggested that the two authors are writing at different levels which really do not clash. In the day-to-day exchanges of the conference the two questions represented different items of the agenda. Mr. Ullman can tell his story with barely a reference to the Franco-German problem. French security was an issue in its own right, though after the Fontainebleau memorandum in March it became increasingly difficult to keep Russia and Bolshevism out of the picture; more words may have been spoken and written about it than about any other item. But Professor Mayer is less concerned to describe what happened between the delegates at Paris than to analyse the pressures, including the pressures of domestic politics, which determined their attitudes; and Mr. Ullman's account complements and reinforces, and certainly does not contradict, this analysis.

The Russian question divided even the French delegation in its attitude towards security against Germany. There were those who, like Churchill, would have liked to rebuild the old Russia as a bulwark in the east; there were those who pinned their faith on a *cordon sanitaire* of smaller states, grouped around Poland and the Little Entente, drawn between Germany and Russia. On the whole, the first solution seemed more desirable, the second more practicable. The British and the Americans were, for the most part, sceptical of both solutions. They thought less in terms of balance of power politics, and more in terms of building up a stable Europe as a barrier against Bolshevism. This meant a stable Germany; and stability in Germany required, though an excited public opinion made this difficult to admit, some relaxation in the penal conditions imposed on Germany by the victorious Powers. From this dilemma the peace-makers at Versailles never escaped: it continued to dog Allied policy for many years after.

It has become a commonplace to say that the peace settlement of 1919 settled nothing and sowed the seeds of all the confusions and errors in Allied policies in Europe for the inter-war period. This is notoriously true in regard to Germany. Allied support of the Russian Whites against the Bolsheviks in the Civil War also set a pattern which proved extraordinarily difficult to break. As has recently been remarked, the Cold War began the moment the hot war stopped, and has gone on, with brief interruptions and relaxations, ever since. The device of playing on western fears of Bolshevism, skilfully exploited by Hitler in the 1930s, was already being used by the German negotiators in 1919; indeed, the British and Americans may almost be said to have invented it for them. As late as 1939, the British faced the dilemma which had confronted the French seekers for security in 1919—whether to invoke Russia or the border states of Poland and Rumania as the counterweight to Germany; and once again fear of Bolshevism was one, at any rate, of the factors in the decision. Mr. Ullman's book, though limited to the narrow field of British diplomacy in 1919, is a valuable contribution to many larger problems.

II

The Anglo-Soviet Accord is the last volume of Richard H. Ullman's magnificient historical trilogy on British policy towards Bolshevik Russia from its beginning in 1917 to the conclusion of the first Anglo-Soviet agreement in March 1921.[2] This volume, which covers the period of one year and one month after the effective ending of the civil war proper in February 1920, relies mainly like its

[2] Richard H. Ullman, *The Anglo-Soviet Accord* (Princeton: Princeton University Press).

predecessors on British documents and memoirs, the available quantity of which has vastly increased while Mr Ullman has been at work. He is now able to record the verdict that only one important collection of papers—the Churchill archive—is still withheld from the historian, and that most of the correspondence in that collection likely to be relevant to the theme is already available in other sources.

The period under review was still dominated by the personality of Lloyd George, who was more often right in his conclusions than in his facts, and whose devious diplomacy often looked in retrospect like the only way to achieve important results in adverse conditions. It was Lloyd George who from the end of 1919, when the bankruptcy of the policy of military intervention was clearly apparent, harped on trade as the key to the Russian problem—and incidentally as a shot in the arm for the injured and faltering British economy. From January 1920, when he first raised the question formally with Allied Supreme Council in Paris, he worked untiringly for a trade agreement, which, as he perfectly well knew, had also political implications, with Soviet Russia. The interval before he finally reached his goal was full of astonishing diplomatic and military episodes and reversals of fortune, which are the subject of this book.

The major barrier in the path of Lloyd George's plan of accommodation with Soviet Russia was Poland. Lloyd George, with his uncanny perception of underlying realities, had long ago sensed that the Poles, with their romantic memory of past glories, with their record of suffering and injustice, and with their boundless ambitions, were an awkward obstacle to any stable settlement in Eastern Europe. In the negotiations for the Versailles Treaty, he had approached Polish claims with obvious distaste and without much understanding. But nobody had foreseen what would happen in the summer of 1920. During the previous winter Pilsudski had kept Polish-Soviet relations simmering, with frontier incidents interrupted by peace negotiations, but showed no signs of serious military activity. Pilsudski liked no Russian Government. But Kolchak or Denikin, once installed in Moscow where they might have enjoyed Western favour and support, would have been a greater menace to Poland than Lenin and Trotsky. So long as the Red Army was still wrestling with Denikin's offensive, Pilsudski held his hand.

It was only when the "Whites" had been decisively defeated, and the pressure on Moscow removed (Wrangel's last flicker of resistance in the South was never serious), that Pilsudski set out to realize a long-standing national dream. Early in May 1920, Polish armies marched into the Ukraine and occupied its capital, Kiev, in preparation for the creation of a nominally independent puppet state in the Ukraine where Polish princes had once ruled. In Western Europe, right-wing opinion, and nearly all French opinion, enthusiastically welcomed the advance, and was buoyed up by the hope that, where Allied intervention had failed. Pilsudski might succeed. In Great Britain, when the campaign broke in on the first stubborn stage of Lloyd George's negotiations with Krasin, the Soviet envoy, liberal and radical opinion was shocked by so blatant an act of aggression; and the dockers, led by Ernest Bevin, threatened direct action, and refused to load munitions for Poland to mount a capitalist assault on revolutionary Russia. Lloyd George temporized. If nothing was done to help the Poles, nothing would be done to hinder them.

The bold enterprise miscarried. The Polish occupation of the Ukraine lasted only a matter of weeks. In June and July the Red Army was driving them in hot pursuit back into Poland, and early in August had reached the outskirts of Warsaw, apparently poised for an assault on the capital. These events faced Lloyd George with an appalling dilemma. The French Government, and the right wing in Great Britain, clamoured for action to save Poland, without being at all clear what action was possible. Nobody, French or British, was seriously prepared to send troops. The sending of munitions was a limited resource, and in any case provoked the implacable hostility of the trade unions and the Labour movement. Meanwhile the confrontation with the Russians was now entirely and inevitably political. Krasin was back in London reinforced by Kamenev. The question was what terms the Russians could be induced to offer the Poles, and what terms the Poles could be induced to accept.

The hurly-burly of these negotiations provides the central and most fascinating section of Ullman's book. Charges of bad faith flew in all directions. The so-called "Curzon Line" established in the Allied discussions in Paris in 1919 had not extended to East Galicia. Perhaps inadvertently, perhaps through the need for some common-sense solution to fill the gap, the line quite independently proposed by the Supreme Council as the western boundary of a hypothetical autonomous East Galicia was now silently tacked on to it. The terms of peace with Poland which Kamenev announced in London did not exactly correspond with those offered to the Poles on the spot. It did not seem anomalous in Moscow to assume that the independence of Poland would be defended not by Pilsudski's army, but by a "militia of workers"; in London the anomaly seemed to make all the difference. If Kamenev was willing to deceive, Lloyd George was probably not unwilling to be deceived. He wanted only to get this troublesome Polish question settled somehow or other, in order to get back to sensible discussions with the Russians on things that really mattered.

An unexpected dénouement rescued him from his dilemma. In the middle of August, when the fall of Warsaw seemed imminent, Pilsudski—encouraged perhaps by the arrival of an Anglo-French military mission which included Weygand, Foch's chief of staff—launched a successful counter-offensive. The roles were reversed; and the Polish Army was soon driving the Red Army back over the way by which it had come. The British and French Governments could now sit back contentedly, and let things take their course. Kamenev was told to go home. It was not till the beginning of October that the Russians accepted the inevitable, and came to terms. The agreed Soviet–Polish frontier was some 200 kilometres east of the old Curzon Line—a piece of greed which caused much grief to the Poles twenty years later.

One fascinating point about this book is that, while still based primarily on British documents, it does, unlike its two predecessors, illuminate Soviet policy and the conditions in which it was formed. This is partly because Soviet Russia, having emerged victorious from the civil war, was now strong enough to have a policy of its own, and was no longer simply reacting to blows showered on it from the outside world, but partly also because Mr Ullman has found in the Lloyd George and Davidson papers (Davidson was Bonar Law's private secretary at that time) transcripts of the telegrams exchanged between Moscow and London in the summer of 1920, which were successfully decoded by the British experts. It must be said that, once removed from the exciting atmosphere of espionage, the content of these messages for all the efforts of the British secret service to inflate their importance, does not add up to anything very sensational. But, combined with documents already published from the Soviet archives, and occasional material from the Trotsky archives, they do illuminate the processes of policy-making in Moscow at a crucial moment.

What emerges is the opposite of the familiar stereotype of Trotsky as the dogmatic revolutionary and Lenin as the practical statesman. Throughout the summer of 1920 it was Trotsky who preached a policy of caution and feeling one's way, Lenin who wanted direct action and no compromise. Trotsky, in a memorandum of June 1920, argued that there was "by no means absolutely one line" in British policy, and that it was possible and desirable by concilatory speech and action to strengthen the hands of those British ministers who sought a rapprochement with the Soviet regime. Lenin overruled this view as "hopeless". Great Britain was helping, and would help, both the Poles and Wrangel. "There is", wrote Lenin with emphasis, "*absolutely only one line.*" And a message was sent to Krasin, duly unravelled by the British code-breakers: "The rascally Lloyd George (the British translated it "that swine Lloyd George") is gulling you godlessly and shamelessly; don't believe a word, and gull him three times as much."

Among leading figures in Moscow, Chicherin was Lenin's most wholehearted supporter; it may indeed have been primarily on his advice that Lenin relied at this decisive moment. Chicherin, like his father before him, had been trained in the Tsarist diplomatic service. This, rather than the shabby treatment he received at the hands of the British Government in 1918, may help to explain his anti-British attitude throughout the 1920s. He, too, now warned the Soviet negotiators not to become "the victims of deceit". When the Red Army was already marching into Poland, Trotsky once more advised acceptance of British mediation to bring about peace. Poland was, after all, an independent state "on whose inviolability we have never made an attempt". Lenin, convinced that, given a minimum of encouragement, the Polish revolution was imminent, pressed on with the advance. It was, perhaps, his greatest, and most uncharacteristic, error.

Once peace was made, without British assistance, between Soviet Russia and Poland, the great obstacle was removed and Lloyd George could resume negotiations with Krasin. A Cabinet meeting on November 18, 1920, authorized him to proceed; according to the records, Curzon, Churchill and Milner formally dissented, and some other Conservatives grumbled. Innumerable minor difficulties had to be resolved, and there was some dragging of feet by those who still hoped to block the agreement. The signature of the agreement in March 1921, coincided with the Kronstadt Rising; it was suggested from the Foreign Office that it might be wise to postpone signature till the outcome of the rising was known.

There is much else of interest in Mr Ullman's book, notably two chapters, once more heavily indebted to the opening of the British archives, on the unwinding of the British–Soviet involvement in the Caucasus and in Persia. But the general reader will find more in the final chapter entitled "Russia, Bolshevism and the Statecraft of David Lloyd George". This contains one of the fairest assessments yet penned of Lloyd George's stature and achievement, seen through independent American eyes. Lloyd George was the prisoner of the coalition formed for the purpose of winning the war. He had split the Liberals; his relations with Labour were his weakest point; and he depended on predominantly Conservative support. For the period of nearly five years during which he remained as Prime Minister after the war he was, broadly speaking, engaged in promoting policies which were actively disliked, or accepted reluctantly, by a majority of his supporters.

This was the essential nature of the prestigious balancing act which he was constantly obliged to perform. Mr Ullman quotes one of A. J. P. Taylor's penetrating epigrams:

He did not browbeat his followers. Instead he led them with much blowing of trumpets in one direction until the moment when they discovered that he had brought them to an exactly opposite conclusion.

Finally the conjurer could produce the illusion no more. Lloyd George went, amid the resentment of those who felt themselves to have been bamboozled. But in the meantime much vital clearing up had been done.

The question whether "such subterfuge" was necessary is raised by Mr Ullman and answered rather indecisively. Implicit in his answer—it could have been made more explicit—is the recognition that Lloyd George was the victim, not only of the domestic political situation, and perhaps of his own temperament, but also of the need to adapt to a totally changed configuration of world forces. Nobody could admit, or even understand, that, after four years of blood and sacrifice ending in a dramatic victory, the result of the war had been the destruction of British supremacy in the world. Most Conservatives wanted to fight the Bolsheviks in Europe; Curzon wanted to fight them in Asia.

The War Office knew that it had no troops, but somehow hoped that somebody else would do the actual fighting. The Foreign Office wobbled and waffled. Only Lloyd George saw clearly that it could not be done, and drew the inevitable conclusion. But he also saw that, in order to reach the conclusion, he must conceal the premise from his constituents.

Should one pass a censorious verdict? Or is this just politics? After all, Churchill, contrasted with Lloyd George both in background and in temperament, but with far less acute perceptions, followed the same path a quarter of a century later. Amid much blowing of trumpets about the British Empire, he paved the way for its dissolution.

5 The German General Staff

In his introduction to *The Nemesis of Power*,[1] Mr. Wheeler-Bennett makes no bones about the moral which he seeks to draw from his study of "the German army in politics" between the debacle of 1918 and the catastrophe of 1945. He begins with the famous quotation from Mirabeau: "La Prusse n'est pas un pays qui a une armée, c'est une armée qui a un pays." He recalls that, since these words were written, German armies have sustained three crushing defeats in war, after each of which "the victors were outwitted to their subsequent detriment", and concludes that "no country has displayed a more phenomenal capacity for military resilience or for beating ploughshares into swords". After these trenchant judgments, he pronounces the rather lame and impotent verdict that the policy of encouraging the rebirth and rearmament of the German army "is essentially the only one to follow under the exigencies of present conditions", hoping rather than believing that "the infection of the virus of the *furor Teutonicus* may at last be eradicated from the body politic of Germany". The book, in short, does not prescribe what we should do, but warns us what to expect on the rather despairing hypothesis that the warning may help us to avert it.

This introductory plugging of a political moral, especially since the author seems to feel so uncertain of his own conclusion, does something less than justice to the book. *The Nemesis of Power* is not a popular tract for the times; nor, on the other hand, is it a profound political or social analysis of the forces which have given the German army its peculiar position in Germany, and which may or may not continue to dominate the German future as they have dominated the past for the best part of 100 years. Mr. Wheeler-Bennett's most outstanding qualities are not those of a historian, but

[1] John Wheeler-Bennett, *The Nemesis of Power. The German Army in Politics, 1918–1945* (London: Macmillan).

41

of a first-rate writer of memoirs. What he has given us is a brilliant portrait-gallery of the German generals who strutted across the stage in the quarter of a century after the downfall of 1918, and a vivid and lucid account of the successive episodes—many of them crucial episodes in German, or even in European, history—in which they appeared. Mr. Wheeler-Bennett has known personally many of the generals of whom he writes and many of the leading figures in German political life during the Weimar republic. He has his strong personal feelings about them, which colour the narrative and give life to it. There is no nonsense about being fair to those whom he dislikes (most of all, Schleicher) or seeing the warts on the faces of those whom he likes (for example, Brüning and Groener). The constant emotional tension, combined with a crisp and pungent style, makes the whole story not merely readable, but fascinating. This is a noteworthy book.

Much of the story has become familiar, but even those parts which have been told most often were worth telling again. The first task of the German General Staff after November, 1918, was to restore order and to restore its own authority. The two operations were indistinguishable in the minds of the German military leaders, notably in that of General Hans von Seeckt; and, since it was the generals who carried them out, their interpretation prevailed. The hapless and innocent leaders of the German Social-Democratic Party were caught in a dilemma which they realized in practice without fully understanding it. If they were to resist the Communists, they must obey the soldiers: instinctively they chose this alternative as the lesser evil. The far-sighted genius of General von Seeckt was proved by a single brilliant intuition which made him the arbiter of the foreign policy, as well as of the domestic policy, of the Weimar republic. Almost alone at first, he rejected the grandiloquent absurdities of the "anti-Bolshevist crusade", and perceived that it was perfectly possible at one and the same time to repress Communists at home and to establish a working alliance with the Soviet Russian Government which would pave the way for a restoration of Germany's military power. Though Mr. Wheeler-Bennett sometimes seems to go rather far in praising Seeckt in order the more effectively to damn Schleicher, and exaggerates the change in the role of the Reichswehr after Seeckt's resignation in the autumn of 1926, it must be admitted that few men of the period saw so clearly, and acted so consistently within the limits of the goal that they had set themselves, as Hans von Seeckt.

After depicting the rise of the Reichswehr to power under Seeckt, Mr. Wheeler-Bennett turns back to examine the early years of National Socialism and its first relations with the military power, succeeding best where the *dramatis personae*—as with Hitler and Ludendorff—stand out in highest relief: nothing could be better than the description of the *"Bierkeller" Putsch* and its sequel. He traces, rather than explains, the gradual strengthening of the hold of the Nazis on the Reichswehr at the end of the 1920s—which was, after all, a reflection of rising Nazi influence in almost every field of German life. It is at the end of the "Schleicher period" that the process of demoralization is completed, and that the army can be sufficiently softened up to accept Hitler's political supremacy and, eventually, its own *Gleichschaltung* into the coils of the all-mastering Nazi machine.

Mr. Wheeler-Bennett's long last chapter is devoted to the conspiracy of July 20, 1944—that feeble and ill-starred plot to assassinate Hitler when the war was already lost, which has been so much over-exploited in the interests of the myth of German resistance. The author has taken immense pains to collect every available scrap of evidence, written or oral, and provides by far the best account of the affair yet published in English—or probably in any other language. It is a record of timidity, bungling and almost incredible inefficiency—with the two principal conspirators dashing in their car to the aerodrome and flying to Berlin without waiting to verify that Hitler had in fact been killed when the bomb exploded. Even the hideous tortures afterwards suffered by some of the participants almost fail to add a note of heroism to so essentially sordid an adventure. But this should perhaps have made another book. For what clearly transpires is that the original begetters of the conspiracy and the few sincere enemies of the régime—the only men whose fate really moves us to pity and terror—were the civilians. The soldiers were concerned only to avenge themselves on Hitler for having brought the army to defeat, and to save what could still be saved—their hopes were probably much exaggerated—from the wreck. This is not so much the story of the failure of the German army—that was a foregone conclusion—but of the failure of the German body politic to produce more than a tiny handful of devoted men who, even in this last hour, were prepared to strike against the main author of Germany's shame.

In so rich and varied a narration, detailed points here and there may provoke doubt or disagreement. Why was the unconstitutional overthrow of the Saxon Government in October, 1923, by military action, because it contained three legally appointed Communist ministers, "a commendable display of forceful action"? Was this not merely one example of the habitual and reckless overriding of the constitution by the soldiers which Mr. Wheeler-Bennett elsewhere so roundly condemns? Is there really any ground for describing Maltzan as "oriental", "not quite European" and "un-Germanic"? It is true that he strongly supported the Rapallo policy. But so did many, indeed most, good Germans; and Maltzan afterwards made a quite successful German Ambassador in Washington. The sources quoted for an alleged offer by Seeckt in the summer of 1920 "for cooperation between the *Reichswehr* and the Red Army 'against Versailles' " are dubious.

More serious, the reader may feel that the author makes unnecessarily heavy weather over Stresemann. While he does not appear to have examined the unpublished Stresemann papers, he rightly assumes Stresemann's full knowledge of the secret military arrangements with Soviet Russia to evade the military prohibitions of the Versailles treaty. Stresemann doubtless did not concern himself with the details, may even have preferred not to know too much about them, and was prepared to lie about them when necessary in public or to his diplomatic opposite numbers. But what Foreign Secretary takes, or can take, any other attitude towards the operations of secret departments of his own Government? And if the sentimental adjudicators on the Nobel Committee offered Stresemann the Nobel Peace Prize for bringing Germany into the League of Nations, is it seriously suggested that he ought to have refused? Stresemann's perfectly clear and straightforward position as a German patriot anxious to make the best of both eastern and western worlds for his country appears to present a moral problem only because of the highly unrealistic view of his policy taken at the time in western countries. This view still persists in unexpected places. Only a few months ago an article in the *Deutsche Rundschau* sought to exculpate Stresemann from complicity in "Seeckt's private foreign policy" towards Soviet Russia. It came from the pen of Stresemann's former secretary, who prepared three volumes of

Stresemann papers for publication in the early 1930s, and was evidently unaware that other parts of the Stresemann archives have survived to tell a different tale.

What, however, one most misses in Mr. Wheeler-Bennett's memorable book is something which he has not professed to undertake—historical design as opposed to the supply of historical material. It will strike many readers that, while the sub-title of the work is "The German Army in Politics", Mr. Wheeler-Bennett has from first to last virtually nothing to say about the German army as such. This is a book about the German generals or, more specifically, about the German General Staff. For the Weimar period, this is perhaps a distinction without substantial difference. Trotsky in a moment of elation once based his hope of a successful Communist *coup* in Germany on the hypothesis that the rank and file of the Reichswehr consisted of "working-class elements who will not defend the bourgeoisie very stoutly." He was doubtless thinking in terms of the pre-war German army. Even so, the hope might well have proved illusory; but, applied to the Weimar Reichswehr, it was fantastic. Formed under the distorting pressure of the Versailles limitations of numbers and insistence on voluntary recruitment, the Reichswehr of the 1920s was a peculiar army. It consisted of an officer corps and of "other ranks," of whom nearly half were former non-commissioned officers. It was an army of *cadres*, which in the meanwhile made an admirably efficient police force. The auxiliaries on whom the Reichswehr relied in case of emergency—the so-called "black Reichswehr"—were professional soldiers, professional adventurers and rabid nationalists. Divorced from the workers, divorced from the masses of ordinary people, it was a perfect instrument in the hands of a military clique. It was no empty boast when Seeckt told Ebert in 1920 that the Reichswehr would be loyal to him.

In the Nazi period, and particularly after the return to conscription, these conditions no longer held good. The Reichswehr of the 1930s was no longer, like that of the 1920s, a private army of the German generals; its loyalties were divided between its commanders and Hitler, with the latter predominating. And this helps to explain one of the paradoxes which Mr. Wheeler-Bennett brings out very clearly, but does not pause to discuss—why the political role of the army was so much greater under the Weimar republic than under Hitler. In this sense it is quite erroneous to describe

Seeckt's Reichswehr as "non-political": it was a superb and highly
serviceable political instrument in the hand of its masters. Hitler, by
creating a mass army, took it away from the generals and made it,
what it never had been under the Weimar republic, a "non-
political" servant of the régime.

But there was surely also another explanation of the paradox; and
here, too, Mr. Wheeler-Bennett provides facts pointing the way to a
conclusion which he does not himself reach. Neither the Weimar
Reichswehr nor its policy can be understood without reference to its
alliance with heavy industry. Hugo Stinnes, the friend of both
Seeckt and Stresemann, whom Mr. Wheeler-Bennett scarcely
mentions, was a powerful influence and a symbolical figure of the
early Weimar period. The blows which Versailles had dealt to the
German army were comparable only to those inflicted on German
iron and steel production. The victims were mutually dependent on
one another and could hope to rise again only if they acted together.
Since Soviet Russia offered the only hope of a revival of German
armament and the only potential market for German heavy
industry, deprived of its pre-war outlets at home and in the west, the
Soviet orientation of the Reichswehr and of heavy industry was not
difficult to understand. Whether under the Weimar republic the
Reichswehr dominated German industry, or was dependent on the
power and influence of the German industrialists, is perhaps a
superfluous question; the two worked harmoniously hand in hand
for what they saw as the greater glory of Germany.

Mr. Wheeler-Bennett has emphasized not for the first time, the vital
part played by German Industry, with Papen as its confidential
agent, in bringing Hitler into power. But he has also shown that one
of the elements in Schleicher's downfall was the disapproval of the
industrialists. Schleicher, a more romantic figure than Seeckt, had
always toyed vaguely with social policies: he liked to pose as an up-
to-date politician who understood the importance of appealing to
the masses. During his brief Chancellorship he made a much quoted
broadcast speech in which he declared his impartiality between
capital and labour and spoke with sympathy of economic planning;
and this attitude may well have contributed more to his ruin than
his much more notorious attempt to drag the rapacity of the Junkers
and the scandals of the *Osthilfe* into the light of day. It is not always a
man's worst actions which call down nemesis on his head.

It was a fortnight after this speech that the bargain between

Hitler and the industrialists was sealed by Papen in Schröder's house in Cologne. This has commonly been recognized as the decisive moment in Hitler's ascent to the throne. It has not always been so clearly understood that what Hitler had done was to outbid the Reichswehr for the support of industry, and that it was this which not only gave him the Chancellorship but enabled him to bring the proud German General Staff to heel with an ease and rapidity which astonished the world. The army, isolated and encircled by the new symbols of Nazi ascendancy, was transformed from a political power into a technical instrument. As an instrument it retained all its old efficiency. But it never again functioned as a power in its own right. The story of the relations of the German generals to successive German political leaders from 1918 to 1945 is varied, dramatic and instructive; and Mr. Wheeler-Bennett has told it superbly. The work which he has done in this field need never be done again; and it is hardly likely that future revelations will add much of value to his careful researches. But it is also true that the story of the German generals is not the history of the German army, and that that history cannot be understood without analysis of the relations of the army with other elements in German society. That is still a task for the historian —as well as for any one who seeks to assess the consequences of the future revival of a German army and a German armaments industry. The rehabilitation of Herr Krupp may yet turn out to be an important date in history.

Part II Essays in Russian History

6 The Pan-Slav Tradition

It is sometimes forgotten nowadays how deeply rooted the revolutionary tradition was in Russian thought long before Marxism had penetrated into Russia and even before Marx had completed the elaboration of his doctrines in the West. While Russia was almost the only country on the continent of Europe which remained in the 80 years from 1825 to 1905 untouched by the practice of revolution, no leading Russian thinker or writer of that time wholly escaped the revolutionary ferment, and many of them were to seek in the idea of revolution the main source of their inspiration. The so-called "Decembrist" insurrection of 1825, pitiable fiasco though it was, set in motion a process of intellectual revolt which found its first coherent expression in Belinsky and the "men of the forties", and in the hands of the men of the sixties and seventies began to crystallize into a revolutionary programme and a revolutionary party. These foundations had already been laid when Marx first became known in the Russia of the seventies, when Russian Marxist groups were formed in the eighties, and when, in the last decade of the century, Marx became a powerful motive force in the Russian radical movement.

In this native Russian revolutionary tradition of the nineteenth century the central place is beyond dispute occupied by the massive figure of Michael Bakunin. Pestel, the most important of the Decembrists, may have been more original; Belinsky was certainly a more profound, and Herzen a more versatile, thinker; Chernyshevsky came nearer than any pre-Marxist Russian writer to anticipating the doctrines which the Russian revolution was one day to make its own; Nechaev did more than anyone to create the tradition of individual terrorism in which this initial Russian revolutionary impulse finally petered out. But it is Bakunin who through his dramatic personality and experience and his intense though dispersed and often misguided activity, touches, reflects and sometimes deflects Russian revolutionary thought at almost every point.

Since the victory of the Bolshevik revolution Bakunin has always been a dubious and embarrassing historical figure in Russia itself. An uninspired and uninspiring biography by Steklov, useful as a collection of material rather than for any freshness of interpretation, appeared in Russian in the 1920s. But a collection of Bakunin's writings and letters, started in the early 1930s, was discontinued after the publication of the first four volumes; and interest in this greatest of all Russian revolutionaries before Lenin seems for the moment to be completely extinct in his own country. It is therefore encouraging to note a revival of interest in Bakunin abroad, and especially in France, where the latest contribution to Bakunin studies is a volume of essays by M. Benoit-P. Hepner under the title *Bakounine et le Panslavisme Révolutionnaire*.[1]

Bakunin is a many-sided phenomenon and could be studied in many aspects and from many points of view. He is—rightly, on the whole—regarded as the father of anarchism; for William Godwin, to whom the title is sometimes awarded, never left the plane of abstract theory, and the anarchism of Proudhon took on the special concrete mould of syndicalism and exercised a lasting influence on French politics and French thought mainly in that guise. Bakunin was the apostle of liberty in its absolute form—a liberty which, as M. Hepner remarks, had nothing in common with Hegel's conception of liberty realizing itself in the State. Yet Bakunin, on the strength of his emphasis on propaganda by deed and of his willingness to appeal to the "evil passions", has often been convicted of an affinity with the movements which ultimately issued in Fascism. He was always ready to subordinate theory to the spontaneous character of the revolutionary impulse; in this respect he was a revolutionary empiricist and stood at the opposite pole to Marx. When Lenin in 1917 announced that, in spite of the rudimentary progress made by the Russian bourgeois revolution, the socialist revolution was at hand, the Mensheviks—and some of his own followers—branded him as a disciple of Bakunin and not of Marx.

M. Hepner's learnedly discursive essays touch on many matters of interest to the student of revolution in nineteenth-century Europe; the first of them is devoted to the influence of French precept and

---

[1] Benoit-P. Hepner, *Bakounine et le Panslavisme Révolutionnaire* (Paris: Marcel Rivière).

practice on early Russian revolutionary thinkers, not leaving out of account the freemasons, the Rosicrucians and the "Martinists"—followers of Saint Martin, the first French theosophist. But he has devoted a large part of his attention to one aspect of Bakunin's work which is certainly not the least important—his cult of the Slavs and his belief in the solidarity and in the united mission of the Slav peoples. It is not surprising that this theme should now appear particularly topical. A French book by M. Albert Mousset designed to show that pan-Slav "solidarity" is no more than a tool of Russian policy has just been translated into English under the title *The World of the Slavs*.[2] It provides a useful recapitulation of the steps taken from Moscow during the war to organize and exploit Slav loyalties and Slav antipathies to the German aggressor; but its treatment of the historical background is cursory and not very profound. Here, M. Hepner is by far the sounder guide.

The essential feature of Bakunin's advocacy of the solidarity and brotherhood of the Slav peoples was its revolutionary basis. It would be madness, he told the Slav congress in Prague in 1848, "to expect help for the Slavs or their salvation from contemporary Russia". In his *Appeal to the Slavs*, which appeared a few months later, he ingeniously attempted to exculpate the Russian People from the charge of oppressing the sister Slav nations. The oppression was the work of Nicholas I, "a Holstein-Gottorp on a Slav throne, a tyrant of foreign origins". The liberation of the Slavs could come only through the liberation of the Russians themselves:

> It is at Moscow that the slavery of the peoples subjugated by the Russian sceptre and that of all the Slav peoples will be broken; it is there, too, that all European slavery will be buried in its own ruins. From the ocean of blood and fire there will arise at Moscow, high in the firmament, the star of revolution to become the guide of liberated humanity.

While it would be idle to minimize the gulf which separated Bakunin from the main apostles of the Slavophil movement in nineteenth-century Russia, Bakunin's "revolutionary pan-Slavism" was none the less a legitimate branch or variant of the Slavophil tradition, which itself had revolutionary origins and did

---

[2] Albert Mousset, *The World of the Slavs*. Published under the auspices of the London Institute of World Affairs (London: Stevens).

not acquire its orthodox and conservative colour till well after the middle of the century. Križanič, the seventeenth-century Croat priest, who generally passes as the progenitor of pan-Slavism, boldly predicted a future age of Slav culture and Slav predominance in Europe. But his main concern was with language and religion, and he played in Slav development somewhat the same role as Herder in the history of German nationalism.

It was the work of Napoleon to fan the flame both of German and of Russian nationalism. But Russian nationalism burned far less fiercely and devouringly than its German counterpart; and when it began to receive from the early Slavophils, Khomyakov and Kireevsky, its first extension to the Slav world, it still retained much of its cultural, religious and non-political character. It is not unfair to say that Bakunin was among the first to conceive Slavophil doctrines in a purely political context. The Slav peoples were to look to Moscow not only for enlightenment, but for liberation; and their liberation would and must be a product of the Russian revolution.

In Bakunin's own thought the transition was not difficult from the liberation of the Slavs by the process of a Russian revolution to a general championship by Russia of the Slav cause. As things stood in mid-nineteenth-century Europe, with nationalism as one of the main tenets of the radical and revolutionary programme, the most urgent and practical item on the agenda of the Slav peoples might well seem the liberation of those suffering under the yoke of German rule. In the events of 1848 in central Europe, the issue of Slav *v.* Teuton was never far beneath the surface. The Slav congress at prague was convened as a sort of counter-blast to the German national assembly at Frankfurt; the relations of the Slavs to the Habsburgs and to the lesser German States were the chief bone of contention at the congress. Meanwhile the Frankfurt assembly was facing, with more embarrassment than generosity, the awkward issue of Prussian Poland. The German revolution of 1848–49 left Bakunin, as well as many other observers, with a bitter conscious-ness both of the weakness of the German radical and revolutionary impulse and of the tenacious antagonism between Slav and German as a force in European politics.

It was this second factor which figured most prominently in the extraordinary "confession" which Bakunin wrote for Nicholas I in the Schlüsselburg prison in 1852—a document compounded of a strange blend of sincerity and calculation, in which the prisoner threw into relief those genuine elements of his variegated creed which were likely to appease and placate his imperial captor. Into this confession Bakunin poured all his enthusiasm for the Slavs and all his venom for the Germans, here depicted without too much straining of facts and probabilities as the principal enemies of the Slavs. He found among the Slavs "incomparably greater innate intelligence and energy than among the Germans". Moreover, "the predominant feeling of all Slavs is hatred of the Germans"; the phrase 'accursed German" was common to every Slav language and dialect. From this it was only a short step to invoke the might of Nicholas, as he had formerly invoked the power of the revolution, for the liberation of the Slav from the Teutonic yoke. Bakunin's *volte-face* was part monstrosity, part absurdity. Yet one hesitates to attribute it exclusively either to cunning calculation or to the unnerving and demoralizing effects of prolonged captivity when one remembers Proudhon's salute to the enlightened and progressive intentions of Napoleon III or Herzen's profoundly sincere acceptance of Alexander II, only a few years later, as the "Tsar liberator". Those who recoiled in disgust from the imperfections of western democracy often turned to strange allies in their pursuit of the path of liberation and revolution.

From the time of Bakunin's imprisonment and release and escape from Siberia, these pan-Slav and anti-German propensities remained deeply rooted in all his thought and writing. They played their part in his famous quarrel with Marx. Bakunin was the first to discover in Marx those supposedly Germanic or Prussian traits of rigid organization and authoritarian discipline which have often done duty since his time in critiques of the founder of "scientific" socialism. Bakunin himself was not above demanding blind obedience and discipline from the followers whom he enrolled in his fantastic and usually quite unreal secret revolutionary organizations. But in his less esoteric activities he preferred to dwell on the alleged Slav preference for living in loose voluntary "federations" of communes which were the condition of true political freedom, and to contrast this with the centralization and standardization which crushed individual initiative and was the typical expression of the Germanic spirit. But after his escape to western Europe there was no return to his momentary idealization of the liberating propensities of the Russian Tsars; he shared none of Herzen's short-lived enthusiasm for Alexander II. One of the last and most finished of his later political pamphlets bore a title which swept away both

Hohenzollerns and Romanovs in a single contemptuous gesture—
The Knouto-Germanic Empire.

What then remained in the end of Bakunin's "revolutionary pan-Slavism" was a contempt and hatred of all things German and a belief that the Slav peoples were destined in the immediate future to carry on the torch of civilization, which he identified with revolution—"Ex Slavia Lux", in the words of one of M. Hepner's chapter-headings. This was a long way from the later orthodox "pan-Slavism" which became a regular feature of Russian foreign policy from the 1870s onwards, reached heights of "jingoism" at the time of the Russo-Turkish War, and disfigured the political writings of Dostoevsky's last years. But both developed the same Slav messianism, the same element of racialism, the same appeal to national animosities; and both rested on the hypothesis, inseparable from any practical creed of pan-Slavism, of Russia's predestined leadership of the Slav peoples. Nor were these ideas in their modern guise altogether divorced from their religious origins, however little Bakunin himself may have cared to admit it. Enmity between eastern and western Europe reflected the old schism between Orthodoxy and Catholicism; when Bakunin accused Marx of imposing a rigid and lifeless discipline he echoed the charges which Dostoevsky, now or a little later, was hurling against the Catholic Church; and political pan-Slavism all too plainly harked back to the quasi-religious vision of Moscow as the third Rome, called by destiny to succeed and supersede the second Rome on the shores of the Bosporus.

Pan-Slavism is thus a coat of many colours and suitable for many kinds of political weather. The one climate to which it could not be readily adapted was that of Russian-German friendship; and so long as that policy prevailed, as it did till nearly the end of the nineteenth century, the Slavophils enjoyed only a precarious and rather lukewarm recognition in Russian official circles. But, as the rift with Germany opened more widely, the exaltation of Slav as against Teuton became a more and more current and popular theme. Such genuine sentiment as attended the outbreak of war in 1914 in Russia was inspired by the slogan of the defence of oppressed Slav Serbia against the hereditary German foe. The change in the name of the capital from Petersburg to Petrograd was symbolic of the rejection of the Germanic in favour of native Slav speech.

The Bolshevik revolution signalized the rejection as a matter of

course of anything that savoured so sharply of racialism, nationalism and even imperialism as the pan-Slav movement and
idea. Some Bolshevik purists even insisted on continuing to speak of
"Petersburg" by way of protest against the Slav sentimentalism of
"Petrograd". Nothing in early revolutionary programmes or
policies suggested any peculiar or exclusive affinity with the other
Slav peoples; all eyes were fixed on Germany, the most "advanced"
capitalist country in Europe, and the starting-point of the impending proletarian revolution in western Europe which alone could
save the revolutionary régime in Russia from being strangled by a
hostile capitalist world. Then, when this dream of European and
world-wide revolution faded out in the early 1920s, the policy of
Soviet-German friendship on a basis of common hostility to the
western Powers and to the Versailles Treaty took its place. Once
more there was no room for pan-Slav sympathies or aspirations. Nor
was the situation in the Slav world propitious. The Bolsheviks had
no more bitter enemies than the Pilsudski régime in Poland—from
the time of the Polish invasion of the Ukraine in 1920 to the time of
Beck's pact with Hitler in 1934; and Yugoslavia, under the
influence of its royal house, was one of the few European countries
which even in the 1930s still refused official recognition, and
diplomatic relations with, the Soviet Government.

The break between Hitler and Moscow in 1934 did not,
therefore, at once pave the way for a pan-Slav revival; and little was
done in the 1930s to emphasize the brotherhood of the Slav peoples
beyond a few cautious appeals, mostly from Litvinov, to Slav
solidarity between Russia and Czechoslovakia. It was only Hitler's
attack on Russia in 1941, following his absorption of almost all the
rest of the Slav peoples into his "new order" for Europe, which
brought back pan-Slavism to the historical stage. A certain distant
coincidence could even be traced between 1914 and 1941: it was
Hitler's overrunning of Yugoslavia in the spring of that year which
led to the first overt move of Soviet diplomacy against him in the
form of an agreement with the Yugoslav Government of resistance.
Once again, wittingly or unwittingly, Russia was courting war with
Germany in defence of a smaller Slav people. After the German
invasion of Russia the note of Slav solidarity was struck loudly and
repeatedly and became one of the most effective instruments of
Soviet propaganda—not least in the United States, the home of 15
million Slavs conscious and proud of their Slav origin.

The mobilization of the united Slav forces of eastern Europe under Russian leadership against Hitler during the war was, however, less successful and effective than their mobilization since 1945 as an outpost and bulwark against the potential encroachments of the western world. This last operation is the main theme of *The World of the Slavs*. As M. Mousset points out, an element of unreality enters into the conception of a Slav group in eastern Europe; for non-Slav Rumania is an uncontested member of the group, while the Yugoslav break-away is a serious derogation from Slav solidarity. This last state of affairs has, however, an interesting precedent. In the nineteenth century Poland, the second largest member of the Slav family, was always the recalcitrant member of the group, resenting the assumption by Russia of leadership over the Slav peoples as a whole. This tradition held good as late as the Second World War, when opposition to Russia among the Slavs was mainly represented by the "white" Poles. Now the situation has been reversed. Yugoslavia, as the result of her successes in the war and of Marshal Tito's outstanding personality, has taken the position of the second Slav nation and of the dissident in the Slav group, whereas Poland has receded into a position of less independence and authority and of greater fidelity to Russian leadership. But the tradition of a jealous and unruly second in the Slav family of nations has been precisely maintained.

The immense strength and predominance of Russia must always be the major, and to some extent distorting, factor in any attempt to realize pan-Slav aspirations and ambitions. On the one hand, the Slav world is and can be nothing without Russia; on the other hand, with Russia it must be always be, not a constellation of stars of like magnitude, but a planet with a group of satellites. But it would be a mistake to deduce from this that Slav solidarity is a myth, a convenient fiction to mask the domination and aggressive designs of Moscow. Western writers and western politicians, making the wish the father to the thought, have in the past few years tended to underestimate the natural pull exercised by Russia on the other Slav nations. Such miscalculations have their dangers. Even Czechoslovakia might have retained a larger measure of independence if western diplomacy, working through a group of westernized Czechs, had not been so eager to draw Czechoslovakia away from the eastern orbit; and too great success by the western Powers in wooing Marshal Tito's favours might easily threaten an upset of the delicate balance of forces in Yugoslavia.

Moreover, in spite of the vicissitudes of the last 50 years, certain aspects of Bakunin's "revolutionary pan-Slavism" still seem to retain their validity. The Slavophil movement of the last half of the nineteenth century was in turn cultural and political, but never social. Masaryk, when he argued that Slav liberation was found up with the cause of liberal democracy, had his eyes focused too narrowly on his own small country, where alone in the Slav world the western liberal tradition had stuck some roots. Paradoxically enough, it is Bakunin's notion, half abandoned by himself, that Slav solidarity would result from a social revolution kindled by Russia, which has come nearest to realization in the contemporary world. For what today, in addition to the military might and prestige of Russia, holds the Slav nations of eastern Europe together is the reality of an agrarian reform and a process of economic reconstruction which could not have been achieved without the impetus of Russian counsel and Russian pressure. The economic revolution in eastern Europe is certainly not the last chapter in the almost fantastically complex and incoherent story of the pan-Slav tradition.

7 Liberalism in Alien Soil

It has always seemed a puzzle, particularly to those who were impressed by the whole-hearted way in which Russia borrowed political ideas from the West, that there was never, at any rate before 1905, a serious liberal movement in Russia. Individuals called themselves liberals, or more often were called liberals by their opponents and critics; tendencies of thought were described as liberal. But there was no clearly identifiable liberal group in the sense in which the *narodniks*, the Social Revolutionaries and the Marxists formed groups. What had become, by the second half of the nineteenth century the prevailing ideology of western Europe and of the English-speaking world seemed to have passed Russia by. No Russian nineteenth-century writer of the first rank carried the liberal label; the one or two second-rank writers to whom it was sometimes affixed carried it in inverted commas.

Professor Fischer's new book on *Russian Liberalism*,[1] in spite of its comprehensive title, does not attempt to provide a direct answer to the puzzle. But, by offering an intensive study of Russian liberalism between 1861 and 1905, he suggests some of the material for an answer. The great reforms of the 1860s which included, besides the emancipation of the serfs, the beginnings of local self-government and the establishment of regular courts of law, had provided a soil in which liberal ideas might have been expected to grow and flourish. It did, in fact, enormously stimulate political thinking in Russia in the next forty years. But this thinking fell far more easily into a socialist or revolutionary than into a liberal mould. The liberalism of these years, which Professor Fischer so carefully analyses, was always at a low pitch. It was patient and sensible and honest. But the inspiration and driving force were elsewhere.

It is perhaps a pity that Professor Fischer should have been

---

[1] George Fischer, *Russian Liberalism* (Cambridge, Mass.: Harvard University Press; London: Oxford University Press).

content to start with 1861; for some of the traditions which then affected the movement went back much earlier. Russian liberalism, like Western liberalism, had its roots in the Enlightenment. Catherine the Great liked to pose as a liberal; Alaxander I in his earlier years was full of liberal professions. It is not enough to dismiss these as humbug or as idle dreams. What was intended was a rationalization of the autocracy. Liberalism was the rule of law—of law promulgated, of course, by the autocrat—instead of the rule of mere caprice. It was only in this sense that the constitution-making schemes of Speransky could be called liberal. Some of the leaders of the Decembrist rising of 1825 did not go much beyond this in their ideas; others seem to have thought more deeply. But they were all agreed—and this was their originality and their significance—that whatever was sought must be sought not through the autocracy, but against it. They introduced into Russian history the equation between reform and revolution, from which Russian society for the rest of the century could find no escape, and which proved fatal to liberalism in Russia in any western sense of the term.

The "liberal" reforms of the 1860s in Russia, unlike liberal reforms elsewhere, came from above not from below—from the will of the autocrat; and the movement which arose out of them receives from Professor Fischer the appropriate, though not particularly elegant, name of "gentry liberalism". (Professor Fischer is addicted to these ponderous composite labels, which are expressive enough for the initiated, but make for heavy reading; for example, he writes in one place of "non-political *Kulturträger* populism".) It was the small or relatively small landowners, the gentry rather than the great nobility, who were most conscious of the breakdown of an agriculture based on serfdom, and saw the necessity of some measure of agrarian reform and, with it, of the modernization of law and administration; and they joined hands with the forces at the centre which, shocked by the *débâcle* of the Crimean war, wanted to bring an element of up-to-date efficiency into the antiquated structure of the Russian State.

This was the background of the new institution of the *zemstvo*. It was, within limitations, an organ of self-government, and to this extent could be called liberal. But it was not "democratic": everywhere it was dominated by the gentry; and it was purely local: any attempt by the *zemstvo* to concern itself with national politics, or to seek association with other *zemstvos* on a national level, was jealously and implacably resisted by the higher authority. The *zemstvo* was up to a point an organ of enlightenment and social progress; the "gentry liberals" were as a whole a sincere and devoted group—sometimes genuine, even naive, idealists. The first steps to bring education and primitive social services to the countryside were taken by them; they were the first to attempt to introduce an orderly system of public law. But the *zemstvo* flourished to the extent that it remained non-political, and did not aspire to challenge the decisions and prerogatives of the central autocracy. If this was liberalism, it was a non-political liberalism—something infinitely far away from the early, rugged, fighting liberalism of the West.

The first surprising conclusion that emerges is the close link between this "gentry liberalism" and Slavophilism—or at any rate one wing of that amorphous, and also largely non-political, movement. The difference between the "liberal Slavophil" Koshelev and the "Slavophil liberal" Shipov (the labels are Professor Fischer's) is mainly that one was born twenty years earlier than the other. It was Shipov who wrote, in purely Slavophil language, of the "fruitful interaction between authority and popular representation" and "the realization and execution by both sides of their moral duty", and who, in the crisis of the 1905 revolution, wanted "a renovated imperial authority on the one hand, and on the other free access to the Tsar of the people's voice through elected representatives". In questions of practical local improvements—what, in the jargon of the period, were called "small deeds"—the "gentry liberals" had between 1860 and 1905 as good a record as anyone. But their predominance in the landscape of Russian liberalism goes far to explain why, in 1905 and in 1917, Russian liberalism was condemned to political sterility and bankruptcy.

But, like all trends of Russian nineteenth-century thought, Russian liberalism had its western as well as its Slavophil face. The outstanding "westerner" among the liberals of the 1860s and 1870s was Boris Chicherin, a collateral ancestor of the later People's Commissar for Foreign Affairs. Chicherin sprang from the gentry class, was a learned and intelligent student of Hegel and of the philosophy of law, and was at one time mayor of Moscow—a tribute both to his interest in public affairs and to his fundamental orthodoxy. Chicherin's liberalism stemmed from that of Speransky. It was concerned above all with legal and constitutional forms. Constitutional monarchy in western usage meant the establishment of a constitution as a bulwark against the monarchy, for the curtailment of its powers. Constitutional monarchy, in the eyes of Russian liberals of the school of Chicherin, meant that the monarchy should constitutionalize itself and, without surrendering its supreme power, express that power in constitutional terms. Thus, just as we find the "gentry liberals" hobnobbing with the Slavophils and speaking a language indistinguishable from theirs, so it is not surprising to find Chicherin, the constitutional liberal, stretching out a hand to Pobedenostsev, the ideologist of unlimited autocracy, who in his way also wanted to legalize and regularize the monarchy. This strain in Russian liberalism also remained influential after 1905 in the person of Maklakov, who was in all essentials a disciple of Chicherin.

But Russian liberalism did not remain wholly static throughout the period from the 1860s to 1905. Professor Fischer's main, and impressively argued, thesis is that these years saw an evolution from the "gentry liberalism" of the *zemstvos* to the "intelligentsia liberalism" of the new professional and managerial class. In the terminology familiar from Turgenev's novel, the hard-headed "sons" of the 1860s had revolted against the idealistic "fathers" of the 1840s, and had plunged headlong into socialism, anarchism and nihilism. Now in the 1880s and 1890s the "grandsons", reacting against the radical extremism of the "sons", and finding themselves comfortably ensconced in the rising professional classes and the new bureaucracy, moved towards a new brand of "intelligentsia liberalism", which concentrated on the demand for reform, but not revolution, and provided a solid social basis for the vague aspirations of Russian liberalism in the past. It was this group from which, after 1905, the Kadet party—the only party in Russian history which could in any sense be called liberal—was to draw its main support.

The first years of the new century saw an attempt to give concrete shape to the movement. In 1902, proceeding by the classic Russian method of a journal published abroad, Peter Struve, the former high priest of "legal Marxism", founded the journal *Osvobozhdenie* (or *Liberation*) in Stuttgart. It addressed itself to "the moderate elements of Russian society not participating in the revolutionary struggle", and hoped to create a "liberal-moderate nucleus of Russian society". In the following year the "League of Liberation" was constituted at a meeting held in Switzerland, and representing "*zemstvo* liberals" and "intelligentsia liberals" alike. The personality of Struve, and the journal which he had created, was clearly the driving force of the new union.

The pre-eminence of Struve was, however, the symptom of a peculiar feature of this birth, or renaissance, of Russian liberalism. Not only Struve but those most closely associated with him were almost all converts either, like Struve himself, from the Marxists or from the *narodniks*. "Ideological disaffection", as Professor Fischer puts it, among the socialists, first appearing in the 1890s, was the principal stimulus to the new growth. This, among other things, explains Lenin's bitterness against the liberals. The most conspicuous of them were renegades from Marxism. But this also reveals the special character, and one of the ultimate weaknesses, of Russian liberalism. It had its psychological roots not so much in antipathy to Tsarism as in antipathy to socialism. Its fire was directed quite as much against the Left as against the Right. In this respect, too, it was far removed from western liberalism in its fighting days.

The outstanding exception to these generalizations, and a unique figure in the history of Russian liberalism, was Milyukov. Milyukov had no affiliations with the *zemstvo* liberals. He was an out-and-out intellectual. But, unlike almost all the other intellectuals of the movement, he had never been in the camp of the Marxists or of the *narodniks*, and had not come to liberalism by way of a reaction against the Left. He may at the outset have been said to belong to the Chicherin school of constitutional liberalism; but he quickly shed its distinguishing features. An early contributor to *Osvobozhdenie*, he soon found himself at loggerheads with Struve, whom he accused of toying with Slavophil ideas, and failing to put forward clearly formulated demands for a constituent assembly, and a parliament. The Russo-Japanese War completed the rift. Milyukov, if not a thoroughgoing defeatist, was at any rate in favour of using the war as an opportunity to drive home the slogan "Down with autocracy". Struve, if not a thoroughgoing patriot, was prepared to temporize with those who were and to postpone the internal struggle for the sake of winning the war.

Professor Fischer gives a vivid picture of the liberal approach to the 1905 revolution. In October, 1904, the League of Liberation held a congress in Petersburg, and decided to organize a series of political banquets in the principal cities—a conscious and rather pathetic invocation of the Paris of 1848. In the following month, a *zemstvo* congress took place, also in Petersburg: owing to an official ban it had to be held in private houses. But, in spite of this odour of illegality, its positive proposals were mild enough—so mild, indeed, that Sviatopolk-Mirsky, the Minister of the Interior, agreed to receive a copy of the resolution on the understanding that it would be presented as emanating from individuals and not from a banned congress. Its most daring demand was that

> the supreme authority should call together freely elected representatives of the people, in order to lead our fatherland with their collaboration on a new path of state development, of establishing principles of law and interaction between state and people.

Thus the liberals played little direct part in the 1905 revolution. But they were swept along in its path; and something emerged of which they had scarcely dared to dream—a political party containing both the words "constitutional" and "democratic" in its title, the "Kadets". Milyukov became its unquestioned leader; and Milyukov stood well on the Left of Russian liberalism. Yet once again the inherent weaknesses reappeared under the new régime. The party was divided within itself; it lacked any broad mass appeal; and it could not function within the limitation even of autocracy in retreat. The old dilemma could still not be surmounted. The liberals could not fulfil their programme so long as they accepted the régime: but they could not effectively attack the régime without ceasing to be liberals and becoming revolutionaries. This period falls outside the scope of Professor Fischer's present work. But the story which he has to tell seems incomplete without it.

Perhaps the chief impression which will remain with the reader as he lays down Professor Fischer's stimulating book is the extent to which history is complicated by the fascination of political vocabulary. The origins of "liberalism" as a term in political thought are almost as obscure as those of "socialism". But liberalism as an historical phenomenon cannot now, wherever the word may have first been used, be dissociated from the "expansion of England" and of the English-speaking world in the nineteenth century. It commits nobody to a narrowly economic interpretation of history to dwell on the industrial and commercial background of this expansion, or to believe that the liberalism of the English-speaking world, and its recognizable counterparts in western Europe, was bound up with a period of unprecedented industrial and commercial development. And this development was in a remarkable degree the product of individual enterprise and initiative. The ideas of Samuel Smiles may not have been specifically "liberal". But nineteenth-century liberalism as an historical phenomenon cannot be understood without taking into account what may be called its Samuel Smiles component.

Liberalism, like any other great political movement, developed its ideology, its creed, its body of doctrine; and these, accepted as the essence of the movement, exercised their appeal not only in countries where liberal institutions flourished but also in countries where such institutions had not been born. In such countries liberalism could become an inspiration, a source of ferment, a remote ideal. But it could not, without striking new roots, become a going concern; and it was precisely those roots which were lacking in Russia. Trotsky, in one of his early writings, made the point with his usual analytical brilliance:

> Pure liberalism with all its Manchester symbols of faith faded in our country before it blossomed; it did not find any social soil in which to grow. Manchester ideas could be imported, but the social environment which produced those ideas could not be imported.

Trotsky was not particularly concerned to do justice to liberalism, or to Russian liberals in particular. But the essence of the matter is here. Professor Fischer is warmly sympathetic to all brands of Russian liberals. But the tragedy of the withering away of imported liberal ideas in Russian soil comes out on every page of his book.

This is, however, not the end of the matter. The failure of liberalism to strike roots in Russia was no mere question of its western origin; for Marxism was as much an import from the West as liberalism. It may well be that Russian Marxism diverged as widely as Russian liberalism from the western prototype. It may be that it was turned, perhaps perverted, to purposes already inherent in Russia's historical development. But the point is that Marxism could be made to serve and that liberalism could not. For Marxism proved to have the appeal which liberalism lacked. And something like the same phenomenon is visible to-day in Asia and Africa, where the national resentments and aspirations, which fifty or sixty years ago began to find expression in the language of John Stuart Mill, are to-day couched in the terminology of Marx and Lenin.

The basic difference which confronts us here is not a difference between ideologies or a difference between countries or continents, but a difference between periods of history. This is particularly apparent in the dilemma of Russian liberalism. The process of economic development with which historical liberalism was associated was development through the initiative, enrichment and expansion of the individual trader or producer. Hence the extraordinarily strong emphasis on individualism in the liberal ideology— on the individual as the antithesis of the State, on the individual liberating himself from the tyranny of state power and building for himself a society in which government is an unnecessary excrescence or, at most, a necessary evil. But the economic development which came belatedly to Russia in the closing years of the nineteenth century was the development of an altogether later period—the period of standardized production and large-scale industry and above all, of an industry which, far from depending on individuals emancipating themselves from state control, invoked tariffs, state subsidies and state orders as the condition of its growth and prosperity. Such was not a soil in which seeds of imported liberalism could flower and come to fruition.

But this meant also that liberalism was soon to be on the defensive even in the countries of its birth, where economic evolution was already bringing new creeds and new ideologies in its train. The liberalism which was imported into Russia from the West at the end of the nineteenth century was no longer so much concerned with offence as with defence. Already, in the western world, liberalism was splitting into two camps, of which the camp primarily interested to conserve positions that had already been won, and values already established, was not the less powerful. It was the same split which paralysed the weak and puny growth of Russian liberalism. No sane analysis can burke the fact that by the early years of the twentieth century Russia was ripe for revolution. It was the dilemma and the tragedy of Russian liberalism that it could not provide the fuel and motive power for that revolution.

8 Rural Russia

It has become a commonplace to recognize the peasant as the uncrowned hero or the principal whipping boy—according to the point of view adopted—of Russian history. This is because a state of affairs once familiar in western Europe—an economy and society which was predominantly rural—survived in Russia down to our own day. Even in 1914, by which time industrialization had begun to make its mark, well over eighty per cent of the population lived on the land and by the land. This eighty per cent was not, of course, an undifferentiated mass. Every extreme of geographical configuration, of soil fertility and of climate could be found in the ample expanse of the Russian Empire.

It comprised a primitive hunting economy in the north; a nomadic cattle-raising economy in the steppes of Asia; specialized dairy-farming in parts of Siberia; cotton-growing on irrigated land in Turkestan; cultivation of fruit, wine and tobacco in the Caucasus and the Crimea; sugar beet in the Ukraine; and large-scale grain-growing with the beginnings of mechanization in the southern European steppe. But all these occupations had a local and limited character. By far the largest part of the population was engaged in near-subsistence farming, producing food crops primarily for its own consumption and for the satisfaction of its immediate obligations to some superior authority. This is the Russian peasant who, throughout the ages, has been the focal point in Russian society and Russian history.

There is therefore every reason to welcome an attempt to retell the story of the development of Russian history "from the ninth to the nineteenth century"—from its first beginnings to the emancipation of the serfs—in terms of the relation of the peasant to the land and to the landowner. It is also reassuring to discover that Dr. Jerome

[1] Jerome Blum, *Lord and Peasant in Russia* (Princeton: Princeton University Press; London: Oxford University Press).

Blum, the author of *Lord and Peasant in Russia*,[1] made his bow some fifteen years ago with a study of the Austrian peasant in the period before 1848. This means that Dr. Blum's initial approach to his present theme has been through interest in the peasant rather than through a specialized interest in Russia: such an approach forms a salutary safeguard against a misleading conception of the Russian peasant as a unique phenomenon without parallel in other countries or in other historical epochs.

It would, of course, be wrong to ignore or underestimate the peculiarities in Russian history, due to the retarded development of the Russian economy and society in relation to that of western Europe. The immense territory in which the Russian nation grew and expanded suffered from extremes of climate and a frequently infertile soil; its mineral resources, though rich, were widely dispersed and difficult of access; and it possessed few of those natural geographical features and divisions which facilitate the building of workable local units. Over this territory the establishment of a settled economy and of an orderly political authority proved an exceptionally arduous task. Consciousness of the time-lag between Russian and western development set up special stresses in relations between them. But it remains broadly true that the great problems of Russian history—and notably the relation of the peasant to the land—were problems which had arisen in the West at an earlier stage of its historical development.

The kinship group seems to have formed the basis of all primitive societies. The first point to notice about the peasant in Russian history, even down to the most recent times, is that the unit with which we are dealing is not the individual peasant, but the *dvor* or peasant household. This is the same elastic unit which was familiar in medieval Europe, and survives today in the *zadruga* of the Balkans, in the Chinese *chia*, and in many other parts of the world. With a natural non-monetary economy and a largely illiterate population, where custom rules and there are few written laws and fewer written contracts, the individual is too unstable and precarious a unit to serve as the formal basis of the social and economic order. The *dvor* provides, throughout the history of the Russian countryside, the element of durability and continuity. Whatever happens to the individual, the *dvor* goes on. On it rests the responsibility for cultivating the land allotted to it. It works as a unit: its earnings and its outgoings are shared in common. By it the necessarily unproductive members of the community, the young children and the aged, are cared for.

The essential function of the *dvor* in the economy is to make the requisite periodical adjustments between land and people. If the members of the *dvor*—the "eaters" in the graphic Russian phrase—become too numerous for the land occupied by it, some of them must be hived off, temporarily or permanently, and found employment elsewhere. Conversely, if the number of "workers" in the *dvor* is insufficient to meet its needs, fresh hands could be recruited by marriage, real or sometimes fictitious, or by adoption. But this necessary flexibility made impossible any strict definition of the scope or extent of the *dvor*. It was not a family in the narrow biological sense; but its character as a family group was never lost. Custom regulated the forms of self-government of the *dvor*. The senior working member, the natural head of the household, was the recognized head of the *dvor*. But the extent of his authority was nowhere defined, though his decisions, regarded as decisions of the *dvor*, were largely enforceable.

In the earliest period of Russian history the cultivation of much of the land was in the hands of slaves of the princes and monasteries who were the great landowners of the day. The free tillers of the Russian soil, when they first came into our view, seem to have been mainly confined to uncleared and unclaimed lands beyond the borders of regular settlement. The two current systems of tillage—the so-called "slash-and-burn" technique and the alternate field-and-grass system—both depended on the unlimited availability of land to be used and discarded when its fertility was exhausted. Such systems implied a population in constant movement. Dr. Blum rightly discards the once popular "nomad theory" as an all-embracing explanation of Russian history. But the habit of mobility long remained part of the traditional make-up of the Russian peasant; and the need to root the peasant to the soil was a recurrent *leitmotif* of Russian agricultural development.

The Mongol invasions and the "Tatar yoke", which lasted from the first half of the thirteenth century to the second half of the fifteenth, left behind them a trail of destruction and depopulation. Their positive results are more difficult to assess. Dr. Blum cautiously observes that "the Russian princes may have decided that it would be easier to collect the tribute demanded of them by the Tatars if they limited the freedom of movement of the people who lived in their realms"; but these developments can also be explained by other motives. What is clear is that the ensuing period was one of growing restriction and tension, which turned primarily on the ownership and possession of land.

Here we reach a characteristic puzzle of Russian agrarian history— not the question, who owns the land? but the question, what does landownership mean? So long as land was abundant and the cultivator tended to move on from place to place, the question was not important. But when, in the centuries after the Mongol invasions, the Muscovite princes laid the foundations of a settled economy and an organized state, a clash occurred between the conception of ownership of the land by the entity or group responsible for its cultivation and the claim of the princes to own all the land in their domains. The distinction between public and private law, between sovereignty and ownership, which provided a solution of this problem in western Europe, was still unrecognized. At a much later date it was never quite clear whether the obligations of the cultivator to a superior authority were in the nature of rent, which conferred a title to the land, or a tax in the domain of public law; and the same confusion lay at the root of the popular theory that the land belonged to the peasant and the peasant to the lord.

But, whatever the theory, the Tsars of Moscow, as they extended their power, successfully asserted their rights over the land. Not only did they confiscate much of the vast estates formerly held by the church, but they bestowed land right and left on their officials, servants and favourites, so that ownership of land became the mark of a new class bound to the service of the Tsar and of the state. And with the land went the peasants who tilled it, who now found themselves for the first time the serfs and bondsmen of the landowner. This process went on from the sixteenth to the eighteenth century. Moreover, by the time of Catherine the Great the class of noble landowners had become sufficiently powerful to emancipate themselves from their formal obligations to the state, while at the same time strengthening the bonds of serfdom in which the peasants were held to an extent which made serfdom virtually indistinguishable from slavery. It was the golden age of aristocracy.

Moral condemnation of these proceedings is commonly expressed both by liberal and by Marxist historians; Dr. Blum roundly accuses Catherine of hyprocrisy in pronouncing panegyrics on liberty and at the same time subjecting more and more peasants to the harsh tyranny of noble landowners. But, while not dissenting from this verdict, and while making full allowance for the success of the nobles in bending the state machine to their will and their interests, it is fair to point out that the initial impetus behind the movement was of a different character. Serfdom did not make Russian agriculture efficient. But during the first two centuries after its introduction agricultural production rose, population increased, and new regions were taken into cultivation. To overcome the previous anarchy in the countryside was a condition of the consolidation of the state. The method was crude, and in the long run perhaps bred greater evils than it cured. But the eighteenth-century state was not a refined institution, and had few tools at its disposal.

A far more obscure and enigmatic product of the same period was the growth of the peasant commune or *mir*, the beginnings of which have long been a subject of acute controversy among Russian historians. In early times a number of peasant *dvors* were grouped in a large unit, the *volost*. Some writers, including Dr. Blum, cause unnecessary confusion by translating *volost* as commune. But the *volost* was an administrative unit; and the word has survived to denote an administrative district down to Soviet times. The *mir*, or commune properly so called, was a union of *dvors* for the purpose of organizing cultivation. By the time the *mir* had become well established in the seventeenth and eighteenth centuries settled non-migratory cultivation was the rule, and the primitive slash-and-burn and field-grass systems had been superseded by the three-field rotation—winter sowing, spring sowing and fallow.

The *mir* performed so many functions in relation both to the peasant and to the landowner that its status is difficult to define. It was an essential part of the attempt to maintain a settled rural economy on the basis of serf labour. This implied a measure of responsibility for the serfs, who went with the land and could not be simply recruited or dismissed to keep pace with changing conditions. Just as it was the business of the *dvor* to adjust land and labour to changing relations within the peasant household, so the main function of the *mir* was the periodical redistribution of land as between households. But the constant division and subdivision of the land in order to provide for its allocation in just proportions to all the households in the *mir* also entailed the direction and control by the *mir* of the current rotation of crops as well as of the common use of pastures, water-courses and woodland.

It is, however, misleading to treat the *mir* as a purely peasant organization. Its origins, like everything else about it, are obscure and controversial. The view which traces its beginnings to a voluntary association of *dvors* is less plausible than the view which regards it as an organ created by landowners and administrators for the more convenient management of the peasant and his affairs. It was the organ through which the landowner received the payments due to him in cash or in kind, and organized the labour of his serfs; later, it was also the organ through which the state collected its taxes and recruited conscripts for the army. Yet, in spite of these apparently oppressive functions, the *mir* enjoyed the respect of the peasant, and was regarded by him as in a certain sense the protector of his interests. As Dr. Blum aptly puts it, it "served as a buffer between the lord and his peasants", and was as necessary to one side as to the other. The tenacity with which the *mir* lived on, not only after the abolition of serfdom but into the Soviet period, is proof of its essential role in the Russian countryside.

For about 100 years before the emancipation of the serfs in 1861 voices had been raised from time to time in Russia against the institution of serfdom. It is not unfair to connect these with the spread among the Russian ruling class of the ideas of the Enlightenment and, in the nineteenth century, of western liberalism and humanitarianism. But this diagnosis remains superficial unless it is seen as part of the new consciousness of the material backwardness of Russia in relation to western Europe and the campaign to emulate the superior efficiency of its economy and institutions. The essence of the Russian indictment of serfdom was that it was obsolete and inefficient, and a bar to the entry of Russia into that modern world to which the West belonged. It is, of course, correct that the protesters failed to see that serfdom was only a single element in the Russian economy, and that its removal would have far-reaching consequences and would not in itself suffice to modernize the economy. But serfdom became the symbol of Russian inefficiency and Russian backwardness. The Napoleonic wars and, finally, the disasters of the Crimean War were decisive landmarks in the campaign against it.

Dr. Blum, whose story ends with the emancipation of 1861, rounds off his narrative with some reflections on the causes of that event. This is perhaps the least satisfactory chapter in the book. Dr.

Blum brushes aside somewhat cavalierly the argument that serfdom had become inefficient in a period of rising capitalism, and the argument that emancipation in the now prevailing conditions was in the interest of the landowners themselves (this surely turned on the unresolved question whether the serfs were to be emancipated with or without land, and with how much land). Even the suggestion that serfdom was got rid of because it was an obstacle to future industrial development is not as far-fetched as Dr. Blum seems to think. In the end he falls back on "the importance of humanitarian and liberal ideas", on "the shock of the Crimean defeat" and on fears of rural unrest as the main motives behind the emancipation.

This lame conclusion is all the more surprising because in the earlier parts of his narrative Dr. Blum has been assiduous in his analysis of economic causes. Indeed, in discussing the processes which led to the imposition of serfdom he appears to dwell almost too exclusively on its economic aspects and to underrate the political exigencies of centralized state building. He even tries to persuade us that "the history of agrarian institutions in Russia would have taken much the same course without the creation of the absolute state". In his study of agrarian reform in Austria, which was published in 1948, Dr. Blum put very strongly the argument for the superior efficiency of hired over indentured labour: and, while he wrote of "the realization of the economic loss involved in the existing landlord peasant relationship" as being only one of several motives behind the reform campaign, he clearly treated it as the main driving force. Why should the economic factors which were apparently all-powerful in seventeenth-century Russia, and dominated the agrarian problem in pre-1848 Austria, be so summarily dismissed in the setting of mid-nineteenth-century Russia?

Notwithstanding its disappointing conclusion, Dr. Blum's study of nearly ten centuries of the life and organization of rural Russia is packed with information and will for a long time remain an invaluable textbook, (though two of the three maps have unfortunately been reversed). The English student of Russian agrarian history is now indeed exceptionally well catered for. For the early period the gaps in Dr. Blum's more general narrative can be filled from Mr. R. E. F. Smith's important monograph on *The Origins of Farming in Russia* published three years ago; and the period from the emancipation of 1861 to the revolution of 1917 is covered in Professor Robinson's *Rural Russia under the Old Regime*, now thirty years old but still without a rival in this field. The period of Russian agrarian history since 1917 has been the subject of an immense amount of polemical writing, and a large corpus of information is available. But nobody has yet attempted to provide a chart to these treacherous waters.

9 Bolsheviks and Peasants

The story of the Russian peasantry in the first decade after the revolution of 1917 is full of reversals of fortune, and full of pitfalls, as Teodor Shanin is keenly aware. The Stolypin reform of 1908 had sought to weaken the authority of the *mir*, or traditional peasant community, by encouraging the most enterprising and efficient peasants to contract out of it, and set up as independent small farmers. It was a bold plan to modernize the structure of Russian agriculture. What would happen to the mass of weaker peasants who remained in the enfeebled *mir* was not very seriously considered. Those who could not keep afloat would have to work as labourers on the farms of their more prosperous neighbours, or starve, or emigrate to America—or perhaps to Siberia.

Steps had been taken towards the settlement of a million or more independent peasants when war supervened and reduced the Russian countryside to confusion. The revolution gave the peasants their heads, with results that the Bolsheviks could not, and hardly attempted to, control. The landlords' estates were looted and taken over. So far, so good. But the Stolypin holdings disappeared also, virtually overnight, and were reabsorbed into the *mir*. The puzzle is, as Mr Shanin points out,[1] that this happened apparently without resistance. The independent peasant abandoned his independence and resumed his place as a leader of the *mir*. Peasant solidarity had asserted itself against the landlord—but also against attempts by the government to organize it from the outside.

The paradoxical result of the revolution was therefore to restore and confirm, through the initiative of the peasants themselves, the authority of a traditional peasant institution which "liberals" and "progressives", even under the last of the Tsars, had come to regard as an obstacle to agricultural reform and to the modernization of the economy. And this was the fundamental problem of a revolutionary

[1] Teodor Shanin, *The Awkward Class. Political Sociology of Peasantry in a Developing Society: Russia 1910–1925* (London: Clarendon Press, Oxford University Press).

regime which had seized power in the cities and military centres of a country of whose population more than 80 per cent were peasants who had never seen a town. In the 1920s a few Bolsheviks still believed that the *mir* could be won over, and used as an instrument for the establishment of Soviet rule in the countryside. But the party leaders more cogently—like Stolypin before them—recognized the tightly knit, inward-looking peasant community as a barrier to any substantial reform of the present economy, or of the national economy as a whole.

Lenin, from the beginning of his career, had brought his Marxist learning to bear on the fundamental problem of the peasant. He believed that capitalism—in the form of a market economy—had already begun to impinge on Russian peasant life: that this must bring with it a process of "differentiation" between the rich and successful peasant and the unsuccessful and indigent; and that this would eventually produce an oppressed and exploited rural proletariat, which, in alliance with the urban proletariat and under its leadership, would carry the revolution to the Russian country-side. This came to constitute, as Mr Shanin points out, a rigid framework of party doctrine. But Lenin was quite as much of a pragmatist in his attitude to the peasantry as to other practical problems; and, in the famous "April theses" of 1917 (a passage which Mr Shanin does not quote), he was notably cautious: "We cannot say exactly how profound is the class cleavage within the peasantry. . . . Such questions can be decided only by ex-perience."

The issue was not doctrinal but practical. The peasantry, in the anarchy of the revolution, had taken things into its own hands with the connivance of the revolutionary leaders (who, indeed, could do nothing about it). How could the newly-fledged regime, run by a pre-eminently urban party with few rural members and no rural experience, impose itself on the "dark", primitive, and formidable mass of peasants? "Divide and rule" was a precept older than Marxism. The obvious tactic was to divide the peasantry and to seek friends and auxiliaries in its ranks; and this, in the light of what had happened in the towns and of the whole revolutionary ethos, could only be among the poorer peasants. But the "committees of poor peasants" set up in the summer of 1918 proved a hopeless failure; they lasted less than six months. The attempt to establish village Soviets to counteract, and eventually to take over the authority of the *mir* was scarcely more successful. It persisted throughout the

1920s, but, with all the power of the Government behind it, did not really shake the loyalty of the peasant to the *mir*.

The introduction in 1921 of the New Economic Policy—a concordat with the peasantry as a whole—solved the immediate crisis of peasant discontent and incipient revolt. It lasted for five or six years. During this time, the wounds of the revolution and civil war had healed. The habits of normal life, and some measure of prosperity, had returned to the towns. The party had consolidated its power, and its bolder spirits were eager to press forward to the first goal of the revolution—the industrialization and socialization of the economy.

But the peasants, also, had recovered from their own nightmare of famine and devastation. Harvests had been good; the well-to-do peasant had accumulated grain stocks in his barns. Everyone was reassured and ready to settle down into the old ways. The upheaval produced by a massive programme of industrialization would be stubbornly resisted. The clash between the innovating processes of the revolution and the traditional peasant way of life enshrined in the *mir*, which had been apparent in the early days of the revolution, now emerged in an embittered and intensified form. The way was open to the tragic battlefield of collectivization.

This complex (and increasingly desperate) situation provided throughout the 1920s a field-day for economists and statisticians. The party economists (supported by surviving economists of the old "classical" school who had been behind Stolypin) demonstrated with a wealth of statistics that the gap was widening between the well-to-do and the poorer peasants. The statisticians were extremely resourceful. Since correct estimates of income were elusive, and areas of land held misleading implications, such items as the possession of animals and implements, and amounts of land leased and labour employed, were drawn into their calculations.

All this was enough to show that a substantial number of peasants had grown richer under NEP. This was, after all, a natural result of reopening a free market for grain; and, when serious requisitions began again early in 1928, the well-to-do peasants had large stocks of grain in their barns. But it was not enough to show that this was the sole, or even the predominant, trend. Nor were these calculations, as Mr Shanin suggests, primarily the product of a rigid adherence to Marxist dogma. They were offered in aid of a policy. If masses of the peasantry were in fact impoverished and discontented, they could be mobilized as allies against the wealthier peasants. Failing this, the prospects seemed—and were—grim.

An alternative analysis seized on the fact that the unit in Russian countryside was not the individual peasant, but the family household or *dvor*. The size and composition of the *dvor* was constantly changing; the number of workers had to be adjusted to the number of mouths to be fed. Moreover, land-holdings were subject to periodic (in some places, annual) readjustments and redistributions by the *mir*, so that, along with economic factors favouring differentiation, an automatic levelling process was going on between *dvors*. In so far as this analysis had political implications, it reflected the old Populist vision of a self-contained peasant Russia consisting of equal family farms clustered round the *mir*, impervious to the turmoil of capitalism and the modern world. In the twelve years after the revolution, the number of *dvors* increased by something like fifty per cent. The causes and consequences of this increase, probably due to social as much as to economic changes, have never been thoroughly investigated. There may well not be adequate material for a full inquiry.

Finally, NEP inspired yet a third school of statisticians, who argued that the tendencies towards differentiation and levelling ultimately cancelled one another out, and that both neglected other factors—variations of climate and weather, changing terms of trade, fiscal policy and even "random oscillations"—all of which were seen as promoting cyclical or levelling movements rather than basic change. This analysis denied both the theory of differentiation between upper and lower strata, and the view that the regime had anything to gain by promoting it, and encouraged the NEP view of the peasantry as a homogeneous whole. In political terms, it favoured the indefinite prolongation of NEP, shying away from the dilemmas this would give rise to.

Mr Shanin has expounded these different types of statistical analyses in great detail, with full reference to the sources, in a way that will make his study very valuable to students of the subject. He himself is a fervent champion of the NEP analysis, which he calls "multifactorial" and "multidirectional". But his argument reveals some of the weaknesses, as well as the merits, of this method. Not only does it lead to no positive conclusion—only to a refutation of other methods—but it inspires scepticism of the validity of the whole statistical approach. What the Marxists and Populists tried to do was to isolate a single factor which they regarded as crucial and dominant, though it need not have been the only factor at work. But an analysis which professes to be comprehensive is always open to the reproach that it is not comprehensive enough. Can one put much faith in "multifactorial" analysis which omits such factors as the extensive migration to the towns, the increase in the number of *dvors*, the wide variations in geographical configurations and types of cultivation, the introduction of more modern implements and techniques?

Consciously or unconsciously, Mr Shanin in his last two chapters, which are devoted to a sensible though rather unsystematic review of the conflicts in rural society under NEP, seems to feel something of the same scepticism. He drops altogether the statistical pre-occupations of the central part of the book, and nearly everything he writes is unaffected by them. It is indisputable that the peasantry, in defiance of Soviet hopes and expectations, presented an almost unbroken front of resistance to pressures from above. But Mr Shanin's assumption that this was somehow connected with what he calls "the absence of socio-economic differentiation" in the peasantry remains unproved.

There is plenty of evidence to show that differentiation did exist, that the poorer peasant was conscious of his dependence on his more prosperous neighbours, and was prudently willing to follow their lead. But this was just as compatible with increasing, as with diminishing, differentiation. It is true that Bolshevik and Soviet leaders "lacked a perception of the real social processes going on in the Russian countryside", but this was not because they lacked statistics or used the wrong statistics, but because statistics were irrelevant. The problem they faced was the age-long problem of the opposition of conservative agriculture to innovatory industrial interests, of country to town. It was not a problem that could be solved by quantification.

Two minor criticisms may be made. Mr Shanin, anxious to establish his credentials as a sociologist, finds it necessary to flaunt what is no doubt the most up-to-date technical jargon. The widening or narrowing of the gap in wealth between different strata of the population is not a difficult concept. What is gained by wrapping it up in the guise of "centrifugal or centripetal mobility", even when we get reminders like "centripetal (levelling)" and "egalitarian (centripetal)", both on the same page, and a nice diagram, twice over, with arrows and circles to explain the difference between centripetal, centrifugal and cyclical mobility?

Take a passage like the following:

> The rural outsiders to a Russian peasant commune could be classified by a three-fold typology: neighbours, strangers, and plenipotentiaries . . . . Plenipotentiary outsiders would be agents of external centres of power acting as their rural transmission belts.

It all means something that could be said so much more simply and clearly.

The other criticism relates to some rather flimsy philosophical underpinning. The Marxists are accused of "economic determinism" and the Populists of "biological determinism", determinism being, of course, a dirty word. But to say that process A leads to result X is no more deterministic than to say that processes A, B, C and D taken together produce X; and Mr Shanin on this showing must be convicted of some kind of cyclical determinism.

The practical point is different. To isolate a single significant cause of a phenomenon is often the first necessary step towards doing some thing about it. Blunders are only to be expected; those who sought to demonstrate statistically the impending split in the Russian peasantry made a tragic blunder—not least in thinking that statistics could settle the issue. But the method itself is not wrong, and may in essence be less "deterministic", or at any rate less fatalistic, than the belief that, since multiple causes—some of them purely random and accidental—were at work, nothing much could be done about it. Mr Shanin has given us an excellent review of the statistical controversy, and shed interesting side-lights on Russian rural life in the period (including an illuminating appendix on peasant laws of inheritance); and his book is very welcome on that account. But his main conclusions leave us just about where we were.

10 The Third International

When Stalin in the summer of 1943 decided to give the Communist International a second-class funeral, that once redoubtable institution had long been dead and forgotten—so long, indeed, that it was difficult to find anything to bury. The Third or Communist International, known to its familiars as Comintern, had been in essence the creation of Lenin. Its heroic period—the period when it had a dramatic life and significance of its own—ended with his active career. What followed later was no more than an embarrassing epilogue, when Comintern became a stage on which the rivalries of the Bolshevik leaders found a secondary outlet and from which, later still, Soviet policies could be proclaimed. Finally, it became embarrassing even to its managers, and the last curtain fell.

The heroic period of the Communist International is the theme of M. Branko Lazitch's new study, *Lénine et la IIIe Internationale*.[1] M. Lazitch was, one may infer, formerly numbered among the elect. But he writes now with a well-informed critical detachment which keeps both hero-worship and detraction equally at arm's length, and does justice to the initial enthusiasm, the blend of sincerity and artifice, the sometimes naïve and sometimes cunning calculations which marked the course of the institution. M. Lazitch has a point of view of his own. Marx was for him a "determinist", Lenin (and, *a fortiori*, Stalin) a "voluntarist"; and the introduction of this deviation into the Bolshevik party and into the Communist International was the great source of error, encouraging ill-considered optimism and revolutionary adventure. M. Lazitch's thesis is, to say the least, over-simplified. But it is possible to accept some of his conclusions without being committed to his premises.

The history of the Third International really begins on 4 August

[1] Branko Lazitch, *Lénine et la IIIe Internationale*. Préface de Raymond Aron. (L'Evolution du Monde et des Idées) (Neuchâtel, Switzerland: Editions de la Baconnière).

1914, which for international socialists is not the date when Great Britain declared war on Germany, but the date on which the German Social-Democratic Party in the Reichstag decided to vote for the war credits demanded by the imperial Government. This decision, which was precisely imitated by the French, Belgian and Austrian socialists and by the great majority of the British Labour Party, was a rank defiance of the declared principles of the Second International. At successive congresses of the International during the past decade the member parties had solemnly proclaimed their determination to oppose all military expenditure; and, since they were everywhere a small minority in their respective parliaments, the ritual of voting against military budgets had been regularly observed without practical consequences and without—in peace time—attracting any particular odium. No socialist expected to see the workers' parties caught up in a wave of patriotism on the outbreak of war. There is a well-known story that Lenin, when he read the news in the German party journal *Vorwärts*, believed that the number had been forged by the German Government.

This development, which ended all solidarity between the parties forming the Second International and ranged their members against one another in mortal combat on opposite sides of the battle-front, seemed to have struck a staggering blow at the International. To faithful international socialists it seemed impossible that the institution could ever recover from this betrayal of its most cherished principle and foundation—"Workers of the world, unite!" In October 1914, both Lenin and Trotsky, acting quite independently of each other, wrote articles proclaiming that the International was dead, and that the task ahead was now to create a Third International. These stalwarts knew their party history. The First International faded away in the 1870s, having never recovered from the break with Bakunin and his anarchists; in the next decade the Second International had arisen to take its place. Now that the Second had succumbed, its successor must be brought to birth. But there was no question of rivalry between a Third and the Second International, any more than there had been between the Second and the First. The demise of the Second International was taken for granted.

It was in this spirit that Lenin, almost single-handed and in face of every discouragement, continued throughout the war to preach the need for a Third and truly Communist International to retrieve the treachery and disgrace of the Second. The demand figured in the "April theses" which he presented to the Bolshevik Party on his return to Petrograd after the February revolution. But when the Bolshevik revolution occurred in October, 1917, the situation was no longer propitious for a new International. Considerations of domestic, as well as of foreign, policy made peace rather than world revolution the supreme immediate need; and after the failure of the peace overtures to the western allies the Brest-Litovsk crisis reinforced the same lesson.

It was the armistice of 1918, with the collapse of Germany and the symptoms of imminent revolution in central Europe, which at length put the foundation of a Third International on the agenda. Up to this time Communist parties existed, often surreptitiously, in the countries immediately bordering on Russia; but beyond these limits there were no more than a few isolated and insignificant Communist groups, lacking both numbers and influence. The first condition for a Communist International was absent. On the last day of 1918 a German Communist Party was founded under the leadership of Karl Liebknecht and Rosa Luxemburg; and so great was the revolutionary prestige of Germany—the country where it was generally assumed that the European revolution would start— that this fact alone appeared to show that the time was ripe to put Communist organization on an international basis. The immediate occasion for convening a congress was significant. The Socialist parties of western Europe announced the intention of meeting at Berne at the end of January 1919, to consider what could be done to revive the Second International. Lenin was determined that the Communists should get in first. The new International was therefore started in a spirit of competition with the Second, which had been no part of the original conception.

The founding congress of the Communist International met in Moscow in March, 1919. The official records are rather tenuous, but can be supplemented by memoirs of several of the participants; and M. Lazitch has succeeded in giving a graphic picture of the occasion. Communications were still desperately difficult, and only a handful of those present had travelled to Moscow specially for the congress. Most of the delegates were foreign Communists resident in Moscow, and their credentials were often dubious. The key to the proceedings, as everyone recognized, was the attitude of the German delegation. Only one of the two delegates sent by the

German party had succeeded in getting through; and he came with instructions to oppose the founding of a new International as premature. The reasons for this caution were not far to seek. If the International were founded at this juncture, before the revolution had ripened in Germany, and before serious Communist parties even existed in the other great countries, its centre of gravity could only be in Moscow. The balance would be distorted, and Russian influence—the influence of the only men who had proved that they knew how to make a modern revolution—would reign supreme.

The Bolshevik leaders were apparently inclined to bow to the common sense of the German objection and to postpone the formal act of creating a Third International. But the delegates of the smaller countries had come prepared for a dramatic occasion, and the congress was stampeded by the oratory of the Austrian delegate, who, though the Austrian Communist Party was an insignificant sect, assured his audience that the whole of central Europe was seething with revolution and that it would be pusillanimous to hold back. Nor was the calculation was wild as it may seem in retrospect. In the spring of 1919 the allied statesmen assembled in Paris were constantly preoccupied by the danger of Bolshevism in Europe. Germany was still in a ferment; in a few weeks' time Soviets were to appear in Munich and in Budapest. There had been a serious mutiny which had led to the forced withdrawal of the French naval forces from south Russia and minor mutinies among the British and American troops at Archangel. Lloyd George displayed particular anxiety about the situation at home and abroad. When Fineberg, a member of the tiny British Socialist Party, who appeared (though without credentials) at the founding congress of the Third International, asserted that the strike movement was "spreading all over England and affecting every branch of industry" and that discipline in the Army was "much weakened", he was saying nothing that was *prima facie* absurd. Arthur Ransome, the only foreign journalist who attended the congress, has recorded that Lenin said to him: "England may seem to you untouched, but the microbe is already there."

It was in this mood that German objections were overborne and the decision taken to found the Communist International, without any great publicity or *éclat*, but in the firm and unquestioning conviction that the European revolution was well on the way. The sequel is well known. The wave of revolution receded all over

Europe; the Soviet in Munich survived for only a few days, in Budapest for a few weeks; disaffection in the armed forces ended with the progress of demobilization; labour troubles remained but had lost their revolutionary potential. Nor had the Communist International any influence or any organization to stay the decline. Cut off in Moscow by a rising tide of civil war, it had few means of communication, even with such Communist parties and groups as existed in other countries. The first nine months of the new International were a period of almost complete impotence and seemed to justify the German view of it as a premature birth.

The change came about the turn of the year. By January 1920, the assaults of the "white" generals, liberally supported by allied supplies and equipment, had all been beaten back, and the civil war was virtually won. The allied blockade was lifted, and tentative attempts were made to re-establish relations. Attempts to re-suscitate the Second International had failed, and Left-wing parties, not yet Communist but beginning to quality as fellow-travellers, were turning towards the new star in the firmament. The Italian Socialist Party, pacifist rather than revolutionary in outlook, voted to join the Third International; the German Independent Social-Democrats inquired about the terms of admission; the British Labour Party and the I.L.P. both sent missions to Moscow. The second congress of the International, which met in Moscow in July 1920, was a great contrast to the first. Communications were now relatively easy, though many delegates, including those from Great Britain, had to travel surreptitiously owing to passport difficulties. But there was a large and heterogeneous gathering of parties and groups of the extreme Left from Europe, America and Asia. This was before a rigid orthodoxy was insisted on: everyone was welcome in Moscow who had made the breakaway from the discredited Second International.

What would have happened if the congress had met in an atmosphere propitious to sober reflection cannot be guessed. But it happened otherwise. In the spring of 1920, with the civil war over, Pilsudski saw fit to launch to Polish attack on Soviet Russia, and in the middle of May had got as far as Kiev. Here he experienced the same fate as other invaders of Russia from the west. His effort was exhausted, his lines were extended, and he waited too long: his armies were caught and could move neither forward nor back. In

June a headlong retreat began and was in full progress when the congress of the International met. Before the congress ended the triumphant Red Army had crossed the Polish frontier and was hotly pursuing the Poles towards the fortress of Warsaw. The panic in the capitals of western Europe was matched by the enthusiasm in Moscow. It seemed certain that Poland was about to turn Bolshevik and that Red revolution would then sweep over the rest of the Continent. A large map hung in the congress hall on which the daily advances of the Red Army were recorded. The *dénouement* of the revolutionary drama was evidently at hand.

With these hopes and certainties prevailing, caution could be thrown to the winds. The Communist International could no longer afford to be a loose federation of Left-wing parties; it must be organized as the headquarters and directing staff of the world revolution. The tolerant period of eclecticism was over. The emphasis now was on uniformity, discipline and centralization. The congress laid down 21 conditions of admission to the International. Member parties (and in future only Communist parties would be admitted) must conform rigidly to all directions from the centre (they were indeed referred to as "sections of the International", as if to deny their independent existence); they must work for revolution in their respective countries both by legal and by illegal methods; and they must expel all members who did not unreservedly accept this programme. It was some years before all these conditions were widely or fully applied. But it was this congress which founded the legend of the Third International as a vast and efficient conspiratorial organization with branches in every country engaged day and night in subterranean plots for the overthrow of the existing order.

It is the paradox of the Third International that it was just getting into its stride at the moment when, in July and August 1920, Bolshevism was making its last serious challenge to Europe—at any rate, for a quarter of a century. The battle in front of Warsaw, when Pilsudski checked and then threw back the Red advance, proved, as D'Abernon called it at the time, one of the decisive battles of the world. As the Third International gradually built up its supposedly world-wide revolutionary organization, the hope or the threat of world revolution was rapidly fading. The attempted Communist *coups* in Germany in 1921 and 1923, in which the International played some active part, and the British general strike of 1926, in which it played none, were episodes which showed clearly that the post-war revolutionary tide of 1919 was in full ebb.

The turning-point in the fortunes of the Third International falls in the interval between the second congress in the summer of 1920 and the third in the summer of 1921. From the standpoint of organization much progress was made. A miniature British Communist Party was formed out of several splinter groups and parties: only a small minority of the I.L.P. came over. A majority of the German Independent Social-Democrats fused with the hitherto small German Communist Party, making a mass party of respectable size. The French and Czech socialist parties split, and a majority in each case was won over to found a Communist Party. In Moscow the Intenational acquired an imposing palace—in the former German Embassy—for its headquarters and a large hotel to house distinguished visitors.

But these external trappings concealed the hollowness behind. The defeat of the high hopes of the Polish campaigns was never wholly retrieved. The attempt of the German Communist Party in March, 1921, was a fiasco. Most important of all, this was the moment of New Economic Policy at home and of the Anglo-Soviet trade agreement as the high-spot of Soviet foreign policy. The avowed purpose of both was a temporary compromise with capitalism: both were based on a tacit, or even open, avowal that the revolutionary shock tactics of the previous year had failed. On the other side, the Second International, after several false starts, was now once more raising its head; so was the old International Federation of Trade Unions—what the Bolshevik derisively called "the yellow Amsterdam International". Both structures were rickety and unsubstantial. But there was nothing unsubstantial about the revived Social-Democratic and Labour parties of western Europe, which now played an active and recognized part in national politics and, as they grew respectable, became less and less revolutionary and more and more implacably opposed to the pretensions of Moscow. The Third International had been created. But the Second had, after all, failed to die.

When the third congress met in the summer of 1921 there was much talk of the "offensive of capital" and of the need to establish contact with the "masses" in order to resist it; and the way was prepared for the policy, which was proclaimed a few months later, of seeking a "united front" with other workers' parties against capitalists and employers. The compromise expressed in N.E.P. and in the Anglo-Soviet trade agreement was thus extended to the Third International. This line was followed throughout 1922, though with no great success; for the parties of the Second International for their part now had little interest in a compromise with Moscow. It was a year of success for Soviet foreign policy: the Genoa conference, the Rapallo treaty and the Lausanne conference had once more given Soviet Russia a place among the great Powers and brought her a powerful, or potentially powerful, ally.

But all this had nothing to do with world revolution, and when the fourth congress of the International met in November 1922, the mood was even more sombre and cautious than in the previous year. It was the occasion of Lenin's last public appearance but one. He was a sick man; and Zinoviev afterwards recalled how, at the end of his not very long speech, he could hardly stand for fatigue and was dripping with sweat. The speech was devoted to a rather rambling defence of N.E.P., the unexpressed implication being that the International, too, must go through its phase of retreat and compromise. The strangest part of the speech was its peroration:

> I think that the most important thing for us all, Russian and foreign comrades alike, is that after five years of the Russian revolution we must study. . . . We are learning in a general sense. They must learn in a special sense to achieve organization, structure, method and content in revolutionary work. If this is done, then I am convinced that the prospects of world revolution will be not only good but excellent.

It was an odd last injunction from the man who had founded the Third International as a great fighting instrument of revolution only three-and-a-half years before.

Here M. Lazitch ends his story. It is a good stopping-place in the affairs of the Third International as well as the end of Lenin's career. When the next congress met after his death in 1924 the rival Bolshevik leaders were already striking bargains with important delegates of other parties on a basis of mutual support in the struggle for power. No further congress met till 1928, when it was convened to give an international blessing to the first Five-Year Plan, to confirm Stalin's presidency and, by marking a turn to the Left, to prepare the way for a settlement of accounts with the "Right" opposition in the Russian hierarchy. Finally, a congress of the

International was summoned for the lsst time in 1935 to proclaim an international united front against Hitler. All this belongs to the history of the Soviet Union rather than of the International as an organ of world revolution. As such the Third International did not survive Lenin—hardly, indeed, survived the failure in Poland in 1920.

Many conclusions can be drawn from the brief dramatic story of the Communist International: some of them are set out by M. Lazitch in his final section. The outstanding one is perhaps the inevitability of the identification, which occurred so rapidly, between the International and the Soviet power. The First and Second Internationals had been groupings of outcast or minority parties and organizations which stood, at any rate in this respect, on an equal footing. The Third International was the creation of a party in power, a party in control of the machinery and resources of a great country, grouping round itself a number of parties whose status was similar to that of the parties of the earlier Internationals. It is not necessary to suppose that the consequences of this disparity were intended or foreseen by the Russian party. When the Third International was founded, the Bolsheviks were all confident of the imminence of the European revolution—and did not believe that they could survive without it. It is not necessary to convict Lenin or Zinoviev of insincerity when they declared that the headquarters of the International were only provisionally set up in Moscow, and that they looked forward to the day when they could be moved to Berlin or Paris.

When, however, the revolution failed to spread beyond the borders of Russia, when the International remained a partnership between a single victorious revolutionary party and a bevy of unsuccessful and ineffective aspirants for power in their respective countries, the picture changed radically. The International was anchored permanently in Moscow, with all the predominance of Russian interests and Russian outlook which that implied; it was materially dependent on the resources of the Soviet State (even the strongest parties could not balance their budgets unaided after the first few years); and, above all, the immense prestige and authority of the Russian party were proof against any serious challenge. It was impossible to reply to the argument that the Russians had shown the capacity and courage to make a successful revolution and that the others had not; and, when the Russian party laid down the law on the way in which revolutions are prepared and made, the rest had nothing to do but to listen and obey.

Thus the Third International was built up on a foundation of Russian leadership, Russian resources, Russian ideas and outlook and Russian methods of organization. When, from 1921 onward, it came to be recognized that capitalism had temporarily regained the "offensive" and that the revolution was postponed to an uncertain date in the future, this process received an irresistible impetus. The Third International gradually became assimilated to the Russian party, to its policies, its interests and its internal disputes and rivalries; and, from being a foreign adjunct of the Russian Communist Party, it was only a short step to become an adjunct of the Soviet State.

The consequence of this process on Communist movements outside Russia was, however, equally decisive. For nearly 20 years before Stalin finally disbanded the Third International the question could reasonably have been asked whether it did not on balance do more to prejudice than to advance the cause of Communism throughout the world. In every important country except Germany the Communist parties had come into being under the direct impetus of Moscow; they bore the Russian stamp as their birth-mark. The mere existence of the Third International with its vast resources and world-wide pretensions stood in the way of the development of an indigenous British, French or even German Communism, which might have responded to national outlooks and national emergencies. The movements that existed could be, and were, justly discredited as puppets whose strings were pulled in Moscow.

For this reason it is, as M. Lazitch points out in a revealing chapter, extremely difficult to assess the strength of Communism in western Europe by counting up the membership of the respective parties, since this was almost always affected, sometimes favourably, sometimes adversely, by extraneous influences. Indeed, the Communist parties of France, Italy, Belgium and most countries of western Europe have been immensely stronger since the abolition of the Third International than they were at any time during its existence: M. Lazitch has some telling figures on this point. Generalizations on this tricky, complex and controversial question are even more rash than most historical generalizations. But it would seem fair to say that, in all countries where standards of living and civilization were far in advance of those of Russia, the assumption of Russian leadership implicit in the organization of the Third International proved detrimental, throughout the period between the two wars, to the cause which it professed to promote.

But, unlike the First and Second Internationals, the Third International—and this is a point which M. Lazitch ignores—was not solely concerned with Europe. It is true that, at the moment of its foundation, the eyes of the Bolsheviks were trained on Europe, the focus of all their hopes and all their fears. But even the manifesto of the first congress did not forget the "enslaved peoples" of Asia and Africa; and from the time of the second congress, of which one of the high spots was a debate on the "national and colonial question" led by Lenin and the Indian Communist Roy, Asia was never far from the centre of the picture. But while in Asia, even more than in Europe, the impetus to the foundation of Communist parties and the inspiration for their action came from Moscow, Russian leadership here carried none of the unwelcome implications which it had for the West. Moscow stood, not for the dictatorship of an alien Power, but for the dawn of a new hope, not for a decline in economic, political and cultural standards, but for an escape from the backwardness and humiliations of the past.

It is because of this fundamental difference of attitude, already apparent in the history of the Third International, that Soviet policy since the war has enjoyed so much success in splitting East and West. Between these two extremes the countries of eastern Europe, where Cominform operates to-day as a sort of bastard posthumous offspring of Comintern, occupy an intermediate position; for here, while western European influences counted for much, the tradition of Russian leadership was also strong—even among the Czechs, the most westernized of these peoples, and the only one among them to develop a vigorous Communist party in the period between the wars. But these conflicting influences were at work long before the Bolshevik revolution, and carry us back to factors far earlier than the beginnings of international Communism.

11 Marriage of Inconvenience

The episode of the Anglo-Russian Trade Union Joint Advisory Council or Committee, founded in 1925 and dissolved after a tempestuous career in 1927, brings out vividly, by pointing up the contrast, aspects of the mentality both of the Russian and of the British trade unions which commonly remain in the background. More significantly, it illustrates the besetting problem of Soviet relations with the Western world for almost sixty years, when formulas of agreement mask underlying discords, and what look like the same words are used with more or less subtly different shades of meaning.

The troubles begin with the conception of the "united front", which goes back to 1921. It is better not to be too censorious about this policy; the Russians are not the only politicians responsible for the framing of policy who do not always know exactly where they are going, and pursue mutually incompatible aims. When the Bolsheviks seized power in the autumn of 1917, they had their own picture of what was going to happen. The Russian revolution would touch off revolutions elsewhere in the more advanced European countries; and these would be their salvation. It seemed inconceivable to them that they could survive for long alone in a capitalist world. A year later, and for some time after, it was still plausible to believe that the prospect of revolution would be realized in Germany and central Europe; and their own survival in the turmoil of the civil war hung in the balance.

By 1921 all this was over. Stabilization and recovery were in the air. The Soviet regime in Russia had survived the strain. But so had capitalist society in the rest of Europe. Nothing catastrophic was going to happen for some time; and it was necessary to establish a *modus vivendi* between the two worlds. The ideology which asserted the desirability and the inevitability of the downfall of capitalism could not be abandoned. On the other hand, communists must try

to make friends—to form a "united front"—with left-wing sympathizers in capitalist countries who might oppose and mitigate the
hostility of their governments to the Soviets. Ambiguities in this
dual policy were apparent from the outset. Lenin spoke of
supporting the MacDonalds and Hendersons "as the rope supports
the man who is being hanged". Karl Radek, rather more elegantly,
wanted to "embrace them in order to stifle them".

The British trade union movement was an obvious field for an
experiment in united front tactics. Marxism had, it was true, made
less impact on British than on Continental workers. But Great
Britain was the most advanced industrial country, and the British
trade unions the most powerful in the world; the omens were not
unpromising. A lot of enthusiasm for the workers' revolution and
the workers' government in Russia had been expressed in fiery
revolutionary speeches by British trade unionists. The British
workers had compelled the British government to abandon its
military intervention in the civil war in 1919, and had stopped the
shipment of munitions to Poland during the Polish-Soviet war of
1920. Fraternization between British and Russian trade unions
seemed assured. It reached its peak in 1924 when both combined to
put pressure on a faltering British Labour government to conclude
the Anglo-Soviet treaty then in course of negotiation. Mikhail
Tomsky, the Russian trade union leader, spoke amid scenes of
enthusiasm at the trade union congress in Hull in September; and
two months later the compliment was repaid when a delegation
from the TUC, led by its left-wing president A. A. Purcell, attended
the Russian trade union congress in Moscow.

It was in this atmosphere that the idea of an Anglo-Russian joint
committee, a standing committee meeting periodically to promote
cooperation between British and Russian trade unions, was first
conceived. By the time it was brought to birth at a special
conference in April 1925, the climate was already changing. The
charge of softness to communists and Russians had helped to defeat
the Labour government in the "Zinoviev letter" election of the
previous autumn. The handful of British communists were making
themselves a nuisance to the Labour party and the trade unions, as
well as to other people. The Conservative government was working
to draw Germany back into the Western fold, and was openly
hostile to Moscow. The trade unions were not insensitive to the
wind of change. Tomsky was once more applauded at the

Scarborough congress in September 1925, and some solid left resolutions voted. But undercurrents of mistrust were coming to the surface. Jimmy Thomas and Ernest Bevin emerged as powerful leaders of a right wing in the trade unions.

The Anglo-Russian committee began to function in a world which no longer had a place for it. Professor Calhoun, in a scholarly study, enriched by extensive research in unpublished TUC archives, has charted its always erratic, sometimes farcical course.[1] The Russians were the active partners, coming up with one proposal after another for joint manifestoes on trade union unity, on aid for the striking miners, on the danger of imperialist war, on whatever issue at the moment bulked largest in Moscow, or seemed most likely to drive a wedge between right and left in the British movement. The committee was a perfect propaganda platform, and a way of showing up those traitors on the British left who now wanted to back out of their fine words about revolution and Anglo-Soviet solidarity.

The British contingent dragged their feet from the start, and especially when the able but skeptical Walter Citrine succeeded to the post of secretary-general of the TUC. It was difficult to find a convenient time and place for meetings of the Anglo-Russian commitee members. When they met, the time available was curtailed by other engagements. They were not empowered to discuss this or that question raised by the Russians. More and more time was spent in recriminations. The intervals between meetings were filled with acrimonious correspondence between Tomsky and Citrine. All too obviously, the TUC had an unwanted child on its hands. The Russians kept it alive, partly in order to exploit British embarrassment, partly because the Russian party opposition in Moscow, and especially Trotsky, denounced the committee as an undignified concession to reactionary British trade union leaders, and it was necessary at all costs to prove the opposition wrong. Finally, it was the British—in September 1927—who at length summoned up courage to make the break.

What lies behind this strange story, and makes it significant, is the total incompatibility and mutual incomprehension existing between the Russian and British unions, not only about aims and

[1] Daniel F. Calhoun, *The United Front: the TUC and the Russians 1923–1928* (Cambridge: Cambridge University Press).

policies, but about what kind of animals they were. The Russian unions had had no effective prerevolutionary organization or experience. They were part of the revolutionary movement. Once the revolution had triumphed, some people wondered what role the unions had still to play and whether they would survive. It was the Soviets of Workers' Deputies, not the trade unions, that now spoke for the workers. They did survive—they were strong enough for that—but at the logical cost of their integration in the state machine. The organs of the workers and the organs of the workers' state could not go their separate ways. It was hard to say whether the People's Commissariat of Labour was an auxiliary of the trade unions, or the unions of the Commissariat. Together they were responsible for carrying out economic policy in so far as this concerned the allocation, remuneration, and control of labor. Any differences between them and other economic organs were ironed out by the supreme party authority, whose decisions were mandatory for all.

The British delegates, brought up to think of trade unions as engaged in a running battle with employers, and with the state which supported them, could make nothing of all this. They constantly sought to identify a special trade union interest, and could not understand that trade union policy and Soviet policy were not even opposite sides of the same coin, but the same side. For a long time they hoped that Tomsky, who alone of the Russian team could speak in something like a Western idiom, might be encouraged to win over his stubborn colleagues to more reasonable attitudes. It was an odd misapprehension of what went on in a Russian delegation. The Russian trade unions were fighting nobody except these obstinate and incomprehensible foreigners who refused to play their revolutionary games.

But this narrative of misunderstandings is most interesting of all in the light which it throws on the complex and rarely discussed mentality of the British trade union movement. The Protestant nonconformist background embedded in its tradition gave it a missionary zeal and fervour in the cause of the oppressed which kindled a lively flame of enthusiasm for the workers' revolution in Russia. But the same tradition also accommodated a respect for a liberal society and the rule of law; the prospect of winning concessions for the workers within that society, and through its procedures, still seemed real. There was nothing here of the anarchist strain which is a common ingredient of the revolutionary spirit.

The Russians, in so far as they were aware (which was not very far) of this duality in the British movement, attributed it to a split between the mass of workers and timid or corrupt leaders who betrayed them. There was a grain of truth in this explanation. It cost the rank and file of trade unionists nothing to demonstrate their enthusiasm for worthy causes. The General Council had the less easy task of translating words into action, and did not always relish it. They were more in touch with "official" opinion, and were sometimes swayed by it. Long after the General Council would have been glad to rid itself of the incubus of the Anglo-Russian Committee, it would have been impossible to get a popular vote for its dissolution. Even in September 1927, when the council submitted to the annual congress a unanimous recommendation to jettison the committee, much vocal opposition—and not only from left-wingers—was heard from the floor; and it required all Bevin's eloquence to push through the resolution by a four-to-one majority. And this was followed by a resolution, which was carried unanimously, deploring the action of the British government in breaking off relations with Moscow.

The general strike of 1926 spotlighted the duality of the movement and the bewilderment of the Russians. The great mass of workers fervently embraced the cause of the miners, and responded eagerly to the call for a strike to support them. The General Council had committed itself too far in words, and was maneuvered into calling a strike about which its leading members were at best half-hearted. The Russians regarded it as political—a revolutionary bid to seize power. What else could a general strike mean? It was nothing of the kind—just an old-fashioned quarrel, though on a mammoth scale, about wages. It was the government that insisted on treating it as an incipient revolution; and, when this became clear, the General Council, full of disclaimers on any revolutionary intention, beat a retreat.

In the eyes of the Russians, it betrayed the workers. But the workers were not altogether unwilling to be betrayed. They too had had a whiff of revolution, and it made them uncomfortable. The miners were abandoned, as they had been in 1921. Six months later, the miners, the last hope of the Russians, also had to concede defeat.

Deep bitterness remained, but no revolutionary movement. A lot of miners drifted into the British Communist Party in the second half of 1926, and drifted out again in the next two years.

Fifty years later, one can still argue whether, in the perspective of a century or more, the general strike should be seen as a first halting step on the road to a British workers' revolution, or a final demonstration that such a revolution is impossible. In one direction Britain has since travelled some way along the Russian road—the integration of the trade unions into the machinery of the government. This has set up tensions between the leaders and the workers on the shop floor—tensions in part fomented, in part cushioned, by the movement of shop stewards, who have sometimes acted independently of union officials. The miners remain a special case. But the ramshackle rickety trade union structure stands intact. Trade union solidarity is still an enormous force, and serves as an unbreached dam against revolutionary currents.

Much in the landscape remains, however, clouded. If Professor Calhoun had had more space—it was marginally relevant to his theme—he might have taken a look at the most promising of the British communist "fronts" of the 1920s: the National Unemployed Workers' Movement. The TUC, involved in it at the outset, backed out on scenting the whiff of communist domination. The communists later dropped it with other united front organizations. When unemployment became the key question of politics in the 1930s, communists were no longer in the vanguard of the movement. Moscow no longer wanted to see a revolution in the Western world. But perhaps even today mass unemployment, more than the wages question, is the Achilles' heel of the British trade unions and of the capitalist economy.

The story of the British and Russian trade unions in the 1920s leads Professor Calhoun in his epilogue to some general reflections. "Had the International not jettisoned the united front in 1928", he remarks, "It is questionable whether Adolf Hitler would ever have come to power in Germany five years later". One of those dubious might-have-beens of history! Professor Calhoun goes on quite sensibly to explain that the change of line in the Communist International was not due simply to a whim of Stalin, or to a calculation of domestic politics, but followed on the failure of the united front tactics to produce results. Perhaps no policy that could have been devised in Moscow would have worked. The story carries its own lessons, and leaves the reader to choose the ones he prefers. It is told here with a wit and irony which show that, in order to be serious, one does not need to be ponderous. Occasionally the writer's sense of fun gets the better of him. The Food and Drink Workers' International may not have been a very important organization. But it was not just a collection of revolutionary waiters and wine stewards.

12 The Legacy of Stalin

It is just about fifty years since the sinister and imposing figure of Stalin began to dominate the Soviet scene. It still does so today, as the figure of Peter the Great dominated the Russian scene through much of the eighteenth century. This does not merely mean that Soviet citizens and Soviet historians, looking back on the recent past, inevitably frame their judgments of that past as verdicts on Stalin and Stalinism, and that currently accepted views of Stalin are an index of policies being pursued today. It means also that political and economic controversies in the Soviet Union still fall into the pattern of arguing about the continuation or rejection of policies inaugurated by Stalin.

Both Alec Nove's *Stalinism and After*[1] and Moshe Lewin's *Political Undercurrents in Soviet Economic Debates*[2] revolve round the cluster of problems evoked by the concept of Stalinism. Both are concerned with the question asked by Professor Nove in the title of one of his earlier writings: *Was Stalin Really Necessary?* And, since no Westerner, and very few people in the Soviet Union, care to answer this question with an unqualified affirmative, the reply turns into an exploration of more or less radical alternatives to this or that aspect of Stalinism. Both these writers—Moshe Lewin even more explicitly than Alec Nove—are concerned with the discovery of a better way than Stalin found of coping with the cardinal problem inherent in the Russian revolution: that of overcoming Russia's age-long economic backwardness and of bringing Russia into the modern industrial world. Here, however, the resemblance between them ends.

Professor Nove has set out to produce a clear and concise account at a fairly elementary level, without scholarly apparatus or statistical tables, and also without the all too common intrusion of complacent moralizing, of the origins, character and consequences

---

[1] Alec Nove, *Stalinism and After* (London: Allen & Unwin).
[2] Moshe Lewin, *Political Undercurrents in Soviet Economic Debates* (London: Pluto).

of Stalinism. His approach is tentative in a way which sometimes leaves a certain impression of superficiality. He sets forth the different factors which contributed to the rise of Stalinism without probing any of them too deeply, and without deciding which should be regarded as dominant. He offers two alternative explanations of the same situation or event with only the barest hint, if any, of which he prefers. One red herring he prudently avoids: the psychological investigation of Stalin's personality. Stalinism is a political phenomenon not explicable in terms of individual eccentricity.

Given his modest objectives, Professor Nove has scored a remarkable success. It will be difficult to find any other outline sketch of this crucial period of contemporary history so firmly concentrated on essentials, so carefully pruned of every excrescence of detail, so free from the element of shrill propaganda characteristic of much current Western writing about Soviet affairs. Indeed so rare nowadays is the attempt to take a balanced view, even to attempt to say what could be said in extenuation of Stalin's attitudes and policies on specific points, that Professor Nove may be in danger of incurring from some of our red-baiters the ludicrously unjustifiable charge of being an apologist for Stalin.

It is worth taking a look at some of the crucial issues in this light. Such achievements as "almost universal literacy, a great expansion of education, a social security system" may be credited to the Revolution, but not personally to Stalin, who like Churchill cared for none of these things. But can it be argued that it was Stalin's "economic strategy"—the forced industrialization at breakneck speed, at the expense of the peasant, of the wage-earner, of the consumer—which "made possible the survival of Soviet Union in a desperate military struggle with Nazi Germany"? Professor Nove states this view cogently and fairly, but leaves the last word to the prosecutor:

> His victims number many, many millions. It is absurd to argue that they *had* to die to ensure the success of Soviet policies. It is arguable that these very policies would have been pursued more effectively if they had not been massacred.

If one cavils a little at this presentation, it is because, to anyone reared in a liberal tradition, there is something mechanical and rather repugnant in this weighing of human lives against material achievement. One would like to believe that the costs of progress can be measured in less brutal terms.

Foreign affairs played their part both in the genesis and in the procedures of Stalinism. Less than due attention is perhaps paid in these pages to the role of the Allies in the civil war and to the long trail of fear and mistrust which it left behind. Professor Nove will not decide whether the war scare of 1927 was "sincere", or whether it was deliberately promoted to support the more radical and uncompromising turn in all Soviet policies from 1928 onwards. It is true that no Western power in the middle 1920s could or would have undertaken military action against the Soviet Union. But it is also true that at no time during the past twenty years could or would the Soviet Union have undertaken military action against Western Europe. Should one nevertheless deny that the fears in both cases were sincerely and deeply felt?

War situations breed strong national feelings and prejudices. It is not often that one comes across in a book published in the West so spirited an apologia as Professor Nove offers, "in the harsh terms of Great Power politics", for the Nazi-Soviet pact of 1939, or so crisp a verdict:

> By twentieth-century international standards of behaviour it was not worse than many other things that were done in and by the West.

But this, whatever may be said for it, was quickly qualified by Stalin's blindness to the consequences of Germany's victories in the west, and eventually to the imminence of the German attack on the Soviet Union.

Professor Nove professes no philosophy of history, and is disinclined to see history as an inexorable succession of events, one growing out of the other. A passing mention of Stolypin prompts the rather jaunty question: "Who knows, perhaps Stolypin was right when he claimed that political stability under Tsardom would come, given time." Another question would have been more germane to his subject. Who knows, perhaps Lenin, had he lived, would have brought the Revolution to a more humane, more fruitful, less bloodstained consummation. Professor Nove does not belong to the school which equates Leninism with Stalinism, and makes one significant point:

It is true that statesmen do not always speak the truth. But others, Lenin included, would have talked about the necessity of sacrifices rather than blandly denying that any sacrifices existed.

Stalin hailed as triumphs, and converted into a system, compromises, concessions and abuses which Lenin, if he had been driven to accept them, would have treated as harsh and temporary sacrifices.

Every historian, however, has his own ideologically conditioned angle of approach; and Professor Nove's standpoint, for all his detachment and impartiality, can be identified. He is no worshipper of Western capitalist society. His ideals are humane, his inclinations socialist. He might perhaps be called in Russian terms a Menshevik, in English terms a Fabian.

But this brings with it a certain antagonism, consciously held in check, to so tumultuous and turbulent an outbreak as the October Revolution. He is more at home when analysing the degeneration of the Revolution under Stalin than in describing the mystique of its early years, which was still a driving force in the years of the first five-year plan, and lived on beneath the surface till it was crushed out of existence by Stalin in the purges.

Professor Nove would probably not call himself a Marxist. But he is alive to the damage done by Stalinism to the cause of Marxism in Russia and throughout the world:

> It is due to the Stalin terror that original Marxist thought atrophied in Russia, and so the recent interest in Marxist ideas in the West and in developing countries has kindled no Soviet contribution or response worthy of the name.

It goes further than that. Stalinism has been widely and effectively invoked to discredit the names of Lenin and of Marx. No weapon has come handier to conservatives of every brand and shade in Western countries than the argument that any radical change in our social and economic system is a step on the road to Stalinism.

The weakness of *Stalinism and After* is perhaps that it gives in too easily to the Stalinist concept of a monolithic orthodoxy. Oppositions appear in these pages, both under Stalin and under his successors, as agents and victims in an all-or-nothing struggle for power; little account is taken of the continuous ferment of ideas going on beneath the smooth and uniform surface. This is the special interest of Moshe Lewin's *Political Undercurrents*. Mr Lewin is concerned to show how, throughout much of the Soviet period, and especially since Stalin's death, substantial and fruitful controversies about the running of the economy have been carried on in the traditional language of subservience to a monolithic authority.

The picture is realistic—far more so than most pictures of what goes on in the Soviet Union today. Pressure groups are at work. Problems of planning (the "command economy"), of agriculture, of the role of the market, are constantly canvassed, and produce varying decisions, and reversals of decisions. Nothing is less plausible than the vision of a monolithic power issuing its unchallengeable edicts from the top. Moreover this economic pulling and hauling has its political repercussions:

> The alternation between "thaws" and "freezes", which has characterised Soviet policies since Stalin's death, externally express [*sic*] the deeper tensions involved. If the system in its current version is in fact "over-extended" and has difficulty coping with the growing maze of problems and social and economic complexities, more revisions, twists of policy, "thaws" and "freezes" can be anticipated.

The Soviet Union is not the only country where economic crises inspire "stop-go" policies. Mr Lewin throws a searching light on some of these processes at work.

This is, nevertheless, an extremely odd book, and one has to guess how it came to be what it is. Mr Lewin seems to have started with an ambition to write an intellectual biography of Bukharin (the first chapter is "Bukharin's life"). He remarks rather ruefully in his introduction that Isaac Deutscher's brilliant biography "has helped to restore Trotsky to the place he deserved in Soviet history, at least in western literature", and he would like to see the same tribute paid to Bukharin. But the character of a biography depends on the subject as well as on the biographer. To present Bukharin as a thinker with a coherent message would be a daunting task.

In the days of Lenin and Trotsky, his agile and impressionable temperament led him constantly to shift his ground, swinging from one extreme to another; under Stalin, he was so often content to revamp the clichés of the official line that his personal image becomes dull and tarnished. In the immense corpus of his speeches and writings, quotations can be found to justify almost any position.

What Mr Lewin has done in his first four chapters (one quarter of the book) is to rewrite, in terms of Bukharin's policies and pronouncements, the history of the crucial years 1925–1928, when the New Economic Policy with its emphasis on the appeasement of the peasant was gradually eroded by the pressures for rapid and intensive industrialization culminating in the first five-year plan. When, after the elimination of Trotsky at the end of 1927, Stalin went over to the industrializers and inaugurated a regime of all-round radicalization and totalitarian pressures, Bukharin, who had embraced the pro-peasant orientation with his customary enthusiasm, was adrift. After a year of rather half-hearted struggle (of the three who now formed a "Right" opposition only Tomsky was a born fighter), Bukharin was condemned and removed from the seats of power—though never expelled from the party.

Mr Lewin believes firmly in the market economy of NEP, has a strong emotional feeling for the peasant, and mistrusts the harshness of industrialization and centralized planning. Bukharin naturally becomes his hero, though even here a good deal of selectiveness and idealization is required. If a prize is to be offered for "a Bolshevik anti-Stalinite", Trotsky is surely a more convincing candidate; and to describe Trotsky in exile as becoming converted to "Bukharinist" ideas borders on the absurd.

Nor does one much care for the credit awarded to Bukharin as the main author (he served on a drafting commission with Vyshinsky as one of his colleagues!) of the "democratic" Stalin constitution of 1936, promulgated three months after the trial and execution of Zinoviev and Kamenev. As an individual, Bukharin was a lovable and gentle character, not a man of action, but an intellectual *pur sang*, a clever and fluent writer and speaker. These qualities give him a special place among the Bolshevik leaders. At present what he needs most of all is to be saved from over-zealous admirers.

But what has all this preliminary matter to do with the valuable core of the book, already described above? Believe it or not, the discussion of the contemporary economic problems of the Soviet Union is also made to revolve round the personality and opinions of Bukharin:

> The phenomenon of "liberal communism" in eastern Europe . . . polycentrism, economic difficulties, reforms, and new ways of thinking in the Soviet Union, especially among the intellectuals there—all rested on the critique of the system created under the aegis of Stalin.

In the words of an American observer of the 1960s: "The ideas of the twenties are far from dead in our days."

In a very broad sense this is true. Centralized planning and decentralized administration, the balance between industry and agriculture, priorities for producer or consumer goods, controlled versus market prices—all these problems were debated in the 1920s, and are still debated today. Themes change, but recur in their changed form. Denunciation of inefficient and oppressive bureaucracy is as much in order today as it was fifty years ago. More broadly still, every-turning-point in the great debate will divide the radicals who demand prompt and drastic solutions from conservatives and cautious liberals who preach the virtues of hurrying slowly. If anyone wants to acclaim the latter as followers of Bukharin, why grudge him the pleasure?

But seriously, on any significant level, this proposition makes no sense. In the Soviet Union for which Bukharin prescribed in the 1920s, nearly 80 per cent of the population lived and worked in the country; today the proportion of the rural population has fallen below 40 per cent. Arguments valid in one situation may be quite inappropriate to the other. If today more ordered and leisurely progress imposes itself, this is partly because the economy has advanced for enough to afford it.

Alternatively, for all the progress made, Soviet agriculture is still desperately backward. Mr Lewin quotes some significant figures. The Soviet Union has eight tractors for 1,000 hectares of ploughed land, the United States thirty-four, West Germany 129. In the United States six million people are working directly on the land and seven million in industries supplying agriculture; in the Soviet Union the corresponding figures are 29 and two million. Soviet yields per hectare are double those under NEP, but half those of the United States and one-third of the German and English. Whatever went wrong in the 1920s, it is difficult to believe that the Soviet Union—or Soviet agriculture—has suffered from too much industrialization. Nor, so far as the evidence goes, do any of the contemporary controversialists in the Soviet Union invoke the authority of Bukharin; it would indeed be difficult today to hymn the virtues of "snail-pace industrialization". Trotsky's name is still alive in the Soviet Union as a target of official popular propaganda; he is still a living enemy. Bukharin's name crops up from time to time in the pages of a learned journal, but otherwise appears to be forgotten.

Let us, however, return to the real value of Mr Lewin's book. He has shown top-level planners, sophisticated economists and practical administrators locked, behind the spurious façade of ideological conformity, in a continuing debate on the fundamental problems of the Soviet economy and Soviet society. He has probed some of the most sensitive points of controversy.

The story of the Soviet economy told by the modern scholar has been simultaneously a story of tensions and accumulating contradictions among the state and social classes and groups, sometimes a straightforward chasm between state and society— a far cry from the pretended harmony between the centralized state and party guidance, and mass initiative and popular sovereignty. . . . For the first time relations among state, society, social groups and economy were scrutinised.

This is a work of imaginative insight as well as of scholarship. If it has been triggered off by the notion that all this has something to do with Bukharin, we should not complain too much. All one need say is that Mr Lewin might have written a more sober, though perhaps less readable, book if the Bukharin bee had not buzzed in his bonnet.

13 Jewry under Bolshevism

Among the hated legacies of Tsarist Russia which the revolution of 1917 was pledged to eradicate, anti-Semitism had a prominent place. Nothing could have been more natural. The association of many Jews with the revolutionary cause had often been cited to justify the prejudice against them and the brutal measures of repression to which they were subjected. After the revolution anti-Semitism was constantly invoked by the Russian "Whites" and their foreign supporters, not excluding a section of the British press, to discredit a regime several of whose prominent leaders were Jews. But anti-Semitism was deeply embedded in traditional Russian attitudes, especially in rural areas; and in this respect, as in others, tradition dies hard. The story of the Jews in the Soviet Union has been one of good intentions gradually submerged by defective, and sometimes vicious, practice. Since about 1930, the Jews have never been able to feel themselves secure in the Soviet environment. The only question that can fairly be asked is whether, at any rate in certain periods, they were less secure than many other sections of the population.

The Jews in Soviet Russia[1] is a collection of solid essays, both historical and analytical, by Jewish writers on various aspects of the problem. Concentration on a single topic may tend to create the impression of too sweeping and one-sided an indictment. But the individual contributors have obviously striven to achieve a high measure of objectivity, and to avoid the pitfalls of exaggeration. Professor Schapiro, who has written an introduction, sets the tone by remarking that "no serious scholar, no scholar of the standing of those whose contributions appear in the pages which follow, would go so far as to equate the position of the Jew in the Soviet Union today with the oppression of the Jew in the Russia of 1883 or 1903",

---

[1] Lionel Kochan (ed.), *The Jews in Soviet Russia since 1917* (London: Oxford University Press for the Institute of Jewish Affairs).

and by discerning "grounds for modified optimism" even in the present situation.

The Bolsheviks—for two reasons which were closely allied—did not regard the Jews as constituting a nation. In the first place, they accepted the Western European rather than the German concept of the nation, which defined a nation by the possession among other things, of a national territory. The lack of this qualification distinguished the Jews from all other national minorities in the Soviet Union. Secondly, the Bolsheviks regarded the differences in racial and religious background between Jew and Gentile as basically irrelevant, and believed that the destiny of the Jew was to be assimilated with the population among which he lived. This belief was common to Bolsheviks and Mensheviks (who had an even larger proportion of Jews among their members than the Bolsheviks). At the beginning of the twentieth century it was, of course, shared by virtually all liberals, and by very many influential Jews, in Western Europe.

This view influenced Party thinking from the earliest days of the Party. While the existence within the Russian Social Democratic Party of, say, Ukrainian and Lettish national units was taken for granted, jealousy and resentment were felt at a corresponding Jewish association—the "Bund"—partly no doubt because it successfully competed with other sections of the party for members. After the revolution, when the Bund was disbanded, it was found necessary or expedient to create "Jewish sections" (as well as other national sections) within the party organization at different levels. These sections continued to exist till 1930. But they were regarded with toleration rather than enthusiasm, and none of the Jews among the prominent Party leaders was ever associated with them. Oddly enough, the only top-ranking figure in the government hierarchy who ever expressed sympathy in public with Jewish national aspirations was the Gentile Kalinin.

A demographic study of the Jewish population of the Soviet Union is contained in an exhaustive and scholarly article by Alec Nove and J. A. Newth, who begin by discussing at length the different criteria that can be applied in attempting to answer the question: What is a Jew? Before 1914; the number of Jews in the Russian Empire probably exceeded five millions. But the cession of territory after the revolution almost halved this number; and in the Second World War Nazi menaces and deportations decimated the Jewish population of the regions where it was most numerous. The census of 1959 returned just over 2¼m Jews, registered as such on the strength of their own statements. It is generally agreed that this is an underestimate of the number of Jews in most senses of the term, which may be as high as 3 millions. Subject to all margins of error and uncertainty, Jews constitute between 1 and 1.5 per cent of the population of the Soviet Union.

The proportion is, however, not uniformly spread. The areas belonging to the old Pale of Settlement—the Ukrainian and Belorussian republics—still have 2 per cent of their population Jewish. But the main variation from the norm results from the flow of Jews into the large cities, which has been going on almost continuously since the revolution. Of the population of Moscow, 4.5 per cent is now Jewish; of Leningrad 5.1 per cent; of Vilna 7 per cent; of Kiev 13.9 per cent. The predominantly urban character of the Jewish population is reflected in such statistics as are available of occupational distribution. It seems clear that the proportion of Jews in the professions is higher than their proportion in the population. Of higher "specialists" employed in the national economy in 1964, 7 per cent were Jews, and of "scientific workers" 8 per cent. On the other hand, Jews appear to have been almost entirely excluded from political life, as well as from diplomatic posts abroad.

History has known anti-Semitism in many different guises, which are categorized meticulously, perhaps a shade too systematically, in an essay by Dr. Weinryb. Russian anti-Semitism was basically a primitive peasant anti-Semitism far removed from the self-conscious, sophisticated racial anti-Semitism of the Nazi Herrenvolk. Like medieval anti-Semitism, it had religious overtones. In the 1920s, when official Soviet denunciations of anti-Semitism were still frequent and vigorous, they were commonly coupled with denunciations of the Orthodox church, and sometimes of the Dissenters; the association was not fortuitous, and there was some justification for it.

The stereotype of the Jew, however, which haunted the Russian country-side was the trader, the usurer, the speculator, the man from the small market-town who, not himself a cultivator of the soil, managed to squeeze a living out of the impoverished cultivator and his products. The picture was partly, but not wholly, mythical; and in these capacities, real or imagined, the Jew suffered all the vagaries of Soviet history. In the civil war the Ukrainian nationalist forces gave short shrift to the Jews: Denikin's armies were only marginally better. The end of the civil war and the introduction of the New Economic Policy in 1921 seemed to promise a regime of greater tolerance for traditional Jewish pursuits. Trade in the produce of the soil was once more permitted and even encouraged. The value of money was stabilized, and credit began to flow again in modest trickles. There was even some easing up in the campaign against religion.

This interlude proved illusory and short. The hint of toleration refurbished the image of the huckstering, exploiting Jew, and fanned again all the old prejudices, so that when in the middle and later 1920s the official machine was put into reverse, a brake applied to N.E.P., and the campaign for planning and intensive industrialization set in motion, the Jews were at the receiving end of all these pressures. The world of trade and finance was squeezed out of existence, or driven underground; the Nepman was denounced and treated as the ally of the Kulak. Internal party politics played their part. Hints appear to have been dropped, even in Party circles, that the leaders of the opposition, Trotsky, Zinoviev and Kamenev, were Jews, and that the upholders of the official line, Stalin, Molotov and Bukharin, were not.

In contrast with what came after, it is fair to say that, throughout the 1920s, the Soviet leaders, Stalin included, continued publicly to denounce and deplore the growth of anti-Semitism, and somewhat half-hearted attempts were made to deal with the Jewish problem. These took the form of projects to settle Jews on the land, and thus give the Jewish population a territorial and agricultural basis. Southern Russia and the Crimea were the favourite areas for these experiments, some of which were backed by American money. In 1927, a Jewish "national district" was organized in the Kherson department of the Ukraine with a population of 16,000, of whom 85 per cent were said to be Jews. But none of these schemes enjoyed more than a moderate success, and they barely scratched the surface of the problem.

Even less success attended a more ambitious project launched in the following year. The large and sparsely populated region of Birobidjan in eastern Siberia was allocated for Jewish settlement, with the avowed intention of creating "a Jewish national administrative unit". But the requisite capital was not forthcoming to reclaim and bring into cultivation an area of forest and scrub with an unpropitious climate. Only a handful of Jews could be induced to make the arduous journey to this remote tract of country, and of these not all remained as permanent settlers. Though Birobidjan was eventually proclaimed a Jewish National Republic, the scheme was an almost total fiasco, and survived only as an unreal symbol of the Jewish national entity in the Soviet Union. According to the 1959 census, Jews formed only 8.8 per cent of a population of 163,000. A learned and exhaustive essay by Chimen Abramsky collects such scraps of information as are available about its present condition.

The failure of such plans to transform the Jews into Russian peasants—and it is easy to find plenty of reasons why they were foredoomed to fail—left the Soviet Jews with nowhere to go. Those who became factory workers were assimilated into the industrial proletariat, and probably suffered no worse than the rest of the workers. But they were too few to make much impression on the magnitude of the problem. A party report of 1925, preserved in the Smolensk archives, on a village in the province of predominantly Jewish population, noted that all the Jews were engaged in one of two things: religion and the flax trade. Neither of these traditional occupations helped the Jews to become integrated into Soviet society. They were differentiated from other national minorities by more than their lack of a national territory.

By the end of the 1920s private trade had sensed the faint and fluctuating line which separated legality from illegality; and Jews were not likely to enjoy indulgences. Driven from legitimate private trade, they either went underground into the black market, which never ceased to offer opportunities to the ingenious, or took refuge in the one non-manual occupation still open to them—the clerical staffs of the ever-expanding administrative economic and cultural institutions. Jews in the later 1920s were said to supply 30 per cent of the personnel of all Soviet institutions in the Ukraine and Belorussia; higher positions in these could still, though in diminishing proportion, be held by Jews. In Moscow Jews were still prominent in professional and intellectual occupations. Kalinin in November 1926, in the most sympathetic speech ever delivered by a Soviet leader on Jewish themes, admitted that the number of prominent positions held by Jews made the intelligentsia "perhaps more anti-Semitic now than it was under the Tsar", and that people asked, "Why are there so many Jews in Moscow?"

The story of the suffering of Soviet Jewry is one not so much of sudden and deliberate decisions as of the cumulative intensification of processes that could be observed from the early years of the regime onwards. If a higher proportion of Jews than their numbers could warrant figured as victims of the purges of the 1920s, this was because the purges fell with greatest severity on the intelligentsia, which always carried a relatively high quota of Jews. The massacres of the war could not be laid to the account of the Soviet Government. The nightmare of Stalin's last years diverged, by its very monstrosity, from any recognizable pattern, and was followed by a certain relaxation, which did not, however, mean an end of persecution, but its reduction to more "normal" dimensions. That the whole process, except perhaps for the Stalinist culmination, is explicable in terms of cause and effect does not make the story any less painful.

A composite work of this kind takes a long time to compile and publish; and many of the essays were probably drafted, or even completed, before the Six-Day War of June, 1967. But it receives guarded mention in several of them, and the final essay by Zev Katz is devoted to its consequences. Zionism in the Soviet Union is treated in an article earlier in the volume by Dr. Schechtman, and another on Hebrew literature in the Soviet Union by Dr. Gilboa. Since the 1890s Zionism had come to compete on an increasing scale with Social Democracy for the allegiance of Jewish intellectuals and the Jewish youth in Russia. It was unlikely to win sympathy from the revolutionary regime and, though not at first formally banned, was soon subject to sporadic persecution both by the authorities and by the Jewish sections of the party. Hebrew literature, disliked both for its religious and nationalist associations, led an underground existence almost from the start, in contrast with the toleration, and even encouragement, extended to Yiddish in the 1920s.

The Second World War led to a temporary relaxation of pressure on the Jews and to the formation of a Jewish Anti-Fascist Committee. But this kept clear of any association with Zionism. It is therefore all the more surprising that the Russian Government, for a brief period in 1947–1948, should have given active support, in the United Nations and elsewhere, to the creation of the Israeli state. It might, of course, be argued that Bolshevik theory had never ruled out the recognition of the Jews as a nation once they acquired a territorial existence. But the main motive at work seems to have been the desire to see the weakening of British Power in the Middle East and the birth of a new state which might be sympathetic to the Soviet Union. If so, it was a colossal miscalculation. Dr. Schechtman may indeed go too far when he says that the Russian Government was disappointed that "Israel showed no inclination to become a Soviet satellite". An Israel belonging to the "third world" might have been acceptable. But the year of the creation of Israel was also the year of the Marshall Plan; and, as the American tentacles spread further and further round a world now divided into two opposing camps, it was only too plain to which camp Israel was bound to pin its allegiance. From this time Russian hostility to Israel grew apace. The Six-Day War merely set the seal on an animosity which was already an ingrained factor in Russian policy.

The question how far the rise and recognition of Israel reacted on the fate of the Jews in the Soviet Union is one on which most contributors to this volume are reticent. The heavy hand of Zhdanov was felt by other minorities besides the Jews. The anti-Semitic frenzy of the last five years of Stalin's life, culminating in the openly anti-Semitic nuances of the Doctors' Plot affair, can no doubt be explained as an aggravation of earlier Soviet attitudes or as the work of a paranoiac dictator. It should also be recognized that the persecution of the Russian Jews was an important factor in sharpening Israeli hostility to the Soviet Union. But it is difficult to believe that the influence was not reciprocal, or that the fury and persistence of the persecution did not owe something to the atmosphere of the cold war and to the increasingly obvious dependence of Israel on the United States.

The same issue arises in an acute form after the Six-Day War. Mr. Katz quotes some remarks of Ilya Ehrenburg recorded by the late Alexander Werth. Ehrenburg is said to have observed that, if the Arabs had massacred the Jews, this would have provoked a wave of anti-Semitism in the Soviet Union, but that there is now a certain respect for the Jews as soldiers". This is a characteristically clever *boutade*, but surely not very plausible. The Russian Jews are in a most unhappy situation. Pressed to disown and condemn the exploits of the Israeli state, they are understandably reluctant to comply; and, if they do comply, they will not be believed. Whatever they do, and whatever they feel, they are doomed to suffer for the victories of Israel. It is difficult to imagine a more excruciating psychological tragedy.

The volume shows signs of excellent editing by Lionel Kochan. It cannot have been an easy job to marshal this galaxy of writers, to avoid overlapping and to give an air of cohesion and unity to the book. The subject is one of continuing interest. It may seem peripheral to the major problems of Israel and the Middle East, but is in fact part of them. It is not only in the Soviet Union that the triumphs of Zionism and the state interests of Israel present dilemmas of increasing complexity to the Jews of the Diaspora.

14 The Non-Jewish Jew

Since this posthumous volume of Isaac Deutscher's essays,[1] all of them reflecting in one way or another on Jewry and on his relation to it, is a highly personal document, it is appropriate that it should have as its introductory item a moving account by Tamara Deutscher of his Jewish childhood—the only part of his life when he was a Jew by religion as well as by race, and lived in an entirely and characteristically Jewish milieu. This account is based on his reminiscences, and is partly in his own words—taken, strangely enough, from an interview given by him on German radio only a few weeks before his death.

Deutscher referred to these years as "the most impressionable years" of his life, and he was surely right. The small town west of Cracow, not far from Auschwitz, almost at the meeting-point of the domains of the three monarchies that partitioned Poland, a town where the population was 75 per cent Jewish, and all the experiences of his childhood, must have seemed to the mature man "so unbelievably far away that they appeared unreal". It was here that, at the age of thirteen, deeply schooled in Talmudic lore, he prepared a dissertation on the kosher quality of the miraculous saliva of a mythical bird, and, wearing a black silk robe and the traditional sidelocks, was hailed as an infant prodigy and received as a rabbi. It was here, too, that he witnessed for the first time the persecution of his people—not only the petty harassments of everyday life, but the pogroms which swept through the town in the first days of the proclamation of an independent Poland after the downfall of the Habsburgs in November 1918.

At the age of fourteen the young Deutscher, in a dramatic and painful act of rebellion, shaved off his sidelocks, ate his first ham sandwich, and turned his back for ever on the Jewish, and indeed on all, religion. But such intense childhood experiences could not have left him unmarked. His father, against whom he rebelled, a printer

---

[1] Isaac Deutscher, *The Non-Jewish Jew and Other Essays* (London: Oxford University Press).

by trade, was steeped in German culture: Spinoza, Heine, and Lassalle were his heroes. He reproached his son with his interest in Polish literature: Polish culture was not international, and was of no use once you went "beyond Auschwitz", the frontier town. The profound, even fanatical, Jewish faith in which Deutscher was reared had no alloy of secular nationalism. It was a faith in the ultimate redemption of mankind; and this faith the young rabbi, when he shaved his sidelocks, did not altogether lose, even though the character of the redemption changed. In our hard-boiled days, Utopianism is a dirty word, and it was thrown often enough in recent times at Deutscher. Perhaps there is some significance in this. The Jew is the archetypal Utopian.

The title *The Non-Jewish Jew* is, of course, provocative; and in these essays Deutscher explores the many facets of Jewishness in its relation to the Central Europe which he knew, to the Russian Revolution, to Israel, and to himself. In western Europe anti-Semitism seemed only a peripheral and occasional phenomenon, and assimilation, with or without retention of the Jewish religion, seemed to many Jews a natural and desirable destiny; their ambition was to play their role in the community and to become indistinguishable as far as possible from its other members. In eastern Europe no such prospect could be even imagined. Ghetto life within boundaries set by custom or sometimes by law made the Jews a people apart, with a separate way of life, a separate language, and the sharp consciousness of a separate identity. The escape of a few wealthy or otherwise exceptional Jews from these conditions did not significantly affect the general picture. In the West, the nineteenth century brought liberation and assimilation to the Jews: "in eastern Europe it was a century of oppression and isolation".

It is in Marxist terms, with due regard to these geographical differences, that Deutscher analysed the Jewish problem. Marx was himself a western Jew, and the little he wrote on the Jewish question was written from a western point of view. The Jews formed "a prominent and spectacular section of the western bourgeoisie". Marx saw the Jewish way of life as essentially a product of capitalism; the Jewish problem was non-existent except as a problem of capitalism. To attack Jews as capitalists was right enough: Marx sometimes liked to make a paradoxical parade of anti-Semitism. But to attack Jews except as capitalists, and in association with other capitalists, was meaningless; Bebel, who was a sound Marxist, called anti-Semitism "the socialism of fools".

In eastern Europe this picture did not hold. The Jews remained a caste apart, so that it was not difficult to stir up enmity against them. They were hardly ever peasants or factory workers. They were small artisans or petty traders—but rarely on a scale that entitled them to count as capitalists. They belonged indubitably to the oppressed classes; since they had more education and more political consciousness than the primitive eastern European peasants, they contributed more than their quota to the growing army of revolutionaries. The vast majority of Jewish eastern European revolutionaries were Marxists, who shared with Marx and with the western Jews the belief that the ultimate goal and destiny of Jewry was unqualified unity with non-Jews in the socialist society of the future. They were consciously Jewish, but did not wish to remain differentiated as such from their fellow-men. This belief was devoutly held by all the Jewish leaders whose names figure in the revolutionary calendar, Bolshevik or Menshevik—by Martov, Dan and Rosa Luxemburg, no less than by Trotsky, Zinoviev and Kamenev.

A minority of eastern European Jews did, however, follow another path. The nineteenth century was the era everywhere of rising nationalism; and the debased nationalism of anti-Semitism began to breed an answering Jewish nationalism. It was here in eastern Europe, towards the end of the nineteenth century, that the seeds of Zionism first began to germinate—generally among the more conservative Jews who remained faithful to the strict religious traditions of Jewry, though Deutscher is undoubtely right in saying that, as late as the 1930s, a large majority of eastern European Jews were opposed to Zionism. It is all too easy now to convict them of error with one overwhelming argument. Had Zionist dreams been realized—and at the time there was, of course, no prospect of their realization—more Jews could have been saved from the holocaust. Hitler provided the vindication of Zionism.

But it is worth looking also at what happened in eastern Europe before Hitler. The Marxist vision of a socialist society which would be raceless as well as classless also proved utopian. Too many of the trappings of the old Russia still clung to the victorious revolution. For more than a decade the Bolshevik leaders struggled against any hint of a revival of anti-Semitism, which was constantly denounced as one of the shameful legacies of the Tsarist regime. But the old feelings died slowly and not only among the peasants. Nor was the process of assimilation as easy and painless as the enthusiasts had pictured it. A small minority of Jews became factory workers. Fewer still became farmers, though much effort and enthusiasm went into the founding of some Jewish agricultural colonies in South Russia— long before the ill-fated experiment of Birobidjan.

Far more Jews clung to the way of life which they knew, and profited by the licence accorded under the New Economic Policy to the small private traders and artisans, so that the campaign against private trade and against the practices of the N.E.P., which began in the later 1920s, hit the Jewish population disproportionately hard. This may well have been a more important factor in the rising wave of anti-Semitism than the jealousies created by the allegedly high proportion of Jews in white-collar occupations, in the universities, and among party and Soviet officials. By the 1930s, things had clearly begun to go wrong with the bright vision of a socialist society in which Jew and Gentile would have no reason to remember their differences.

It is the consciousness of this failure which haunts Deutscher's mind, and pervades the whole book. In a moving and eloquent postscript he confronts the fate of the Jews under Hitler:

> To the historian trying to comprehend the Jewish holocaust the greatest obstacle will be the absolute uniqueness of the catastrophe. . . . We are confronted here by a huge and ominous mystery of the degeneration of the human character that will forever baffle and terrify mankind.
>
> Perhaps a modern Aeschylus and Sophocles could cope with this theme, but they would do so on a level different from that of historical interpretation and explanation.

The horror of the gas-chambers made Zionism inevitable and acceptable. But does it really stand outside history? Can one regard Israel as a unique solution imposed by a unique catastrophe? Is it not rather that in a world of nations, a world which had destroyed the hopes so long nourished by an enlightened international Jewry, and which nowhere offered an equal and honoured place for Jewish tradition and culture, the assertion of a secular and political counter-nationalism was the logical answer?

The tragic dilemma of the Jewish state is the theme of Deutscher's ambivalent attitude. "I have long since abandoned my anti-

Zionism", he writes in 1954, "which was based on a confidence in the European labour movement, or more broadly in European society and civilization which that society and civilization have not justified." Israel had become a "historical necessity". Yet he cannot become a Zionist, and embrace what he describes as "another Jewish tragedy" and "a melancholy anachronism". Thirteen years later, in June 1967, the Israeli–Arab war seemed to have justified his worst apprehensions. He had at that moment only two months longer to live, and never penned a full and considered analysis of what he saw as a deeply disturbing episode. Like some other Jews outside Israel, he reacted very sharply against the mood engendered among the victors by this too easily won military triumph and its probable consequences; and he was less inhibited than many in expressing these anxieties.

The point cogently made by Deutscher is that the Israeli–Arab war intensified Israeli involvement in world politics, and specifically in the duel between the United States and the U.S.S.R. This involvement was, of course, already implicit in Israel's almost total dependence, economic and military, on the United States, and in the corresponding hostility of the U.S.S.R. to Israel and somewhat half-hearted support of the Arabs. But the war undoubtedly highlighted and increased the involvement, and Deutscher's gloomy foresights seem to have been justified by the more recent escalation of Soviet naval power in the Mediterranean, and perhaps by the militarization of Soviet policy elsewhere. Nobody can pretend that the war contributed to a lasting security, either local or global. On the contrary, it seems to have emphasized the precarious situation of Israel as a remote outpost of American power in a predominantly unfriendly environment.

This is not, however, Deutscher's main point. The issue is perhaps moral as well as political. What he deplores, as a humanist of what now seems unfortunately a rather old-fashioned kind, is the replacement of an international commitment which transcended national cultures by a narrow and self-centred Israeli nationalism. He was shocked when Ben-Gurion referred to non-Zionist Jews as "rootless cosmopolitans"—the very phrase coined by Stalin or Zhdanov at the time of the worst persecution of Jews in the U.S.S.R. "The future of Israel", he wrote in 1958 on the tenth anniversary of the state of Israel, "may depend on whether the Israelis are on guard against national conceits, and are able to find a common language with the peoples around them." It is Deutscher's life-long and unwavering vision of the ideal—an ideal compounded of humanist and Marxist and Judaic elements—which makes it so hard for him to stomach the harsh reality.

It is difficult to pursue further the argument between the ideal and the real provoked by this book. Hitler destroyed for a generation much of the idealism of the western world which had survived the First World War. Stalin went far to complete the work. In particular, the sense of Jewish liberation and the outburst of Jewish culture in Soviet Russia which followed the revolution of 1917—and of which Deutscher gives a striking example in a short essay on the painter Chagall, a strange, but characteristic, product of Russian Jewry—was stifled by Stalin. It is fair to see in the Israeli state and in Israeli nationalism the logical and necessary answer; and indeed Deutscher accepts it as such. But realism also has its price to pay. We are not likely to suffer nowadays from an over-supply of idealism. It is the underlying idealism—or should one boldly say utopianism?—of Isaac Deutscher's outlook which makes this an inspiring as well as a disturbing book.

Part III Profiles

15 Kropotkin

Peter Kropotkin, the "anarchist prince", is so good and deserving a subject for a full-length biography that it is surprising that he should have had to wait for one until the passage of time has somewhat dimmed his once immense reputation. Mr. Woodcock and Mr. Avakumović have at long last made a valiant attempt to fill the gap.[1] Kropotkin's own *Memoirs of a Revolutionist*, published towards the end of last century, covered his career down to the moment when he finally settled in England in 1886 at the age of 44; and the existence of this fragment of autobiography makes the task of the biographer of these earlier years in some respects easy, though in others all the more difficult. But for the remaining and more important section of Kropotkin's long life the biographer must build up his picture from Kropotkin's own miscellaneous writings and from the evidence of contemporaries. Mr. Woodcock and Mr. Avakumović have been patient and assiduous collectors of such material. They have not only written the first serious biography of Kropotkin, but have done a great deal of necessary spadework of which future biographers will eagerly avail themselves.

Kropotkin belongs to the distinguished line of Russians of noble family—the so-called "conscience-stricken gentry"—who broke away in revolt from the traditions in which they were born and took up the cudgels for the oppressed classes. He received his education in the aristocratic "corps of pages", members of which were assured of the Emperor's personal interest and of high preferment in the army. Young Peter Kropotkin's first unorthodox move was a request to be posted, on receiving his commission, to an unfashionable Siberian regiment. After some trouble the request was granted. In Siberia Kropotkin not only met many political exiles—he arrived there shortly after Bakunin made his dramatic escape—but undertook those expeditions of exploration and discovery which

---

[1] George Woodcock and Ivan Avakumović, *The Anarchist Prince. A Biographical Study of Peter Kropotkin* (London: Boardman).

first gave him his reputation as a geographer. In 1868 he resigned his commission in the army and devoted himself entirely to geographical pursuits, investigating geological formations in Finland and becoming interested in the prospects of Arctic exploration. Three years later, in his thirtieth year, he was offered the post of secretary of the Russian Geographical Society, but declined. His career was about to take another turn. Thereafter he ceased to concern himself with geography except for the occasional writing of articles for magazines—a way of earning a livelihood—or of papers for learned societies.

The determining fact for young Kropotkin's future was that he had become irresistibly attracted by the revolutionary teachings and activities of the *narodniks*, with their idealization of the peasant and of the peasant commune as the perfect form of social organization. In 1872 Kropotkin went abroad, and visited Switzerland at a time when the First International was being torn asunder between the disciples of Marx, who hymned the praises of orderly centralized authority, and the disciples of Bakunin, who preached the destruction of authority and the organization of mankind in a federation of free self-governing communes. Kropotkin, having sampled both groups in Geneva, quickly found his home with the latter. Much of his time in Switzerland was spent among the watchmakers of the Jura, at this time the core and the cradle of the anarchist movement. Here Kropotkin imbibed the fundamental ideas which he held unaltered for 50 years. What came later was merely the logical development and justification of the central theme of revolt against the authority of the State.

He had not been long back in Russia when his views, expressed with little regard for prudence, brought him into trouble with the police. He was arrested and spent two years in prison in Petersburg. In 1876 he escaped—the methods both of political prisoners and of prison authorities were still highly primitive, judged by any modern standard of efficiency in these matters—and landed in England, the recognized asylum for political refugees. He established a few contacts both in radical and scientific circles, and eked out a precarious living by occasional contributions to newspapers and periodicals. But England was politically dead, and Kropotkin had at this time no intention of remaining there. He spent most of the next few years travelling from country to country in western Europe, maintaining relations with more or less organized anarchist parties, most of them professing allegiance to the name of Bakunin (who had died in Switzerland in the same year in which Kropotkin reached England), and helping to found and edit fugitive anarchist journals. It was the period when terrorism was being widely used and acclaimed by revolutionaries in Russia: Alexander II himself fell to one of their bombs in 1881. Western anarchists applauded or condoned such exploits, or at least did not condemn them, and were subject to increasing measures of police persecution. Kropotkin himself spent two years in a French prison, and was released only after the presentation of a petition which represented, as Mr. Woodcock and Mr. Avakumovič say, "a fair cross-section of the world of learning in Victorian England", and included the names of Swinburne, Watts-Dunton, Leslie Stephen, Frederick Harrison, Arthur Russell Wallace and John Morley. It was this episode which finally decided Kropotkin to settle permanently in England. From 1886 to 1917 he resided in successive houses in St. John's Wood, Harrow, Bromley and Highgate.

This period finally confirmed Kropotkin's reputation and gave him a unique place both in the international anarchist movement and in the radical society of late Victorian England. He wrote and published assiduously on both geographical and political themes; he travelled and lectured widely in western Europe and on the North American continent; at home he received innumerable visitors, foreign and British, representative of almost every radical school of thought except Marxism—for the Marxists remained, by mutual consent, his implacable opponents. Belfort Bax, Bruce Glasier, Philip Snowden, Bernard Shaw, and H. N. Brailsford were among those who consorted with him and paid tribute to the charm and sincerity of his personality. It is from the testimony of those who knew him rather than from anything he left behind him in the way of published teaching or of concrete political achievement that posterity will have to assess the influence which he exercised on his own generation.

The concluding episode of his career had in it something of tragedy and something of the macabre. Contrary to the doctrines he had so often preached, and to the dismay of most of his disciples, he adopted in 1914 a "patriotic" attitude towards the war, accepting the official view that Britain and France were fighting a defensive war against a specifically German form of authoritarianism and imperialism. His love of France and long-standing dislike and distrust of everything German—from Marx to Wilhelm II—played their part in what was, after all, a natural decision for one who had become identified with so many aspects of British and western European life. But participation in international war was difficult to reconcile with any fundamental rejection of State authority as the root of all evil; and this *volte-face* undoubtedly weakened his moral authority, not so much in Britain, where a serious anarchist movement could scarcely be said to exist and where most radicals took the patriotic line in 1914, as on the continent of Europe, where anarchism and opposition to war seemed almost synonymous terms.

As things turned out, this was not a very propitious prelude for Kropotkin's last adventure. Like almost all the Russian political exiles of whatever colour, he hailed the February revolution of 1917 and the downfall of the Tsar as the dawn of Russian freedom and hastened back to Russia in the summer of that year. He was now 75 and had had one or two serious illnesses; his constitution was no longer equal to any severe political strain or to great physical hardship or exertion. He supported the war effort and addressed the so-called State conference in Moscow in' August, 1917. But this exertion appears to have exhausted his failing powers; and he made no appearance on the political scene during or after the Bolshevik revolution in October.

In June 1918, Kropotkin retired to the country 70 or 80 miles from Moscow, and there he remained until his death in February, 1921. His attitude to the Bolsheviks was what his attitude to Marxism had always been; the victorious revolution seemed to him to present all those features of centralization, rigid discipline and State authority which were for him the obnoxious hall-mark of the doctrines of Marx. He encouraged the initiative of the local cooperatives and worked on his last treatise—on ethics—while his wife cultivated the garden. He saw Lenin twice to plead the cause of arrested and imprisoned anarchists; he condemned the support given by the allies to the "Whites" in the civil war. Otherwise he remained wholly aloof, and, when he died, had become a symbol rather than a living force. His funeral in Moscow was followed by crowds of sympathizers, and was marked by a gruesome wrangle with the authorities, who promised to release some of the imprisoned anarchists for the day to attend the funeral. The procession became in a certain sense one of the last public demonstrations of opposition to the Bolshevik régime ever tolerated in Moscow. His former house in Moscow was turned into a Kropotkin museum and kept as such till his wife's death in 1938.

Thirty years after Kropotkin's death, it is already difficult to recapture the extent of his significance, or to realize the immense prestige which he enjoyed among his contemporaries. The difficulty is well illustrated by the shortcomings as well as by the merits of this new biography. It must be admitted that for all the wealth of material presented, and the orderly care with which it is set out, Kropotkin the man never comes fully alive in these pages, and that the nature and content of his teaching remain equally blurred and unsatisfying.

The slight sense of disappointment which this picture of Kropotkin's personality leaves with the reader is perhaps no fault of the biographers. Kropotkin's sincerity, devotion and singleness of purpose are never for a moment in question. His earlier career is not lacking in signal acts of courage. His prison escape from Petersburg, while not lacking touches of light comedy, required determination of purpose and vigour of execution. During his last years in Bolshevik Russia he never wavered or compromised. Yet the years in England, the central and longest part of his career, and that part in which his reputation was built up and fixed, somehow contrive to leave a final impression of Kropotkin as a tamed lion, a king of the jungle domesticated by Victorian England and acclimatized to the dimensions and atmosphere of a suburban drawing-room. Thus we see him as ruthless in precept but always gentle in practice, impatient yet infinitely benign, abounding in good works, yet often—the word is too strong, but no other quite conveys the impression—slightly fatuous, the Mr. Cheeryble of the revolution. His stature is somehow not heroic, but domestic. He has to be portrayed—as befits a Victorian worthy—not in Shakespearian, but in Dickensian colours.

At a banquet of the Royal Geographical Society he remained seated during the toast of the King (we have already reached the Edwardian epilogue), half fearing and half hoping to create a scandal, but was nonplussed when his gesture was ignored with well-bred indifference, and his own toast proposed in a speech of eulogy for the distinguished foreign scientist. When he travelled to France in 1902 a police officer awaited him at Dieppe to inform him that he would not be admitted to France and must return by the next boat. He offered to return next day, spending the night in a

Dieppe hotel. The police officer patiently informed him that if he attempted to land he would be put in prison. Kropotkin declared himself ready to go to prison for his principles. At this point the police telephoned to the Minister of the Interior at Nice and obtained permission for Kropotkin to spend the night at a hotel with two gendarmes occupying the next room. Whereupon, Kropotkin, having gained his point, stayed triumphantly in the ship and returned to England that night. The story abounds in incidents like these. Unfortunately, the exploits of the brothers Cheeryble make notoriously dull reading.

Somewhat similar doubts arise about Kropotkin's teaching, of which Mr. Woodcock and Mr. Avakumovič give a fair, thorough, and informative account. In some respects Kropotkin showed a perspicacity and insight not common in his day. He published an elaborate study of the French revolution designed to demonstrate that its real origin was to be sought in the economic distresses and discontents of the people and that, although it had destroyed political absolutism and economic serfdom, it had failed to satisfy the inarticulate demands of the masses out of which it had arisen. He perceived that the developments of modern society had rendered obsolete the "anarchist individualism" of Proudhon. Now less than ever could man seek liberty in isolation and in the rejection of cooperation with his fellow men. Kropotkin always described his doctrine as "anarchist communism" which he contrasted with the "authoritarian communism" of Marx. Though he always professed himself an anarchist he derived perhaps less from Godwin and the other early anarchist writers, who denounced the State, than from Utopian socialists like Fourier and Cabet, who were more or less indifferent to the question of State power and sought salvation in imagining or founding model communities in which the members held all things in common and cooperated freely for the common good without the whip of compulsion.

It is difficult, however, to avoid the feeling that in this mild latter-day anarchism of Kropotkin something has been lost of that fierce dynamic of revolt which animated the anarchism of Bakunin. Bakunin's indignation at the wickedness of the tyrant was no doubt accompanied by a naïve faith in the constructive capacity and untutored goodness of the masses. In Kropotkin this faith has got mixed up with the Victorian belief in the inevitability of progress. His anarchism, no less than Marx's communism, claimed to have a scientific foundation. It was "more than a mere mode of action or a mere conception of a free society"; it was "part of a philosophy, natural and social", and "must be treated by the same methods as natural sciences". In pursuit of this conception Kropotkin wrote what was once probably the most famous of all his works, *Mutual Aid*, in which he demonstrated, in contradiction to the Darwinian theory of progress through the struggle for existence, that animal life, as well as primitive human societies, survived not through processes of mutual destruction but through processes of cooperation. Towards this conception human society was constantly and continuously evolving. To-day such conceptions seem as faded and irrelevant as the pseudo-scientific political applications of Darwinism which they were intended to refute. And with them goes the pseudo-scientific optimism about the progressive evolution of human nature which was the basis of Kropotkin's anarchist creed.

For the moment therefore Kropotkin's life and work are in eclipse, and the present generation is little inclined to listen to his message. But so striking and picturesque an expression of the times in which he lived is unlikely to be forgotten; and Mr. Woodcock and Mr. Avakumovič may be congratulated on a pioneer piece of work which, partly because it pays so little tribute to contemporary moods and fashions will not lose its interest when they have passed away. Their hero moved in so many different circles that his biographer can hardly hope to be equally familiar with all. But the patience with which every allusion has been investigated and every trail followed up makes this an unusually solid and praiseworthy book. A few errors and omissions may be corrected in a subsequent edition. "The economist A. Blanqui (against whom Proudhon polemicized)" is, to say the least, an inadequate description of one of the most remarkable, though least studied, of nineteenth-century revolutionaries; to compare Azev, a cunning and treacherous adventurer who served his own advantage by combining the roles of revolutionary terrorist and police spy, with Gapon, an honest but foolish man who got caught up in events too big for him to understand or cope with, is absurd as well as unjust; Herzen's mother was a south German, not a Prussian; and Robert Michels was surely a German, not an Italian, and Kennan an American, not an Englishman. The book has a useful though not exhaustive bibliography of Kropotkin's writings and of publications about him.

16 Milyukov

Paul Milyukov was an outstanding figure in Russian political life on the eve of the great revolution of 1917. Hurricanes of this violence and intensity sweep everything before them, and seem to reduce those who stand in their way to puny dimensions. Milyukov's reputation has suffered in this manner. In the 1920s many of his compatriots in exile bracketed him with Kerensky as the two "guilty men" who had opened the way to the victory of Bolshevism. Piquancy was added to this conjunction by the extreme animosity felt by the two men for each other. But, though Milyukov was a member of the Provisional Government only for the first two months of its existence, his role in it was important; and the view which makes him one of the symbols, if not one of the causes, of its failure cannot be lightly dismissed. Milyukov was an altogether larger and more significant figure in Russian history than Kerensky. He did not make, like Kerensky, a conspicuous and ignominious appearance on the historical stage at the moment of the final *débâcle*. But his whole career was involved in the bankruptcy of the idea of constitutional government in Russia.

No formal biography of Milyukov has been written, and perhaps none is required. His *History of the Second Russian Revolution*, written in the years immediately after 1917, takes its place with Trotsky's *History of the Russian Revolution* as a striking example of autobiographical history. Now, upwards of twelve years after his death, his memoirs have been published in two volumes in the United States in the original Russian.[1] They are on any showing a remarkable achievement. Milyukov began to write them in September, 1940, at the age of eighty-one, in Montpellier, whither he had fled from Paris before the German invasion. He wrote from memory, or with the aid of such books as he could find in a provincial town in war-time

---

[1] P. N. Milyukov, *Vospominaniya (1859–1917)*, two volumes (New York: Chekhov Publishing House).

France or borrow from friends. When death overtook him two and a half years later he had reached June, 1917, and was about to embark on the crisis which led up to the formation of the second coalition and to the Kornilov rising. Some notes covering the period down to the October revolution were apparently written, but were unhappily not in a condition to warrant publication. Since, however, Milyukov had resigned office as Minister for Foreign Affairs in May, the memoirs cover his whole active period as a politician.

The memoirs are written in a fluent, unfaltering style. The writer never seems at a loss and rarely stumbles over a fact: minor inaccuracies in names and dates have been silently corrected by the editors, who have also cleared up in discreet footnotes a few—very few—ambiguities. The writing bears no marks of fatigue or old age. An occasional touch of venial vanity was characteristic of Milyukov even in his prime, or was frequently imputed to him by his enemies. It was exhibited in the famous remark (which he records in the memoirs by way of establishing its authenticity) when he heard that placards were being carried in the streets of Petrograd demanding his resignation: "I was not afraid for Milyukov, I was afraid for Russia." It forms indeed the core of his argument, the theme round which his *apologia pro vita sua* revolves, that his forced resignation in May 1917, marked the end of any attempt at strong government in Russia, and thus of the last chance of averting the final catastrophe. But strong government presupposed a body of men possessing both the will and the capacity to govern. Men possessing these qualifications were not to be found in the constitutional camp.

The distorting effect of the absence of constitutional government on the structure of nineteenth-century Russian society has been frequently remarked by historians. Those whose lively intelligence or reforming zeal might in western countries have found a natural outlet in political careers were driven by the Russian ban on politics into the world of letters or of learning. Milyukov's unusual career illustrated a converse process, which would hardly have been possible before the turn of the century. He was a brilliant student, and seemed destined for a distinguished academic career. To be influenced by Comte suggested a certain, but not impermissible, tinge of radicalism; but to be a follower of Danilevsky was a guarantee of belief in the destinies of Russia. Vinogradov and Klyuchevsky were among his teachers. His future wife was also a pupil of Klyuchevsky; and it was Klyuchevsky who guided him into the path of Russian history as his specialization, but later broke with him.

The universities were traditionally the home of radical opinions and aspirations; and Nicolas II's accession to the throne in 1894 was hailed as the promise of a relaxation of the strict censorship of opinion which had prevailed under Alexander III. As a young lecturer, Milyukov shared these hopes. He is not very specific about the opinions he held or expressed at this time. Perhaps no precise charge against him was ever formulated. But in 1895 he was accused of exercising a bad influence on the students, and was dismissed from his post in the university and prohibited from living in Moscow. The next ten years were spent in foreign travel, in journalism and—after further trouble with the police—in two short spells of imprisonment. In 1903 Milyukov paid the first of three visits to the United States. When the revolution broke out in 1905 he was already a politician.

The twelve years from 1905, when, in October, he participated in the founding congress of the Constitutional-Democratic (Kadet) Party and became one of its leaders, to 1917, when his active political career ended for ever, were the important period of Milyukov's life and work. It is on the record of these years that he must be judged. He sat continuously in all four Dumas as a Kadet representative, and spoke in nearly every important debate in the name of the party. He visited London with the Duma delegation in 1909, met Grey and Winston Churchill (who "made on me the impression of an uncorked bottle of champagne"), and caused some scandal in his own party, which was professedly republican in sympathy, by participating in the singing of the Tsarist national anthem. In the spring of 1916 he was in the three allied capitals— London, Paris, Rome—as member of another Duma delegation. By this time he had emerged as the authority of the constitutional Left in foreign affairs. When the Provisional Government was formed after the February revolution of 1917, no appointment was so obvious or so little contested as that of Milyukov to be Minister for Foreign Affairs.

The sequel brings us to the key question of Milyukov's success and failure and of his role in Russian history. Two months after his appointment his note to the allies endorsing allied war aims, as recorded in the secret treaties, including Russia's claim to the

Straits, and upholding the policy of a war to the finish, was received with general execration on the Left and without sympathy from a majority of his colleagues, and he was forced to resign. His downfall was a clear case of lack of confidence in his policy, and constitutionally correct and inevitable. Yet there is something also to be said for Milyukov's view that his dismissal heralded the doom of constitutional methods in Russia. For Milyukov, though his fall was brought about from the Left, stood well on the Left of his own party. It was impossible to move farther to the Left without passing outside the constitutional framework altogether. In this sense Milyukov's career was a test-case for Russian liberalism.

The Kadet party was an amalgam of people who thought of themselves as "moderates", rejecting unlimited autocracy on the one hand and the standpoint of the extreme radicals and revolutionaries on the other. It had the weakness of a party which defines its position by dissent from others rather than by positive aims of its own. The core of its support was to be found among the smaller landed gentry and members of the professional classes who, ever since the reforms of the 1860s, had been the leaders of the *zemstvo* movement, and sought to build on a foundation of local self-government and social progress. Though they disliked the autocracy, both as an institution and as a source of policies inimical to progress as they conceived it, their social background made them irrevocable enemies of revolution; and they were therefore left with the uphill task of extracting concessions by peaceful pressure from a firmly ensconced imperial power. The party had little backing in industry or commerce, which, in a country where both depended in a major degree on Government patronage, were not disposed towards liberalism. This was perhaps the most fundamental difference between liberalism in Russia and liberalism in the west.

Two trains of thought blended in Russian liberalism and in the Kadet party. The first, perhaps numerically the weaker, though it counted Milyukov among its adherents, stemmed directly from the west. Milyukov and those who thought with him sought to model the party on the liberal parties of western Europe, and particularly of Great Britain. By inclination most of them were probably republicans, though they did not in principle exclude constitutional monarchy. But they were democrats who believed that the constitution must emanate from the people: popular sovereignty was an essential part of the conception. The other train of thought was much more distinctively Russian. Since the days of Alexander I and Speransky, enlightened Russians had been repelled by the apparently capricious character of autocratic rule: it seemed shocking to them that laws could be made or unmade from one day to the next by the mere *fiat* of the Tsar. What they sought therefore was to establish a constitution or fundamental law. This involved no conception of popular sovereignty: the Tsar himself would promulgate the constitution, consisting of the rules and principles according to which government would in future be carried on. He would make the rules, though he himself, like everybody else, would be bound by them. What mattered was not so much the content of the constitution as the fact that it was a constitution. This was the tradition which inspired the constitutional thinking of the *zemstvo* liberals. They were passionate believers in the rule of law, in what German jurists, who were impeccably conservative, meant by a *Rechtstaat*.

It was, therefore, no accident that the Kadets called themselves by the dual name of Constitutional-Democrats. Half of them were democrats who regarded the constitution merely as a natural expression of democracy and a means to the establishment of popular sovereignty; the other half wanted primarily the constitution, and were content to see in the existence of a constitution, whatever its origin and character, a sufficient justification of the democratic label. Difficulties soon arose. The foundation of the party coincided with the issue of the "October manifesto" of 1905 in which the Tsar, frightened by the progress of the revolution (a Petrograd Soviet of Workers' Deputies had just been established), promised a constitution and a Duma. Unlike the revolutionary parties of the Left, the Kadet party had never led an illegal existence. It waited to be born until political parties were legalized. But it was born into an era of revolution; and this made its career precarious from the outset.

The crucial issue at once arose of the attitude to be adopted to the Tsar and his manifesto. Were the Kadets to accept this promise of a constitution granted from above at its face value, and to regard it as their mission to make this constitution work? Or were they to proclaim that only a constitution brought into being by the will of the people was truly liberal, and that the first business of a Duma would be to turn itself into a Constituent Assembly? Milyukov, in a statement which was often quoted and criticized in later years, took the second view. The October manifesto, he argued, changed nothing: "the battle continues". In the same spirit he refused Witte's invitation to participate in the formation of a government: this would still be a government responsible to the Tsar and not to the Duma or to the people. From the standpoint of western liberalism, the case was irrefutable. But, from the standpoint of those Kadets who put constitutionalism first, it was the betrayal of a great opportunity. Maklakov, the most prominent of these constitutionalists, in his copious writings between the two world wars, and in his memoirs published a few years ago in New York, drew up an indictment of Milyukov's attitude which, on this view, prevented cooperation between moderate men and the forces of authority in a policy that might have staved off revolution. This case, too, does not lack cogency. But the arguments are pursued on different planes, and never really meet. The division was the tragedy of Russian liberalism.

A reproach which might have been levelled at Milyukov from the opposite flank was that, having started with these resounding declarations of principle, he nevertheless allowed himself throughout the next ten years to take part in a parliamentary game which, in successive Dumas became less and less real, and thus compounded with the sham constitutionalism which he had at first so emphatically denounced. It is easy to see how he was drawn into the position as principal spokesman of the "legal" opposition, and even played the game with a certain relish. Self-esteem was flattered by the role, which seemed a good deal more important than it was. Nor could it be shown that, before 1914, Milyukov moved perceptibly to the Right in the process. It was the coming of war which united all Kadets, whatever their differences on internal affairs, in support of the national cause. They reacted equally against the defeatism of the extreme revolutionaries and against the pro-Germanism of some Right groups.

It was the peculiar constellation of forces after February 1917, which made Milyukov appear as a chauvinist and a man of the Right; and the circumstances of his resignation and the eloquence of Kerensky for a time fastened this false reputation on him. After 1917 he played no further role in active life. For nearly twenty years he edited a Russian newspaper in Paris and wrote assiduously for it. He was at all times an excellent writer; some might say that he returned in these last years to his true *métier* as a man of letters. He judged the Bolshevik revolution, first as a mere insurrection of discontented soldiers and peasants, later, in 1921, as a democratic revolution gone wrong which might yet double back on its tracks and bring democracy to Russia. Later, with his Russian patriotism still strongly alive, he became less unsympathetic to some of its achievements. But in all this there was little that was original; and he contributed nothing fresh after 1917 to the store of Russian political thought.

Milyukov was a distinguished and likeable man of high intellectual calibre and principles. For several years he was an outstanding figure in political life. Yet his career must be written down a failure. Among its causes some personal deficiencies can be diagnosed. Milyukov was that not unfamiliar, but rarely successful, phenomenon, the intellectual in politics. He was lacking in any specifically political sense—a failing common enough in a country where so few opportunities were available of acquiring political experience; Witte, a first-rate administrator, was also no politician, as both his own memoirs and Milyukov's references to him clearly show. But Milyukov was also a townsman to his finger-tips. He spent the first thirty-five years of his life in Moscow; from 1905 to 1912 he lived in Petersburg; he travelled widely abroad and was fluent in foreign languages. But he scarcely knew the Russian countryside at all. The problem of the Russian peasant, who made up 85 per cent of the population, was something that he read—and wrote—about in books. It was another facet of the same shortcoming that he was a whole-hearted westerner. The parliamentary democracy which he contemplated for Russia, and to which he pinned his unswerving faith, was patterned on a purely western model and adapted to the conditions of western society. It was a key point in Maklakov's case against him that his aspirations were wholly unrealistic and unsuited to Russian conditions.

Milyukov's personal failure was, however, in a real sense, the collapse of Russian liberalism; and for this profounder reasons must be assigned. Russian liberals are often critical of the explanations given by historians of the bankruptcy of liberalism in Russia, as if these explanations were intended to imply some innate incompatibility between liberalism and the Russian political genius, some inherent reason why Russians could never be liberals. Herzen, it is true, did once say something of the kind. But any such explanation is unnecessary and, strictly speaking, absurd. The true reason lies elsewhere. Liberalism in western Europe reached its peak in the

1860s and 1870s. Owing to the enormous strength of British industry and commerce, and the unique dependence of Great Britain on foreign trade, liberalism in Britain survived unchallenged till the turn of the century, and held on, thanks to the shot in the arm administered to it by Lloyd George from the medicine-chest of social-democracy, till 1914. But even this was exceptional. From the 1880s onwards economic nationalism and imperialism were slowly gaining strength everywhere at the expense of the forces of liberalism. A new era was at hand.

When therefore the power of the autocracy was first shaken and then broken in Russia in the first two decades of the twentieth century, the time for building new and durable liberal institutions on a western model was past. In the twenty years before 1914 the Russian economy developed at an extraordinary rate, and new-born modern industries made enormous advances. But the economy was geared not to the procedures and pre-suppositions of mid-nineteenth-century liberalism but to those of late nineteenth- and early twentieth-century *étatisme*. Nor, in the period and in the country where these advances took place, could they have been achieved in any other way. The fact that the development of the Russian economy and of Russian political institutions came with a long time-lag after the corresponding processes in western Europe meant that the development occurred in a totally different climate. It was a vain, though not ignoble, dream of Milyukov and the Russian liberals that the history of the western liberalism could repeat itself on Russian soil.

Another aspect of this time-lag in Russian economic and political development more directly influenced the course of events. In the west liberalism had risen to power at a time when the working class was still voiceless, unorganized and unconscious of itself. In Russia, 1905 saw not only the formation of the first effective liberal political party, but the first appearance on the stage of the militant proletariat. The simultaneity of these two events profoundly affected every subsequent move. The liberals were from the outset confronted by an inescapable dilemma: whether to seek allies on the Right or on the Left. Though they appeared at first to divide on this issue—a rift which weakened the party—the conclusion was not in doubt. No liberal—not even Milyukov, who was as far to the Left as any of them—could embrace the revolutionary or the proletarian cause. The Kadets remained a party of order, and were in the long run obliged to seek the shelter, and share the fate, of whatever order existed. Milyukov failed, and was bound to fail, because his ideals and policies did not belong to the time and place in which his lot was cast. But, as one of the gallant defeated, he has his place in history; and his writings remain as a worthy record of what he believed in, and what he attempted.

17 Colonel House

The formidable mass of source material now available for the study of the peace conference of 1919—official documents, the contemporary press, diaries, memoirs—will deter any but the most venturesome from attempting a synoptic presentation and interpretation. Yet this was an event which occupied a unique place in modern history. It stands on a watershed between two worlds. What it did, and still more perhaps what it failed to do, illuminates the cardinal problems created, or revealed, by the First World War—problems which mark the transition from the compact and confident nineteenth-century civilization to modern times.

The subject cannot be left alone; and what contemporary scholarship can most usefully offer are detailed studies of different aspects and angles of this vast agglomeration of material. After all, none of those who participated in, or were witnesses of, the peace conference of 1919 could have embraced in their view its whole vast compass; and all the evidence about it, however official and however authentic, is one-sided. The history of the peace conference has still to be written. Historians have not yet got much beyond the preparatory class.

Perhaps the most obvious and promising approach to the theme is through the avenue of American policy. It could be argued that the most significant feature of the conference, though one not widely recognized at the time, was the emergence of the United States as the most important single factor in determining its course, as potentially, if not actually, the predominant Great Power. It is not for nothing that the enigmatic figure of Woodrow Wilson plays so large a role in every book on the subject. Some not very profitable attempts have been made to penetrate the psychological complexities of his personality. The enigma is there. But the enigma which interests the historian is the enigma of American policy, reflected in the policy and behaviour of the American President.

President Wilson was not the only American in Paris in 1919 whose views and attitudes have to be taken into account in any evaluation of American policy. *Colonial House in Paris*, subtitled "A Study of American Policy at the Paris Peace Conference 1919",[1] revolves round the role of Wilson's confidant, adviser and factotum. Inga Floto, in making a most thorough and detailed analysis of every available scrap of information recorded by, or about, House, has in fact probed deeply into the ambiguities of Wilson's own attitude, and of American policy, during a critical period of the conference.

House has proved a difficult figure to assess; and discordant verdicts have been pronounced on him. Before the conference had run its course, a coolness—amounting almost to an open breach—had sprung up between him and the President; and in the hectic negotiations of the last four weeks before the signature of the treaty he played no part. Controversy has ranged round the causes and the precise moment of the rupture, which seems to have been a process rather than an event. Opinions have since been divided between those who put a high rating on House's role and think that Wilson went to pieces when deprived of his prudent and well-informed counsel, and those who regard House as Wilson's evil genius leading him into policies of compromise in defiance of the principles for which he stood. Dr Floto meticulously sifts the unwieldy mass of conflicting evidence (this is the great merit of the book), and comes down, rather more heavily than the balance of evidence warrants, on the adverse side.

Colonel House belonged to a type familiar in many periods of history—the *éminence grise*. It is a regular characteristic of this ambiguous figure that he holds no official position (House was, in fact, one of the American Commissioners at the peace conference, but this was irrelevant—the other Commissioners were nonentities), bears no responsibility, but is known to be in the confidence of his chief. He provides a two-way channel through which opinions can be filtered without the handicap of formal commitment on either side. The ambiguities and temptations of such a position are notorious. One can think of nobody in recent times who has filled it with complete success, except perhaps the incomparable Tom Jones; and even he did not escape the imputation of promoting causes which he himself had at heart.

[1] Inga Floto, *Colonel House in Paris*. Translated by Pauline M. Katborg (Aarhus: Universitetsforlaget).

The severest charges against House—notably the charge of "disloyalty" to the President—rest on a misapprehension of his role. He was, in virtue of his position as well as of his own inclinations, a fixer, a manipulator, a go-between, whose function it was to canvass solutions of intractable disputes, to bring the two sides together. Had he been content merely to reiterate the President's opinions with unyielding rigidity—especially the opinions of so stubborn and inflexible a thinker as Wilson—he would have performed no useful function at all. If on the other hand, in this delicate balancing act, he went so far in the direction of compromise as to lose touch with his chief, his function was at an end. One of several explanations of his breach with the President was that he toyed briefly with the idea that a treaty could be pushed through quickly only by detaching it from the projected Covenant of the League of Nations; and this, for Wilson, was the sin against the Holy Ghost.

House has on the whole fared well at the hands of British writers. When he visited Europe as Wilson's emissary during the war, he was patently sympathetic to the Allied cause, and established particularly good relations with Grey. The so-called House-Grey memorandum, recording a conversation between them in February 1916, has come in for a good deal of criticism. The gist of it was that, if at some undefined time in the future Wilson received encouragement from the Allies to do so, he would offer his services as mediator; and, if then his offices were accepted by the Allies and rejected by the Germans, the implication was that the United States would enter the war on the side of the Allies.

The whole thing was hypothetical and unreal, and the British Government was in no mood for mediation. But the war situation was approaching a desperate crisis; and Grey was not likely to be foolhardy enough to return a dusty answer to the President's eagerness to mediate. It was better to make sympathetic noises, and put off the embarrassing question to some future period. Whether House, who was still young in the ways of diplomacy, was alive to what was going on in the mind of the British Government, may be doubted. But to brand him, on the strength of this episode, as a dupe would be as harsh as to call Grey a trickster.

House never got on terms with Lloyd George, who, unlike Grey, seems to have disliked or despised him, and preferred to deal direct with the President. When House arrived in Paris, however, he succumbed rather unexpectedly to the fascination of Clemenceau, who detested Wilson and found the go-between more sympathetic.

House lacked intimates in the British delegation (Balfour was too aloof, and Philip Kerr had not quite the standing), but established a fairly close contact with Wickham Steed, who was always ready to promote friends' causes, and inspired a flaming eulogy of House in *The Times* in April 1919. This contact perhaps did little credit to House's discrimination, and certainly did not help him with Wilson.

In the American delegation he incurred all the jealousies inseparable from the role of an *éminence grise*. Lansing, the Secretary of State, not unreasonably felt that his authority had been usurped. Ray Stannard Baker, the head of the press section and a fervent admirer of Wilson, might well have aspired to the position which House had pre-empted. House had imprudently secured for his brother-in-law Mezes the appointment of head of the "Inquiry", the team of experts appointed in 1917 to advise on American policies for the peace negotiations; here too House found enemies. It was inherent in his position that it depended solely on the good will of the President; when that was withdrawn, he was friendless and helpless.

In the relations between the two men it is difficult to withhold some measure of sympathy from House. To say that Wilson was never an easy man to serve or to work with is an understatement; his vanity, his secretiveness, his readiness to take offence, need no documentation. Moreover, if we seek the cause of the rift in the familiar contrast between Wilson, struggling to be loyal to his principles, and House, prone to seek devious compromises with expediency, we are bound to recall that some of Wilson's most glaring derogations from his principles came in the very last weeks, when House was no longer advising him.

Ultimately, however, it is more profitable (and Dr Floto's study encourages this attempt) to go behind these personal quarrels and frictions, and examine the deeper causes of the intractable divisions both in the President's own mind and in the policy of the American delegation. The French objectives at this conference were crystal clear; all that remained open was the tactical question how to proceed in order to achieve as many of these as possible. The British were divided between the desire to crush Germany and the desire to preserve Germany as a counterweight to overweening French ambitions and as a stable factor in a turbulent continent. But this issue was at least clear, and Lloyd George could be seen manoeuvring dexterously between the two incompatibles.

American policy, by contrast, was from top to bottom inchoate and indeterminate. No other delegation talked so much about principles; but in no other delegation was it so difficult to discover any coherent principle governing the formulation of policy. The complaint that the American delegation was at sixes and sevens because the President failed to disclose or explain his intentions was constantly heard from its members. But this was not simply a failure of communication. It was the result of a basic ambiguity and uncertainty about what the United States really stood for.

The United States at the end of the First World War was passing through a traumatic experience. The reluctant entry of the country into the European war showed that it could no longer afford to remain indifferent to what was happening in that distressful continent. The peace conference ended the farce of pretending that it was not one of the "Allied Powers"; it was in fact the most powerful of them. Traditional attitudes like isolation from Europe and the avoidance of entangling alliances were no longer consonant with the new status, the new world-wide interests and pre-occupations, of the American nation. Yet they could not be abandoned without a struggle. The need to straddle the old and the new paralysed the emergence of a coherent policy.

Cynics might have claimed that the one thing necessary was to invent the right words and the right forms. For twenty years the "open door" in China had meant the right of Americans to share in the privileges extorted from the Chinese over a period of years by the military action of the imperialist powers. To "make the world safe for democracy" was soon to mean no more than to make it safe for American trade and enterprise. The League of Nations might have been thought to provide a suitable cover for American intervention in any part of the world where American interests required it, the Monroe doctrine or reservation making it clear that this did not imply the reciprocal right for other countries to intervene in the affairs of the American continent.

Unfortunately the exigencies of domestic politics in the United States did not allow it to work out in this way. Woodrow Wilson was not only the President but also the leader of the Democratic Party, and as such a target for attack by Republican rivals. Paradoxically the League of Nations might have stood a better chance if it had not been Wilson's personal fetish. But, once he made it the essential focus of his crusade, the cornerstone of his whole policy, it became mandatory for the Republicans to assail and demolish it. It was twenty-five years before the United States could take its proper place as founder-member and main driving-force of another world-wide organization.

The year which saw the end of American isolation was marked by another fundamental transition in American ways of thought. The United States of America had been born of a revolution. The American Revolution and the French Revolution had stood over the cradle of the modern world. Liberty, Equality and Fraternity had perhaps been more effectively realized in the American nation than in any other. The revolutionary ferment had mellowed with time and prosperity. But America was still the land of the free, upholding the true liberal and radical tradition in face of a conservative and retrograde "old world".

In 1919 the American people found themselves—for the most part, quite unconsciously—in mid-stream, in a process of transfer from one shore to the other. Conservation had become as compelling a purpose as innovation. The United States had stood firm as a rock when all Europe was threatened with ruin and disintegration. Wilson had gone to Europe in December 1918 as the great innovator, the prophet of a new order. Six months later, when the treaty with Germany was signed, the prophetic image had faded away—to the disillusionment of some, to the derision of others. What the United States now wanted, and now stood for in its new role as the predominant Great Power, was security and stability.

The key factor in the change—its catalyst, if not its cause—was the Russian Revolution. Revolution had already presented itself to Wilson's consciousness as a baffling phenomenon in Mexico. The American entry into the war had occurred during the troubled interval between the February and October revolutions in Russia— a symbolical intertwining of two great challenges to the American way of life. The Fourteen Points, destined to play a momentous part in the conclusion of peace with Germany, were originally devised as a counter to the revolutionary propaganda of the Bolsheviks. Dr Floto quite reasonably devotes a well-documented appendix to the treatment of Russian question at the conference.

Contemporary American commentators were significantly more alive to its importance than those of other countries. Veblen, that acute Mid-westerner, observed that resistance to Bolshevism was not written into the text of the peace treaty, but was "the parchment upon which that text was written" at the conference itself. Ray

Stannard Baker took the view that "Russia played a more vital pary at Paris than Prussia!". The French solved the problem by embracing Germans and Bolsheviks in a common hatred, though the Russian issue was always subsidiary to the German.

On the British side, Lloyd George's uncanny powers of perception gave him a deeper insight into the realities of the revolution than was possessed by any other leading figure at the conference. Any British action about Russia emanated from Lloyd George's secretariat, not from the representatives of the Foreign Office. But he was too preoccupied with more immediately pressing issues to give it consecutive attention. Of famous British commentators on the conference, Maynard Keynes was exclusively concerned with Germany; and Harold Nicolson, who actually visited Budapest with the Smuts delegation during Béla Kun's brief term of power, regarded the whole affair with a well-bred disdain which prevented him from taking it seriously.

The initiative was in the hands of the Americans. It was an American diplomat, Buckler, who was sent to meet Litvinov in Copenhagen in December 1918 and brought back a proposal for a "truce" on the basis of existing military fronts which was promptly buried and forgotten. By the time the conference opened the various émigré Russian "governments" in Paris were exercising powerful pressure on the French delegation. It so happened that the first substantive decision of the conference was about Russia.

This was the fantastic Prinkipo proposal—an invitation to all the warring Russian groups to meet in conference on that remote island. It was in fact a compromise between the bad conscience of Wilson and Lloyd George, who felt that something must be done about Russia, and the determination of the French to have nothing whatever to do with the Bolsheviks. The fate of the proposal was a foregone conclusion. It was accepted by the Soviet Government, and broke down on the veto of the émigrés.

The next and more promising attempt was the Bullitt mission of February–March. This time the initiative came from Lloyd George, the details being worked out in his secretariat by Philip Kerr. Bullitt was to put before Lenin what were virtually the same terms which had emerged from the Litvinov–Buckler meeting in the previous December. Wilson was by this time absent in the United States, and American approval was conveyed by House, apparently without consultation with other members of the American delegation. Wilson knew that Bullitt had been sent to Moscow. It is doubtful whether he knew that the emissary had been empowered to discuss terms with Lenin or what those terms were.

When Bullitt returned to Paris, carrying Russia's broad agreement to the terms, on 25 March 1919, the whole situation had changed. This was the real turning-point of the conference. Wilson was back from the United States, knowing that he had to fight for the League of Nations, and for his political life, against an increasingly fierce Republican opposition. To this end everything else was now subordinated. The President could no longer afford to risk further involvement in controversial or potentially unpopular causes. Bullitt had been enthusiastically welcomed by House. Wilson expressed a total lack of interest, refused to see him, and ran off on a quite different and anodyne proposal to send relief supplies to Russia.

Meanwhile Lloyd George had made up his mind. Impressed, now that Wilson was back in Paris, with the need to break the deadlock over Germany, he resolved to reject the French demand for a crippling "Carthaginian" peace in favour of a solution which would leave open the hope of keeping Germany, weakened but not totally crushed, as a focus of order and stability in central Europe. This was the gist of the famous Fontainebleau memorandum circulated to the conference on the very day of Bullitt's return from Moscow. It charted the course which, with many ups and downs, and with much hard bargaining on points of detail, the conference was henceforth to pursue.

By an inevitable reaction, a mood of leniency towards Germany implied the converse mood in relation to Russia. For those who believed in the importance of preserving a stable Germany as a necessary condition of stability in Europe, Germany became "a bulwark against Bolshevism"—a theme which the more astute of the Germans, had harped on in their dealings with the Allies ever since the armistice. Within days of the Fontainebleau memorandum, the establishment of Béla Kun's communist regime in Hungary gave a fresh fright to the Allied statesmen in Paris, and drove home the lesson. Perhaps, as Field-Marshal Sir Henry Wilson was reputed to have said at one point, the Bolsheviks were more to be feared than the Boches.

From April onwards, therefore, the spirit of the conference slowly and imperceptibly changed. The missionary fervour radiated by the President on his first appearance in Europe and at the conference table had evaporated. Order and stability were now the watch-word, and revolution was a word of fear. Bullitt was disowned not only by Wilson, but—less excusably—by Lloyd George. The French fought a stubborn rearguard action to retain what they could of the original conception of a "Carthaginian" peace, and at the last moment received some support from the unpredictable Wilson, with the *éminence grise* no longer at his elbow. Nobody thought any longer of making peace with the Bolsheviks. It was only the timely defeat of Kolchak by the Red Army which saved the Allies from recognizing his regime in Siberia as the future government of Russia.

Dr Floto's survey makes no pretence of covering the whole complex of multifarious activities which made up the Paris peace conference of 1919. The narrative virtually comes to an end when House bows out from his confidential role several weeks before the treaty was signed. But, apart from its illumination of what went on in the American delegation and of the eccentricities of Wilson's thought and behaviour, it provides an acute critical commentary on most of the fundamental issues at stake, and on the still unresolved question of the significance of the conference in contemporary history.

18 Karl Radek

Radek is a secondary figure in the portrait gallery of the Russian revolution. But his non-Russian origins, his fluency in many languages, his wit, his jaunty and jocose manner, his total lack of pomposity and even of seriousness—all these things made him accessible and attractive to Westerners who found it hard going with the ordinary Soviet functionary. Add to this that he had a variegated career full of incident, and that something—not much, it is true—was known of his private life. It is surprising that he had not already found a Western biographer. Warren Lerner has done a predictable job very well—not in any great depth, but the facts are there, and the sources are stated, so that the few myths that have been allowed to creep in can be sorted out.[1]

Radek was born into an "emancipated" Jewish family in Lvov (or Lemberg), then a city of the Habsburg empire. His first language appears to have been German, not Yiddish or Polish; but growing up in a completely multilingual environment, any language came easily to him. Russian, according to his own account, he learned comparatively late—at the age of twenty or so—when imprisoned as a Polish revolutionary. His revolutionary role in Poland ended in 1908, when he moved to Berlin at about the same time as Rosa Luxemburg, whose career and opinions exhibited some striking parallels to his own. They were, however, divided by fundamental differences of character. Rosa always had an uninhibited and uncharacterisitc aversion to him, which may have been connected with an accusation, brought against him on the eve of his departure from Poland and never proved or withdrawn, of having been less than scrupulous in the handling of trade union funds entrusted to him. Even if Rosa believed the charge—which seems probable—this does not, of course, necessarily prove that it was true.

[1] Warren Lerner, *Karl Radek, The Last Internationalist* (Stanford, Calif.: Stanford University Press; London: Oxford University Press).

For the next four years Radek was principally associated with German papers on the extreme left of the Social-Democratic Party. In 1914 he consistently adopted an anti-war position, and moved to Switzerland, where for the first time he came into contact with Lenin and other Bolshevik leaders. Radek was not a dissident for nothing; and he quickly crossed swords with Lenin on the issue of national self-determination. The Russian group of which Bukharin, Pyatakov and Radek became the most articulate spokesmen believed, like Rosa Luxemburg, that national self-determination was emotionally a bourgeois ideal, and that revolutionaries should have nothing to do with the division of the world into national units, which socialists were struggling to supersede. Much ink was spilt on this question in obscure journals in the two years preceding the Russian revolution. When the revolution occurred, bygones were bygones, and Radek was accepted as a good (and useful) Bolshevik.

Most of the time between the February and October revolutions of 1917 Radek spent in Stockholm, then the centre of an incredible amount of pushing and pulling between socialists and revolutionaries of the most varied hues, in some of which agents of one or other of the warring Powers took a hand. Mr. Lerner documents Radek's multifarious activities, but does not perhaps fill in quite enough of the background to make them fully intelligible. It was in Stockholm that Radek developed that genius for intrigue which made, and marred, the remainder of his career. His consistency as a revolutionary is not in question. But it is sometimes uncertain what revolution he was seeking to promote and by what means. What is clear is that it was only the success of the October coup which finally committed him to the Bolshevik, and Russian, cause, and that he did not cease for many years to be an essentially German revolutionary at heart. But the same was of course true of other Bolsheviks in that early period.

The next three or four years were the busiest of Radek's political life. He edited a newspaper in German for the German troops. He was a spokesman for the Bolshevik propaganda line at Brest-Litovsk, though he afterwards disputed with Lenin on the necessity to accept the "shameful" peace, and was once more associated with Bukharin in a group of "Left" Bolsheviks. After the armistice he was the only one of a group which set out from Petrograd for Berlin to elude the patrols and reach his destination. There he argued against Rosa Luxemburg in favour of the immediate creation of a German Communist Party, and attended its founding congress in the last days of 1918. On some rather uncertain evidence Mr. Lerner attempts to show that Radek was less whole-hearted in his support for and more sceptical of the prospects of revolution than he appeared. Radek's attitudes were rarely clearcut and straightforward.

After the assassination of Rosa Luxemburg and Liebknecht in January 1919, Radek was arrested by the German police, and spent the rest of the year in prison or under house arrest. It was the oddest and perhaps most important episode in his career. Throughout 1919 Soviet Russia was almost entirely isolated by revolution and civil war from the Western world. Radek's contacts with Moscow must have been tenuous in the extreme. But the Germans, as their fear of revolution at home receded, and as their humiliation at the hands of the Allies became more and more galling, groped blindly for some balancing force in the East. Radek seemed the one tangible link with the Soviet world, and he was treated—unofficially—with constantly increasing consideration.

During this time he received visits from representatives of every colour in the German spectrum—revolutionaries, socialists, businessmen (Rathenau among them) and, above all, army officers. All these submitted to the fascination of the unknown Russian colossus and of Radek's witty and brilliant talk. What exactly they said to him, or he to them, will never be known. Intrigues galore, sometimes inconsistent with one another, were no doubt woven in Radek's fertile brain. By using hindsight, one can discover in these conversations the seeds of many aspects of future German-Russian collaboration. Whatever was in the conscious minds of the participants in these conversations, the picture is not wholly false. Here was the beginning of a relation which assumed increasing importance in the international scene of the 1920s.

Radek's merit, as well as his demerit, in the eyes of the Soviet leaders was his irresponsibility. Lenin certainly recognized the value of so intelligent and imaginative a flier of kites which were so obviously unauthorized, and could be disowned if necessary. Back in Moscow, his usefulness was limited by his notorious lack of discretion and reluctance to abide by instructions. But he played a part in initiating the Russian negotiations for military collaboration with Germany; and, once more in Germany in 1923, he hatched the bizarre plan of a united front between German communists and the extreme Right—the incipient elements of the Nazi movement. Later in the same year he played an active, but somewhat ambiguous, role in organizing the abortive Communist rising.

It was perhaps inevitable that Radek, after Lenin's death, should have gravitated towards Trotsky, the most Western, and at the same time most independent-minded, of the remaining leaders. It was no doubt this association rather than the German fiasco which earned him the bitter enmity of Zinoviev (which was mutual) and led to his downfall. At the beginning of 1924 he was formally censured for his mishandling of the German affair, lost his membership of the Central Committee, and was henceforth numbered in the ranks of the opposition.

His disgrace was not yet absolute. Stalin appreciated his talents and was more indulgent to him than Zinoviev. In 1925 he received the apparently safe and politically innocuous appointment of rector of the newly founded university for Chinese workers, the so-called Sun Yat-sen University. But Radek's tongue, as Stalin said, always ruled his head. At a session of the Communist Academy, he could not refrain from poking malicious fun at Stalin's doctrine of socialism in one country, then a contentious novelty. Presently he came out as one of the most vocal opposition critics of Stalin's and Bukharin's Chinese policy—a highly vulnerable target. This sealed his fate. He was expelled from the party with the rest of the opposition at the Fifteenth Congress in December, 1927, still uttering cries of protest, and exiled to Siberia.

This was the end of that part of Radek's career for which one can feel admiration, and in which, for all his conspicuous defects, he was at any rate himself. What is left of the story earns only our pity and sympathy. He had not been three months in Siberia before he began to quarrel by correspondence with Trotsky. Exile and inactivity were intolerable to his restless nature, and he was soon looking for ways and means to work his passage back to the centre of things. There was after all the argument that Stalin, now firmly committed to intensive industrialization, was only carrying out the programme which the opposition had been the first to demand. It took Radek just about a year to reach his goal. The price was to bend the knee unconditionally to Stalin; and this he did. His recantation was accepted and published in the summer of 1929. For the next six years he had a twilight existence on the periphery of the party, unmolested, gratified by minimum assignments of work, but never really restored to favour.

The most exciting of these assignments was his attachment to the Russian disarmament delegation at Geneva in 1932. Here Radek assiduously peddled the Soviet propaganda line, a not ineffective one, consorted with foreign journalists, and thoroughly enjoyed this brief return to the international world which he had once known. Mr. Lerner offers a picturesquely exaggerated glimpse of surveillance by the OGPU. It is more likely that the two plainclothes men who followed him everywhere in a car were Swiss rather than Russian agents. Ever since the assassination of Vorovsky in Lausanne ten years earlier, the Swiss Government had been terrified of having another Soviet diplomat murdered on Swiss soil. Litvinov, during his visits to Geneva, was under constant police surveillance for his own protection.

The final tragedy was Radek's involvement in the purge trials, and his condemnation in 1937. Unfortunately, it is only too probable that he earned his relatively light sentence—ten years' imprisonment—by implicating others. He was the first, at any rate in public, to point a finger at Tukhachevsky. Much earlier, in 1929, when Blyumkin, an OGPU agent, visited Trotsky surreptitiously in Turkey, and was caught and executed, circumstantial evidence suggests—nothing is of course proved or certain—that Radek was intentionally or unintentionally responsible for betraying him. In truth, after his recantation Radek was only the shadow of his former self, and the shadow of a man. A note in a Russian publication gives the date of his death as 1939. None of the numerous stories about the manner of his death wins any credence.

Mr. Lerner deserves high credit for his patience and pertinacity in running to earth every available source relating to Radek, and to those people associated with him at any given moment. In dealing with a career which touched contemporary politics at so many different points, it is difficult to be fully at home in every situation. Occasionally one feels that Mr. Lerner may have got the emphasis wrong through failure to understand completely the background of his hero's activities; occasionally an opinion is attributed to Radek which seems to have been a commonplace of the period. More can be found about Radek in the German archives than Mr. Lerner has discovered—in particular, it would be worth looking at the Brockdorff-Rantzau papers. But nobody has yet fully tapped this almost inexhaustible source. In general, the reader who wants to know the facts about Radek's life need not really go beyond the covers of this book.

In his last chapter Mr. Lerner tackles the question why Radek never belonged to the inner circle of the Bolshevik leaders. Here he is a little on the defensive, and propounds some rather strained explanations. It may have been some handicap to be a non-Russian—but so was Dzherzhinsky and, for that matter, Stalin. Mr. Lerner's insistence that Radek's Jewishness was somehow different from that of other Jewish members of the leadership does not carry conviction. Later on Stalin was certainly anti-Semitic. But, like other anti-Semites, he had his pet Jews: Radek might have been one of them had he been a different man—it was not for want of trying. It is more to the point that he was distinctively a Westerner and an internationalist in his outlook and affiliations. But this at the outset was no drawback; and even under Lenin Radek never looked like achieving Politburo status.

Ultimately one must come back to the kind of man he was. He was a fervent revolutionary; but one never knew where one would find him on any particular issue. He bubbled over with ideas; but he seldom knew how to distinguish between good ideas and bad ones, or between the time to be silent and the time to talk. All this created an impression of unreliability and lack of principle. A politician, unless he is in the very top flight, has to run in harness; and this, before his downfall, Radek could never learn to do. He was a chronic dissenter. But, unlike Trotsky, he found no followers, since he had no dissident principles or creed.

His personal relations were, for the most part, political relations. He was capable of generous impulses, but here too he had no firm or abiding loyalties. He was too clever by half; and his wit was often tinged with malice. He was kept at arm's length because he was generally felt to be irresponsible and unreliable. This is why, though on many occasions his outstanding gifts stood the regime in good stead, he never reached any position of influence or power. Nobody, except perhaps his enemies, took him quite seriously. He shone brightly, not to say flashily. But he was never as important a star in the Soviet constellation as most foreigners thought him.

19 The Legend of Bukharin

Bukharin has in the past few years become a focus of attention for American and British writers on Soviet affairs. The reasons are multiple, and some of them obvious. Endless denunciation of everything and everybody connected with Bolshevism or with the Russian Revolution has become tedious. Bukharin was a Marxist, a Bolshevik and a revolutionary. To display a sympathetic interest in his career and his ideas proves at any rate that one does not belong among the case-hardened veterans of the Cold War.

More important still, Bukharin's background makes him readily accessible and attractive to writers steeped in the Western tradition. He was a Moscow intellectual *pur sang*, his father a mathematics graduate of Moscow University, his father and mother both school teachers. Except for four years of his early childhood spent in Bessarabia, he grew up exclusively in Moscow. His background provided no contact with Russian provincial life, with Russian peasants or—until, presumably, as a youth of seventeen he began to engage in political agitation—with Russian workers.

The fruitful formative years from 1911, when he was twenty-three, till the Bolshevik revolution six years later—the period when his economic and political ideas took shape, and his literary career began—were passed in Western Europe and the United States. He was fluent in German and French, and had a good reading knowledge of English. It might be truer to say of Bukharin than of any other leading Bolshevik that his intellectual formation was more characteristically Western than Russian.

Bukharin was a gentle and lovable character of singular personal charm. Contemporary evidence is virtually unanimous on this point; and the same charm surrounds his image in the eyes of posterity. Bukharin seems the only Old Bolshevik at whom no stone can be cast. Lenin was the leader in a revolution and civil war which involved inescapable occasions of terror and ruthlessness. Trotsky is credited with the platitudinous but ruthless-sounding aphorism that a revolution cannot be made in kid gloves. In this fearful period no action of Bukharin is anywhere recorded. At no time did he hold an administrative office. He was a brilliant speaker and a brilliant spinner of words and ideas, not a man of action. Unlike any other Bolshevik leader he had a perfectly clean, because perfectly empty, sheet. He alone wears the halo of innocence.

Finally Bukharin's end can never lose its unique elements of pity and terror. After Lenin's death he faithfully followed Stalin's rising star, and played a full part in the campaign of calumny against Trotsky, Zinoviev and Kamenev, expelled from the party at the end of 1927 and sent into exile. Then the pace grew too hot for him. He had wanted to drive Trotsky out of public life, but not to persecute him personally. He wanted to industrialize, but not as fast and furiously as Stalin. He disliked the savage pressure on the grain-holding peasants. He began to write notes for the Politburo, and then in very guarded language articles in the press, expressing his uneasiness. But he never came out publicly against Stalin.

This did not save him. In the summer of 1929 he was denounced and demoted, though not expelled from the party. He humbly accepted his disgrace, and for several years faithfully performed the minor functions assigned to him. Trotsky, and even Zinoviev, had at least earned Stalin's hatred. Bukharin did not. Bukharin did not speak or act against him. Stalin left him to the last, then he had him arrested, tried, and shot like the rest. It is a horrifying story—even against the whole horrifying background of the purges.

Stephen Cohen, a young American scholar, has paid tribute to the cult of Bukharin—and, indeed, done much to promote it—by writing the first scholarly, full-length biography of Bukharin in English, or probably any other language.[1] The work has been in preparation for several years and Mr Cohen has thoroughly combed everything available that has been written by or about Bukharin, besides using occasional oral reminiscences of the few survivors who had had contacts with him. Mr Cohen in his preface shows awareness of the temptation that besets biographers "to overstate the importance of their subject", and one need not cavil too much if Bukharin occupies a more central or more honoured place in this volume than in the pages of history. Many good biographies are inspired by a special sympathy or affinity between the author and his hero.

Not that Mr Cohen seeks to depict a hero without flaw or

[1] Stephen Cohen, *Bukharin and the Bolshevik Revolution* (Wildwood House).

blemish. On the contrary, his Bukharin is like one of those classic heroes of Shakespearian tragedy who, in Bradley's famous phrase, "contributes to the disaster in which he perishes". At the end of 1923, as editor of *Pravda*, he set the pattern for the long process of hounding Trotsky out of the party in an article in which he "diligently recited the history of Trotsky's factional sins, each of which he also had committed". What Mr Cohen justly calls the "outrageously demagogic passages" of the article were only a foretaste of innumerable articles and speeches directed during the next four years, not only against Trotsky, but also against Zinoviev, Kamenev, Radek and other Communists, Russian and foreign, who dared to challenge party orthodoxy.

It is not quite true to say, as Mr Cohen does in one place, that "it was characteristic of Bukharin to assume that political differences need not influence personal relations". One of the most shocking as well as the earliest examples of the political vindictiveness of which Bukharin was capable was the way in which he rounded on his old friend, co-author with him of the famous *ABC of Communism*, Preobrazhensky, whose analysis of "primitive socialist accumulation"—not a polemical tract, but an acute essay in economic analysis—was answered by Bukharin in terms of crude political demagogy. In an eloquent passage Mr Cohen quotes a letter addressed to Bukharin in November 1927 by a former colleague denouncing him as "a jailer of the best Communists". The letter published in a Menshevik journal abroad, ended:

> Take care, comrade Bukharin. You have often argued within our party. You will probably again have to do so. Your present comrades will then give you comrade Agranov [an OGPU official] as your judge. Examples are infectious.

So presented, the story of Bukharin assumes the dimensions of a great historical tragedy. The pity and terror of its culmination redeem, and seem almost to blot out of our consciousness, the faults of character, the sins of commission and omission, which helped to bring it about. It is the last act which constitutes the essence of the tragedy and gives it its meaning. But to judge a biography in this way is to approach it as a work of literature, not of history; and this is clearly no part of Mr Cohen's intention. He draws, and wishes us to draw, political conclusions from Bukharin's active career. His biography purports to be a contribution to history. But this confronts the historian with a nagging question. Suppose Stalin had died twenty years earlier than he did. Suppose Bukharin, removed from the political scene, had been allowed, like Molotov and Khruschev, to pass his declining years in inconspicuous retirement. Would the legend of Bukharin as a great lost leader ever have been born?

The material on which the biographer of Bukharin has to work has many pitfalls. Like all the other leading Bolsheviks, except Lenin and Trotsky, he left, so far as is known or is ever likely to be known, nothing in the way of personal papers or correspondence; and what we can glean of his private life and thoughts amounts to nothing significant. His published work—books, pamphlets, articles and innumerable speeches—is voluminous. It is unlikely that it will ever be collected. But a fairly comprehensive bibliography has been published in both German and English editions.

Confronted with this mass of raw material the most conscientious biographer faces the task of selection. Bukharin was a compulsive writer and speaker, fluent, clear, and compelling. But nobody could write and speak on so many controversial issues over such an extended period without sometimes falling into inconsistencies and contradictions. Even as forceful and self-assured a personality as Lenin did that; and Bukharin's opinions were notoriously flexible and volatile. Of his major theoretical works, Mr Cohen does justice to his *Economic Theory of the Leisure Class*, written in Vienna before the First World War as a riposte to the fashionable Austrian "marginalist" school; discusses his *Imperialism and World Economy* in the context of his relations with Lenin; treats the *Economics of the Transition Period* rather dismissively as a product of the utopian attitudes of War Communism and does not apparently mention his later polemic against Rosa Luxemburg, though he lists it in his Select Bibliography.

The only one of Bukharin's theoretical writings analysed in detail by Mr Cohen is his *Historical Materialism*, published in 1921, and for several years accepted in the party as a major authoritative text. Mr Cohen usefully observes that a work later condemned for its rightist orientation was written almost simultaneously with the *Economics of the Transition Period*, which represents the extreme left in Bukharin's intellectual output. He also shows that it is directed in part against Bogdanov, whom Bukharin had once supported against Lenin. The book is full of illuminating points; and for the student of the vagaries of Bolshevik theory in the 1920s a variety of ideas can be read into it.

But a careful reading of Mr Cohen's commentary, as of the work itself, fails to make it clear exactly where Bukharin stood. His acute and agile mind, his long study not only of the Marxist corpus but of current Western economists and philosophers, made him an authority in a party whose leaders, at any rate after 1917, had little time for abstract theory. But as an original thinker, as a twentieth-century critic and expositor of Marxism, he stands far behind, say, Rosa Luxemburg or Gramsci.

Bukharin's reputation rests therefore on his role in the politics and economics of the Soviet Union in the 1920s. It is here that the widest divergences of opinion prevail, and that one's judgment is likely to dictate one's selection from the multifarious evidence of documents and reminiscences rather than the other way round. Bukharin's personal virtues are not in question. More human traits are recorded of him than of any other of the leaders. He liked to doodle and draw caricatures; he loved birds and animals. Whatever his theories, he recoiled instinctively from drastic or violent action.

But there is another side which also cannot be blotted out from the record. It is difficult to deny that he was a weak man whose political actions constantly belied his inclinations. When Trotsky taunted him at the Party Congress of 1925 with having acquired a taste for the persecution of his adversaries, he wrote to Trotsky in a strangely ambivalent phrase: "From this taste, I tremble from head to foot." Mr Cohen calls Trotsky's picture of Bukharin sobbing on his shoulder "apocryphal". Why? Kamenev's description of Bukharin's condition of nervous hysteria during their secret meeting of July, 1928, penned within a few hours of the event, makes Trotsky's picture perfectly plausible. (Incidentally, Mr Cohen, in quoting from Kamenev's "elliptical notes" of the meeting, omits this passage.) These all-too-human moments of weakness do not alienate our sympathy from Bukharin the individual—it was a malign fate which cast so gentle a nature into a maelstrom of revolution. But they are bound to colour our judgment of him as a political leader.

Any study of Bukharin's political career must start from his relations with Lenin, which were established in Cracow and Vienna between 1912 and 1914. Of the young Bolsheviks more or less closely associated with Lenin in emigration, Bukharin had incomparably the keenest intelligence and the most thorough schooling in Marxist theory; and Lenin was also evidently attracted to the charm of his personality ("the favourite of the whole party", he called him). Lenin's first serious difference with Bukharin arose when the latter moved in 1915 to Stockholm, and there threw in his lot with a group headed by Pyatakov who, like Rosa Luxemburg and Radek, regarded socialism as an essentially international programme which should have no truck with any form of nationalism.

Since Lenin at that time had committed himself to national self-determination as an important stage in the march towards revolution, a clash was inevitable; and it grew sharper when Bukharin developed views on the role of the state which Lenin described as "semi-anarchistic". At this point what Mr Cohen calls Lenin's "well-known cantankerousness" took charge. Lenin in 1916 pronounced the first of his verdicts on Bukharin—that he was "credulous towards gossip" and "devilishly unstable in politics". On the former count (which related to the Malinovsky affair) it may fairly be said that Bukharin was right and Lenin wrong. On the latter count, everything that happened later showed that Lenin was perceptive and right.

These disputes did not permanently embitter relations between the older and the younger man. Mr Cohen may be a trifle over-zealous in tracing his hero's influence in Lenin's major wartime treatises, *Imperialism, the Highest Stage of Capitalism* and *State and Revolution*; but they certainly reflected a convergence in the two men's ideas. After the revolution, however, Bukharin joined the so-called "Left opposition" in the party, vehemently opposing the conclusion of the Brest-Litovsk peace treaty with Germany, and finding an ideological justification for the measures of War Communism. This was the period of the writing of that classic utopian textbook *The ABC of Communism*.

The next occasion which provoked Lenin's wrath was an attempt by Bukharin to mediate in the fierce struggle between Lenin and Trotsky at the end of 1920 on the future of the trade unions. Perhaps Lenin felt that Bukharin had fallen too much under Trotsky's personal influence; perhaps he was simply irritated by the intervention of a junior lightweight in a contest between heavyweights. But it was this occasion which produced the most penetrating of Lenin's judgments:

We know how soft Bukharin is; it is one of the qualities for which we love him and cannot help loving him. We know that more than once he has been called in jest "soft wax". It appears that any "unprincipled" person, any "demagogue", can make an impression on this "soft wax".

The sequel was unexpected. With the introduction of the New Economic Policy a few months later, Bukharin swung over from positions on the fat left of the party to positions well on the right. The transition to NEP, which for Lenin was a "retreat", meant for Bukharin "the collapse of our illusions", the disappearance without a trace of "the illusions of his childhood period". There is no reason to suppose that Lenin ever lost his personal affection for Bukharin. But some stories repeated by Mr Cohen of the closeness between them during the last months of Lenin's life rest on dubious second-hand reminiscences, and may safely be relegated to the apocrypha of the Bukharin legend. The contemporary political record is clear. It was to Trotsky that Lenin turned in the last weeks of his conscious political life for support against Sokolnikov's and Bukharin's attack on the monopoly of foreign trade and against Stalin and Dzerzhinsky in the Georgian affair.

Lenin's appraisal of Bukharin in his "testament" has often been found confused and contradictory. Bukharin, besides being a "favourite of the whole party", was its "biggest and most valuable theorist". Yet, "his theoretical views can only with very great doubt be regarded as fully Marxist, for there is something scholastic in them (he has never studied, or, I think, fully understood, the dialectic)". Mr Cohen plausibly connects this with Lenin's comments on Bukharin's attitude in the trade union dispute as being "eclectic" and not "dialectical".

If the dialectic is the key to the "unity of theory and practice" on which Lenin strongly insisted, then perhaps what he was saying was that Bukharin excelled in abstract theory, but did not know how to translate it into practice—in short, that he was an intellectual and not a man of action. There is much to be said for such a verdict.

It is, however, on Bukharin's policy for agriculture from about 1924 to 1928 that his claim to be treated seriously as a political leader and a statesman must principally rest. This was the cardinal dilemma of Bolshevism—how to effect a proletarian, or any kind of industrial revolution in a country where 80 per cent of the population were still fairly primitive peasants. NEP was primarily a necessary step to appease a peasantry on the verge of revolt; the "scissors crisis" of 1923 hammered home the same lesson—the peasant could not be squeezed any further. In 1924 Zinoviev proclaimed the dramatic slogan, "Face to the countryside". Bukharin followed the same path to its extreme limit, with his undiplomatically frank appeal to the well-to-do peasants to "enrich themselves"—an uninhibited acceptance of the principles of a market economy.

From 1925 to 1927 what may be reasonably called Bukharin's policy, the gearing of the rate of industrialization to the capacity of the peasant, was quietly pursued. Bukharin, in another rash moment, called it "snail's-pace" industrialization. It was opposed and denounced by Trotsky and the so-called party "left"; and this assured it the full weight of support from Stalin and the party machine. Bukharin threw himself *con amore* into the fight. Trotsky's alleged indifference to the peasant was one of the principal cudgels with which he was battered into defeat.

When Trotsky and the opposition were finally expelled at the Fifteenth Congress in December, 1927, the reckoning was at hand. Bukharin's one positive contribution to agrarian policy during these years was his advocacy of producer cooperatives. But this was in essence a *narodnik* utopia as abstract as the Bolshevik utopias with which he had toyed so eloquently a few years earlier, and did not touch the heart of the problem. Who was to pay for the grain, and provide the "riches" which the successful peasant had been invited to covet? And who, meanwhile, was to feed the factory-workers and the towns? By the end of 1927, after two good harvests, the grain was piled up in barns, sheds and any convenient hiding-place. The currency was depreciating; there were few things anyhow to buy. The well-to-do peasant drew his conclusions, and did not bring his grain to the market.

It was this crisis which dealt the death-blow to Bukharin. The "wager on the peasant" was defeated not by Trotsky, and not by Stalin, but by the inherent impossibility in NEP conditions of inducing the peasant to part with his grain. Famine threatened the towns. In the first weeks of 1928 all the principal leaders from Stalin downwards toured various areas of the Russian countryside organizing the campaigns to bring in the grain—by persuasion if possible, by force if necessary. It was a unique occasion, and a vital turning point in Soviet history. Only Bukharin stayed behind in Moscow to explain to the foreign delegates at a session of the executive committee of the Communist International, at which nobody mentioned the grain crisis, that the leaders of the European socialist and social democratic parties were the worst enemies of

Communism, and that any truck with them was now a mortal sin.

The grain-collecting campaign was, in the short term, a brilliant success. The grain was there, and it was collected. But, in the circumstances of the Soviet Union in 1928, the margin between persuasion and coercion was narrow enough; and the campaign was the beginning of the "civil war" against the peasant which Bukharin had dreaded, but which his policies were powerless to avert.

The deceptive ease of the collections (which could never be repeated, since the large reserves were exhausted, and the peasants better prepared to resist) went to the head of the "super-industrializers" in Moscow, who believed that nothing more than an effort of will and ruthless determination was required to bring about the intensive and rapid industrialization of their backward country. The regime was launched on the policy of total coercion which ended in the horrors of forced collectivization of the peasantry.

The slow agony of Bukharin's humiliation—which lasted from the summer of 1928 till November 1929, when Bukharin, Tomsky, and Rvkov signed a declaration confirming that their views had been mistaken, and promising to struggle against any future deviations from the party line, "above all, against the right deviation"—can be traced in detail in these pages. Mr Cohen does his best for his hero, rather over-playing the gestures of dissent and resistance, always behind closed doors or in cryptic language accessible only to the initiated, and passing over the futile and sometimes almost farcial attempts at appeasement and compromise. Trotsky's comparison of Bukharin's utterances of this period with "bubbles emitted by a drowning man" was harsh, but not far removed from the truth.

In reviewing Mr Cohen's work one becomes aware of certain factors which—probably quite unconsciously—have helped to shape it. He refers twice in his preface, without naming it, to Isaac Deutscher's biography of Trotsky. One has the impression that he has more or less deliberately accepted the challenge, and sought to do for Bukharin what Deutscher has done for Trotsky. Unfortunately the challenge by its very nature works against Mr Cohen. He has instituted himself the biographer and advocate of Bukharin, and in this capacity earns high commendation. But his theme never transcends the personal tragedy of Bukharin. The unique merit of Deutscher's masterpiece is that Trotsky's personal achievement and personal tragedy are seen as an integral part of the unfolding of a great historical upheaval. It is this sense of history, of an overwhelming historical background, which is missing in Mr Cohen.

The comparison leads, moreover, to a still more unfortunate claim, implicit in the preface and explicit in the blurb, which can scarcely have been prepared without the author's approval. Here the author is said to "demonstrate that it was Bukharin rather than Trotsky whose vision and leadership most crucially challenged Stalinism".

It would be difficult to think of a more fantastic claim. Trotsky had faults of temperament, and made serious errors of judgment. His shortcomings as a political leader may have been as great as those of Bukharin, though of a totally different kind. But on one point his credentials are beyond cavil or challenge. From the moment of Stalin's rise to power till the moment of Trotsky's assassination in Mexico fifteen years later, one theme, one obsession, pervaded and coloured everything, that he did and wrote. He was the supreme adversary of Stalin and of everything Stalin stood for.

The comparison is unkind to Bukharin's memory, but the reviewer of Mr Cohen's biography can hardly avoid it. For the three or four crucial years when Stalin was building up his impregnable hold over the party and the state and beating down the opposition, Bukharin was his zealous henchman. The most charitable explanation is that he was indeed "soft wax" in Stalin's hands. In the first months of 1928 Stalin, having routed Trotsky, knew that he had won, and no longer needed the support of Bukharin; and Bukharin became increasingly uneasy at the drastic and brutal course of Stalin's policies. Who first made the break? All that can be said with certainty is that it was Stalin who called the tune, and set the pace. So far as public record goes, Bukharin did not at any time speak or write a word directly attacking Stalin: a handful of phrases have been reported from secret sessions or private conversations. Bukharin's virtues were not those of a fighter.

Nor did Stalin ever treat Bukharin as a serious rival. Unlike Trotsky, Zinoviev and their supporters, and unlike the Ryutin group later, Bukharin was never expelled from the party, or even removed from Moscow. After his recantation, when he had been deprived of all his responsible functions, he continued to serve the regime faithfully in humble capacities. As editor of *Izvestia* from 1934 to 1936, he rendered honourable service in the campaign against Hitler following the entry of the Soviet Union into the

League of Nations. Less impressively, he was one of the principal authors of the famous Stalin Constitution of 1936. It was no act of disloyalty to Stalin on the part of Bukharin, but a paranoiac streak of almost motiveless vindictiveness, which caused Stalin to sweep him into the blood-bath of the last great purge trial.

A second and more agreeable factor may also have been at work in Mr Cohen's assessment of Bukharin—the desire, especially strong among American liberals, to believe that nice men make good political leaders. Cynical observation may throw doubt on this conclusion. In our own century, Lloyd George and Franklin Roosevelt were superb political leaders, but not perhaps very nice men. George McGovern and Edmund Muskie are exceedingly nice people, imbued with humane ideals and unimpeachable principles. But if a biographer of one or other of them fifty years hence seeks to depict his hero as a lost political leader, frustrated only by the devilish machinations of the wicked Richard Nixon, he will be seriously distorting history. And this is what has happened to Mr Cohen over Bukharin.

So much having been said, it seems fair and proper that a reviewer who cannot share the author's perspective on his hero's career should end by paying tribute to the thoroughness and accuracy with which he has marshalled his material and documented his narrative. (The persistent refusal of publishers to recognize that the only tolerable place for source notes in a work of scholarship is at the foot of the page cannot be laid at his door.) It is only in a few passages, notably those relating to the last months of Lenin's life and the last months of Bukharin's own life, that he has resorted to dubious hearsay evidence recorded many years after the event. The student of the period will have reason to be grateful for the vast amount of work done by Mr Cohen even after the currently fashionable view of Bukharin's place in history has been superseded.

20 James Headlam-Morley

James Headlam-Morley was a not untypical product of the last
adult generation before 1914, whose predictable career was sharply
and unexpectedly diverted by the great upheaval of the First World
War. Recruited into the Political Intelligence Department of the
Foreign Office, he became a distinctive and important member of
the British delegation to the Paris peace conference. *A Memoir of the
Paris Peace Conference* contains a rather scrappy collection of letters
and diary entries written by him in Paris in the first six months of
1919, prefaced by a short memoir of his life by his daughter, Agnes
Headlam-Morley.[1]

Headlam-Morley (*né* Headlam) was born in 1863 into a family
of churchmen and classical scholars. Eton and Cambridge (first
class in both parts of the classical tripos) were followed by a
period of research in Germany. Here he encountered two sisters,
distinguished musicians who in their childhood had had piano
lessons from the aged Liszt. The elder already had a circle of English
friends and admirers. Headlam fell in love with the younger and,
after winning a fellowship at King's, married her in 1892. From his
marriage he derived a lifelong knowledge of German language and
literature. His wife never learnt to speak fluent English, and
remained an impenitent German nationalist—without, however, in
this respect influencing her husband in the slightest degree.

The promising classical career was gradually overlaid by wider
interests. Headlam's first book on *Election by Lot at Athens* was
followed by a life of Bismarck in the once famous "Heroes of the
Nations" series. His first concern with education seems to have been
a report written for the Bryce Commission on Secondary Education,
about secondary education in Germany. He became one of the first
Inspectors of Education on the establishment of the service in 1902.
On the outbreak of war he was transferred to the newly constituted

---

[1] James Headlam-Morley, *A Memoir of the Paris Peace Conference 1919.* Edited by
Agnes Headlam-Morley, Russell Bryant and Anna Cienciala (London: Methuen).

Propaganda Department and from there through some intermediate stages to the Foreign Office.

It was Headlam's anomalous status which accounted for his unique and valuable role at the peace conference. The Political Intelligence Department had never been wholeheartedly accepted by the traditional Foreign Office departments; it housed too many eccentric intellectuals. When he arrived in Paris, it was not even certain that he would be listed as a member of the Foreign Office delegation. Time and common sense soon settled that. But what gave him his chance was the almost complete breakdown of relations between the Foreign Office delegation and the Cabinet Secretariat, which was Lloyd George's personal office. Lloyd George had a great mistrust of professional diplomats, which was thoroughly reciprocated. Headlam quickly established close personal relations with Philip Kerr; and for some time this proved the most effective link between the two organizations.

The documents in this volume, while they do not add up to a complete picture, give glimpses of the sections of the peace treaties in which Headlam was active. He was largely concerned in the complicated regulations for the temporary regime in the Saar coal basin, and for the Slesvig plebiscite; and he was almost solely responsible for devising and carrying through the project of a Free City of Danzig when a complete deadlock had occurred on the Polish demand, supported by the Foreign Office and resisted by Lloyd George, for its annexation by Poland. He was the dominant figure in the New States Committee, which drafted the provisions which newly created or recognized states were required to assume for the protection of national minorities, including Jewish minorities within their borders. He successfully opposed the imposition of the same obligations on Germany, on the ground that it would be invidious and humiliating to expect Germany to assume obligations which would be accepted by no other Great Power.

Something of Headlam's personality—though perhaps hardly enough to fix the attention of a reader who never knew him—comes through in these pages. He was the strongly marked product of a classical education and of the British civil service in its heyday before the First World War. He was considerate, enlightened, rational and commonsensical, averse from every extreme, from every fanaticism, from any emotional indulgence. Everything he wrote has the same high-minded and rather aloof quality. Even the letters in this volume (nothing of a personal nature is included) read like first rate departmental memoranda. Comparing his diary jottings with those of Harold Nicolson, made at the same time, one sees that he altogether lacked Nicolson's literary flair, and Nicolson's intense interest in putting across what he was doing. A spice of vanity is needed to make a good diarist. Headlam was the most modest and least vain of men.

What does emerge, and constitutes the main attraction of the book, is the standpoint of the generation of liberal intellectuals which flowered before 1914 and enjoyed a brief Indian summer in the 1920s. Headlam, in spite of his German marriage and interest in German civilization, seems to have paid little attention to international relations—who in that generation did? His daughter gives no clue to his attitude before 1914; but one suspects that, unlike Eyre Crowe, who had a German mother as well as a German wife, and who was neither a liberal nor an intellectual, he nourished no deep-seated suspicion of German designs. The war must have come as a great catastrophe, both personal and political.

Faced with this catastrophe, Headlam unconditionally accepted the official thesis of German guilt, but believed that its sources were to be found in the bungling or wickedness of individuals or small groups, which could be revealed by the disclosure and study of the official documents. His outstanding book, *The History of Twelve Days*, published in 1915, was a minute examination, on the basis of every document then available, of the diplomatic exchanges of the twelve days leading up to 4 August 1914. Headlam never belonged to the Union of Democratic Control, and was probably shocked by some of its more extreme manifestations; he did, broadly speaking, share their view that the war was the fault of "the old diplomacy". And, though he never became one of the devotees of the League of Nations, he believed with them that the solution of the problem of war and peace was the setting up of a better machinery for the ordering of international relations.

Headlam was an able and altogether admirable representative of a powerful group in the life and thought of the period, the ripples of whose influence can still be felt from time to time. Yet the total collapse of the Paris peace settlement in the space of twenty years spelt the bankruptcy of everything they had stood for. One inevitably searches this book for clues to how this happened. Headlam believed that the Germans were, by and large, to blame for the war, that barriers must be erected against the repetition of any such misconduct, but that a vindictive settlement would merely sow the seeds of future trouble. He came to hold the view that some of the clauses imposed on Germany at Versailles were unjustifiable in themselves, and that some contravened the assurances on the strength of which Germany had signed the armistice.

Today the question how far this was true or false, like the question about the rights and wrongs of Danzig or the Saar, seems no longer worth asking. The debate has become irrelevant. This is not really what the war was about. Headlam grew up in an age of optimism; and it would be easy to accuse him and his contemporaries of a strong disposition not to look at things that seemed too bad to be true. But it would be fanciful to censure them for not realizing that what had happened in 1914 was no mere passing accident or disaster, but heralded a breakdown of the civilization in which they lived and moved·and had their being, and to which no alternative could have appeared or even now appears—conceivable. The very magnitude of the events struck contemporaries with blindness.

Yet one can in this book trace some of the blind spots. For Headlam the whole issue in 1919 was really one between Britain and Germany—after all the making of peace with Germany was what the conference was primarily for. France was sometimes troublesome, but peripheral; time would moderate its more extreme pretensions. The United States hovered in the background in the enigmatic figure of President Wilson, sometimes embarrassing but on the whole reassuring. The smaller powers would fall into line once the German question was settled. Asia and Africa were places on the map. The "colonial question" in the 1920s was the question whether Germany should or should not get back its colonies.

The enormous gap was Russia. The Russian Revolution of course presented a problem for a select band of experts. But it did not impinge at all on Headlam's view of the peace settlement, except that it rendered decisions about the eastern frontiers of Poland or about the Baltic states difficult and provisional. (Neglect of things Russian extends to the editors of the book: Sazonov appears variously as Zazanov, Zazonov and Sazanoff.) It is more excusable that China's odd refusal to sign the treaty because it endorsed Japanese encroachments on Chinese territory rates only a casual mention; yet this was the starting-point of a movement which thirty years later transformed, and continues to transform, the face of Asia.

Headlam-Morley died, relatively young, in the autumn of 1929, when optimism about the fate of the West was still easy, and before any strong compulsion had arisen to modify views expressed ten years earlier. He lived and flourished in what might now be thought of as an age of illusion. But history is a record of illusions; and this was a noble, if too simple, one deposited by a great civilization. *A Memoir of the Paris Peace Conference* is a tribute to a man and to a generation. But the moment has perhaps not yet come to get these events into their proper perspective; and to read it now inevitably seems like a visit to a tomb bedecked with laurels that have faded.

21 Harold Laski

Oliver Wendell Holmes, Jr., Judge of the American Supreme Court and the most distinguished American lawyer of recent times, commonly referred to as "Mr. Justice Holmes", to distinguish him from his father of the same name, the author of *The Autocrat of the Breakfast-Table*, had reached the age of 75 in the year 1916 when Mr Felix Frankfurter, head of the famous Law School of Harvard, brought to visit him at his summer residence in New England a remarkable young Englishman in his twenty-third year. Harold Laski was the son of Orthodox Jewish parents of Polish origin settled in Manchester. He had gone up to New College, Oxford, with a scholarship at the age of 18. As an undergraduate he celebrated his emancipation from his background by marrying, in defiance of all family opposition, a non-Jewish girl. On the outbreak of war in 1914, having been rejected for military service, he obtained a teaching appointment at McGill University, Montreal. A year later he became a junior instructor in the Department of Government at Harvard.

The respectful pilgrimage of the enthusiastic young neophyte to the home of the great man in his declining years is a theme familiar in history and literature. Rarely can such a visit have produced so startling a result as the two massive volumes of correspondence exchanged between Holmes and his young visitor over a period of 19 years, and now published in a model edition by a Harvard scholar.[1] Both meticulously filed and preserved the letters, so that very few seem to be missing from the collection. It is now presented to the world in its entirety. The omission of a very few proper names, presumably necessitated by the law of libel, does not detract from the extraordinary frankness and flow of the correspondence. The

---

[1] *Holmes–Laski Letters: The Correspondence of Mr. Justice Holmes and Harold J. Laski, 1916–1935.* Edited by Mark DeWolfe Howe, in two volumes (London: Oxford University Press; Cumberlege).

Laski letters passed into the possession of the Harvard Law School after Holmes's death in 1935. In 1949 Laski, a year before his own death, dispatched Holmes's letters to the same destination. He had intended himself to supervise their publication, but never found time to approach this task.

This dramatic encounter of minds which began at Beverly Hills Farm, Mass., in July 1916, clearly fulfilled on both sides some deeply felt need. This is at first sight less understandable on the side of Holmes than on that of the young disciple. Holmes's letters are, in the nature of things, far less copious and less revealing than Laski's, and contribute far less to the total picture of the man. For real insight into Holmes's mind the correspondence with Pollock, which belonged to the prime of his life and in which his partner was a contemporary and a fellow-lawyer, is far more rewarding than the correspondence with Laski. But of the warmth of Holmes's feeling for the young man, and of the unfailing eagerness with which through the long period of years his letters were received and answered, there can be no doubt whatever. "You may be sure that it was as much refreshment to me," he replied to Laski's first, bread-and-butter, letter, echoing a word which Laski had used, "to see you as it can have been to you to come here"; and later in the same letter he invoked a quotation from Morley, which spoke of "the mixture of flattered vanity and genuine love of the young" as exactly expressive of his feelings. Almost every letter to "my dear Laski" (or once, at least, "my beloved Laski") opens on a note of exultant pleasure at a letter received. "As always," one letter begins in 1921, "I go off bang when you pull the trigger."

The spectacle of old age captivated by the wide-eyed admiration and the boundless energy of youth is no novelty and no mystery. But what is remarkable about this correspondence is the extent to which it does in fact bridge the gap in years. The relationship of master and pupil, of great man and aspirant to greatness quickly falls away, and gives place to an eager volley-like exchange of ideas from which all suspicion of inequality or patronage has been eliminated. It is the more remarkable in that the two men were not really in political agreement; and it is politics which, directly or indirectly, haunts almost every page of their letters. Quite often—and usually on Holmes's side—the disagreement becomes specific. Holmes found Laski's Home University Library text-book on *Communism* "interesting not only in itself, but in suggesting the rationale of the differences between us", and went on:

> I have no respect for the passion for equality, which seems to me
> merely idealizing envy. . . . I think the robbery of labour by
> capital is a humbug. . . . Some kind of despotism is at the bottom
> of the seeking for change.

And Laski, while admitting "a real disparity between us on
intellectual problems", replies composedly:

> A good deal of our difference is, I think, due to our different
> civilizations. You are living amid a system where the classic
> principles of capitalism still work successfully, I amid one where
> the growing inadequacy of that machine is most obvious.

In spite of these divergences, however, a common ground of
political belief, not often explicit and not perhaps very clearly
recognized on either side, did exist between them. This was not only
because Laski, for all his socialism, remained all his life, in many
respects and in a somewhat confused way, a liberal, but also because
Holmes was in American terms a progressive, and liked to think of
himself as such. He was a reformer—in his way, a great radical—
who had rationalized and reshaped much of American legal
thinking. He was proud of his role; and he recognized in Laski a
kindred flame of reforming zeal, quite independently of the
particular objects on which that flame would be directed. Even in
his old age Holmes had not, as his letters bear witness, shed his
restless, critical spirit; the correspondence with Laski nourished and
rejuvenated it. No minor disagreements could affect the relish—the
"refreshment", to use the word which had figured in their first
exchange—that Holmes continued to the end to receive from his
correspondent's outpourings. Holmes's last recorded letter to Laski
is dated November, 1932, and ends:

> You see how hard I find it to write—my affection is unabated, but
> I can no more. *Please* keep on writing to me.

Laski's letters, interrupted only by two further visits to the United
States, end in February, 1935, three weeks before Holmes's death.

For the biographer of Holmes the Laski correspondence is peripheral to his career. In Laski's life the correspondence occupies a central place. These letters belong to the best, most active, most productive years of his life, before the Second World War again darkened the academic horizon and before the ill-starred political excursions and political frustrations of his last years. These letters will be vital to any future assessment of Laski as a man and as a thinker and teacher. One is indeed tempted to place them higher, and to assign to them a more lasting value, than to his more formal writings; for here the gusto, the ebullience, the versatility—together with their obverse quality, a certain slipshodness of thought and expression—which were characteristic of everything Laski wrote or said can find free rein without spoiling the reader's enjoyment or provoking his resistance. It should also be said that few men so soon after their death have had their memory exposed to so severe a test as the publication of so vast a volume of their personal and unconsidered correspondence. If Laski's letters, when put through the sieve of an exacting criticism, prove him to have been not exempt from human frailties, it may fairly be asked whether the reputation of many other men who had exposed themselves by writing so fully and frankly would have stood up better to such an ordeal.

Unhappily Laski died, and the obituary notices and commemorative articles and summings-up were written, at a moment when the tide of opinion was ebbing sharply away from nearly all the positions which Laski had occupied. His temperament and his training—he grew up before the First World War—made him throughout life a confirmed and unrepentent optimist, a fervent believer in human nature and in the ultimate triumph of reason over obscurantism and illusion. Politically his hopes centred on the Labour Party: its spectacular rise to power coincided almost exactly with his career. The record of the Labour Government in the last five years of his life confronted these hopes with intractable political realities; and hard-headed working Labour politicians, including the trade union leaders, turned away in irritation and mistrust from their would-be intellectual mentor. Thus, at the end, Laski's renown had suffered, not only from a revival of Conservative opinion in the country at large, but from a hostile current in his own party. Even in the academic institution where he worked, a certain eagerness was manifest in some quarters to live down its reputation, which he had done so much to create, as a home of "advanced" and radical thinking.

When Laski died, therefore, in March 1950, an unwontedly strong note of criticism was at once sounded; and this was renewed on the publication of Mr. Kingsley Martin's biography of Laski early in 1953. The critics—some, it would seem, a little waspishly—fastened on a notorious shortcoming which, in other men or in other circumstances, might have been treated as venial or even as endearing. In most respects English to the core, Laski in one way violated a sacrosanct English convention. The Englishman is not expected to remain within the limits of the truth when discussing his prowess as an angler, his strokes at golf or his *coups* at the bridge table; but on more mundane matters he observes an obligation of reticent understatement. Laski was no sportsman, and he romanced quite shamelessly on two subjects which lay near to his heart—his purchases of rare books and his encounters with the great and the famous. The first idiosyncrasy might have been forgiven him: the second was not. Mr. Edmund Wilson has recorded that, before Laski returned to England from his first American sojourn in 1920, the *New Republic* group had already discovered his romantic habit of speech. Naturally it ended by defeating itself; and the reader of the Holmes-Laski correspondence will probably be tempted to overdo his scepticism about particular incidents. Even the editor of the present volume has not altogether escaped the temptation. It was, no doubt, his duty, when Laski reports to Holmes a casual meeting in Germany with "von Below, the mediaevalist", to record that the only traceable German professor of the name was an economic historian who had died three years before the reported meeting. But is it not more plausible, as well as more charitable, to suppose, not that Laski had invented a not very striking conversation, but that he had simply misheard or misremembered the name?

It is a pity that this minor eccentricity, which never carried with it the slightest trace either of malice or of self-seeking, should have intruded so conspicuously on estimates of Laski's career and influence. For here there is still much to be said. It is plain that Laski had none of the qualities of the practical politician. In more than one of his letters to Holmes he appears to show an understanding of his limitations in this respect and an unwillingness directly to enter the political arena. In the sense that he never attempted to enter Parliament he maintained this attitude to the end. But in the 1920s he had done far more than any other individual to mould the thinking of the intellectual wing of the Labour Party, many of whose members had risen to high office in it; he had been elected year after year by overwhelming majorities to the Party Executive; he had toiled without sparing himself in its service. After 1945 he found himself in a situation where he could not have effaced himself from a position of influence in party affairs, even had he so wished, but where equally he had no direct authority and no responsibility. Superhuman tact would have been required to navigate these treacherous waters without shipwreck; and this Laski did not possess. He became an easy target for the enemy, a liability rather than an asset to his friends; and the end came in bitterness, prejudice and frustration which eclipsed his immense services to the party in the past—services which will one day again be remembered and honoured.

If Laski was not, in any ordinary sense of the word, a politician, he was also no thinker. He had an unbounded verve and versatility in the acquisition of knowledge. But, where he skimmed everything, he never plunged deep. The extent of his reading was colossal, even if one assumes that he did not more than turn the pages of some of the works which he mentions. "Of books I have read but few in the week," he reports to Holmes in October 1923, and proceeds to enumerate five quite solid titles, including Charles Reade's *Hard Cash* and Plato's *Republic* "reread for work". But in the letters, as in his published works, it is difficult to discover not merely a consistent political philosophy, but any real search for a political philosophy at all. Laski had strong emotional attitudes towards politics—many of them the characteristic emotional attitudes of the ordinary Englishman who is not politically minded; and he had immense wealth of learning in many fields. But he wrote and spoke and taught so much that he never gave himself time to find a permanent resting-place for his ideas, or to bring the vast uncoordinated mass of his knowledge under a single roof. In this respect Laski had many of the qualities of perpetual youth—always curious, always seeking, always enthusiastic over some new discovery that might provide just the key which he had been wanting to the problems of the universe.

It was these qualities which were perhaps the secret of his greatness as a teacher. For this cannot be denied him; and to this a whole generation of students bears witness. Laski founded no school, and left no body of disciples to carry on a specific line of thought or investigation. He did both more and less than this. It may be true that the most mature and profound of his students ended by travelling beyond him. But few teachers have been so uniformly successful in inspiring and fertilizing the minds, not merely of a select *élite*, but of a whole group of students. Hardly any student who passed through his classes failed to learn from him or to catch something of his infectious enthusiasm. Outside the formal classes he was unstintingly generous with his time, with his interest and—on occasions—with his money, of which he had not much to spare. His students were drawn from Asia as well as from Europe and from every part of the English-speaking world; and his close associations with the United States gave his teaching a certain breadth of outlook and made it stand out against the insular background which still distinguished much of British education in the 1920s. Laski was probably one of those whose names are more widely known outside their own country than at home.

Paradoxically the Holmes correspondence provides a better key to Laski's achievement than the numerous text-books into which his lectures were distilled and which ran through many editions in his lifetime. For the way in which he fired and stimulated the aging American judge must have been in many ways similar to the impact which he made on his students. Almost every letter which he wrote to Holmes contains what is in effect an annotated reading-list and was awaited and welcomed by its recipient as such; and the unending flow of discoveries, ideas and anecdotes with which he regaled Holmes was not at all unlike the characteristic approach to his students. Laski was always himself. He did not keep his different interests and activities in separate compartments; and his success with students was partly due to his enviable capacity to establish contact with them as human beings. His text-books and other writings belong to their own time and will scarcely outlive the present generation. But his letters to Holmes contain so much of the essence of a remarkable man and of a remarkable friendship, and present so vivid and many-sided a picture of the intellectual life of a period that has already passed into history, that they may well prove to have a more durable quality. They merit survival, both for their own intrinsic interest and as a fitting—if unconventional— memorial to a great and inspiring teacher.

22 Karl Mannheim

Karl Mannheim occupied—unhappily for all too brief a period—a unique place in this country in the world of social and political ideas. Born and educated in Budapest, he spent the earlier years of his life as a teacher in German universities, Heidelberg and Frankfurt. Driven out, like so many men of learning of Jewish birth, by Hitler, he settled in London, becoming a lecturer in sociology at the London School of Economics. Sociological studies were then just beginning to take root in this country; their extension and development since that time, though modest in comparison with the attention devoted to them elsewhere, have been due not least to Mannheim's fertile mind and influence. The war, and the ferment of ideas which it engendered, brought him into contact with wide circles of men and women interested in social and political thought, including many whose fundamental outlook differed entirely from his own; and both he and they gained in the process. The most remarkable of his concrete achievements was to found and edit that unique series of volumes known as "The International Library of Sociology and Social Reconstruction", which introduced to British readers the work of a large number of foreign scholars settled in this country, including Mannheim himself. At the time of his premature death in 1947 he was Professor of Education in the University of London.

Mannheim was never an elegant writer. Even his German style may have suffered from the fact that German was not his first language. Both his spoken and his written English always had a strongly marked Continental structure and colouring. The translation of his writings into English has varied in quality, but has never altogether succeeded in making the transition from one idiom to the other. Rarely can the reader escape altogether from the impression of German words with English endings. Unfortunately, the later translations of his works have shown no improvement at all in this respect: the posthumous volume of essays contains some of the very worst specimens of Germanic English. This is still an insular country, and it is not fanciful to suggest that the language difficulty has been a serious obstacle to the spread of sociological thinking here. American sociologists, with a national tradition of greater stylistic tolerance to help them, have been content simply to anglicize the German idiom or to invent a still more fearful jargon of their own. It may be suspected that nothing would do more to promote sociological studies in British universities than a vigorous presentation of up-to-date findings in the subject in a thoroughly English idiom.

The present volume,[1] the first of two, is designed to reveal the development of Mannheim's thought through a series of papers originally published in German periodicals during the formative, and probably most creative, period of his career. It is well adapted to this purpose; and since few of these papers had been reprinted in German or were easily available in their original form, it is an important addition to the corpus of Mannheim's work. Dr. Kecskemeti, in a useful introduction, provides the necessary bibliographical information, and briefly indicates the significance of the essays presented in the growth of Mannheim's ideas and interests.

Mannheim was a member of the disillusioned generation which came out of central Europe at the end of the First World War and, under the stimulus of the Russian Revolution, found in Marxism a potent antidote to the spiritual and intellectual void. Hungary contributed heavily to the first post-war efflorescence of Marxist intellectuals, and though Mannheim was never a Marxist, the Marxist foundations of his thought went deep, and he made no attempt to disguise them. He came to Heidelberg at a time when the teaching of the social sciences there was still dominated by the school of Max Weber; and it was in this school that Mannheim received his sociological training. A sociological view of history is inherent in Marxism. But Mannheim himself was less interested in the economic interpretation of history than in a conception of *Geistesgeschichte* which went back ultimately to Burckhardt, and sought to interweave the history of culture, art and ideas with the

---

[1] Karl Mannheim, *Essays on the Sociology of Knowledge*. Edited by Paul Kecskemeti. International Library of Sociology and Social Reconstruction. Editor: W. J. H. Sprott (London: Routledge & Kegan Paul).

history of events as depicting the essential character of an epoch. Mannheim was an undogmatic thinker who was singularly receptive to new ideas and continued to learn and to develop his thought throughout his career.

The "historicism" to which Mannheim gave his allegiance and to which the longest and most important essay in this volume is devoted, was therefore more broadly based than some professions of faith which have been current under this name. His allegiance was, however, wholehearted and uncompromising:

> Historicism is neither a mere fad nor a fashion; it is not even an intellectual current on which we construct our observations of the socio-cultural reality. It is not something artificially contrived, something like a programme, but an organically developed basic pattern, the *Weltanschauung* itself, which came into being after the religiously determined mediaeval picture of the world had disintegrated, and when the subsequent Enlightenment with its dominant idea of a supra-temporal Reason had destroyed itself.

The Enlightenment was "the expression of a mental and spiritual attitude most nearly appropriate to a capitalist society". The French Revolution destroyed the would-be universalism of the Enlightenment, and created a "polarization of modes of thought and attitudes", which substituted the dynamic and the dialectical for the static and the dogmatic. The supposedly "timeless" values of the medieval world and of the Enlightenment—based in the one case on supernatural dogma and in the other on a deified supra-temporal Reason—have given way to values which we recognize as rooted in time and place. The study of the "conditioned" nature of our judgments in all the sciences relating to human behaviour arises directly out of our acceptance of "historicism".

From historicism Mannheim passed on by a short and natural step to the "sociology of knowledge". It was probably in this field that Mannheim made his most original and important contribution to contemporary thought: this was the subject of the first of his writings to be translated into English some 15 years ago under the title *Ideology and Utopia*. Here Mannheim's function was to explore and systematize a body of ideas which had hitherto been tolerated rather than received in polite academic society—not denied admittance but also not accepted with all its implications. The proposition that thought is influenced and conditioned by the situation of the thinker in time and place had been repeated so often as to become trite and boring. Yet in practice the history of philosophical or political or economic ideas could still be discussed and taught as a self-sufficient entity in which one "school" succeeded another without regard to that social background whose changing character determined the changing patterns of thought.

Mannheim laboured to show that the history of ideas, like other kinds of history, could not be studied in isolation from the society in which the ideas were born and flourished—in other words, that political and economic theory as academic disciplines must be closely wedded to sociology. The sociology of thought is rooted in the Marxist doctrine of base and superstructure. Mannheim does not deny the debt. But he refuses to attribute any specifically economic character to the base; and he specifically rejects as narrow and misleading the hypothesis that "an intellectual attitude is dictated by a material interest". The function of the sociology of thought cannot be merely to "unmask" or "debunk", however necessary and legitimate this process may sometimes be. Nor do we seek to "relate an intellectual standpoint directly to a social class". What we have to do is to investigate the whole "style of thought" of a particular group at a particular period, to relate its thinking to the whole social order. Like Marx in his later years, Mannheim would freely admit a process of reciprocal interaction between base and superstructure.

There was therefore in Mannheim nothing of the crude de-terminism which seeks to isolate a single material factor in human history and make it the foundation for an all-embracing theory of human affairs. He struggled hard against the imputation of "relativism", arguing rightly enough that the charge can be made good only by those who accept *a priori* an absolute standard. He believed that the essence of reality is dynamic, and that to seek any static point within it from which to deliver "timeless" judgments is a fundamental error. The individual's apprehension of this ever-changing reality is necessarily partial and relative. He can see it only from the perspective of time and place in which he finds himself; and even this partial view is of something which is in process of continuous change as he looks at it. It makes no sense to describe the one as "relative" to the other. Reality consists in the constant interaction of subject and object, of man and his material environment.

This searching attempt to find a sort of middle ground between a no longer tenable absolutism and an intolerably negative relativism is designed to offer a way out from many of the dilemmas of our time. As Mannheim points out, Socialism since Marx has split on this vital question of the quest for an absolute. Socialism in the English-speaking countries has simply relapsed into the old belief of the Enlightenment in a supra-temporal immanent Reason, and become philosophically indistinguishable from Liberalism (with the political consequences which that entails). Marxism, at any rate in the interpretation given to it by Lukács (and no other Marxist philosopher has carried the argument so deep), identifies the class-interest of the proletariat with the interest of society as a whole, and therefore treats proletarian class-consciousness as the self-sufficient and absolutely "right" form of consciousness in which the non-proletarian has only to merge himself. Neither of these absolutes is acceptable to contemporary western man; and western progressive thought, lacking any firm philosophical basis, fails to-day to perform its proper function of offering a convincing and faith-creating ideal (in Mannheim's language, a Utopia) to the world.

The point at which Mannheim's middle ground is ultimately most vulnerable to attack is the difficulty of providing a standard of value. Mannheim toyed long and lovingly with the idea that, in his quasi-relativist world, a hard core of independence could be found in a body of detached intellectuals (what he called *die freischwebende Intelligenz*) which would remain the custodian of a residuum of quasi-absolute truth. But the idea is put forward in a tentative and hesitant manner which suggests not so much a modesty in pleading *pro domo sua* as an innate doubt whether the idea will in fact work. Even since Mannheim began to think and write, the belief that intellectuals were better equipped than any other section of society to resist the ideological or the economic pressures of current orthodoxy has been put to the test in more than one country, and shown to have only the slenderest foundations. Lenin seems on the whole to have been right when he argued that the intellectuals do not form a class.

But this is not the real difficulty. The question is not where we are to find the standard-bearers, but where we are to find the standard. If none of us—and the point seems irrefutably established—can hope to gain more than a fleeting and conditional view of reality, then by what token can it be judged whether one man's view is better or "truer" than another's? Or must we assume that one man's view is as good as another's, and that any dispute about the respective validity of different opinions is not merely futile but meaningless? Clearly the absolute scepticism of such an attitude is intolerable; and Mannheim, for all his "relativism", has no leanings towards scepticism. To our question he seems to give two answers, one explicit, the other implicit. The first answer is that the right view is the one which enables us to understand and cope with reality in its existing (and *ex hypothesi* transient) form. "Truth in a perspectivic sense means that within one historical constellation only one perspectivic conclusion can be correct." We know that it is the right key because it fits, and because we see the man with the wrong key battering helplessly at a closed door.

It is, however, difficult to acquit those who propound such views of the charge of a nakedly pragmatical belief in power—whatever succeeds, is right—unless we also accept the other answer which Mannheim never directly gives, but unmistakably implies throughout all his teaching. A passage at the end of one of these essays shows his reluctant and apologetic, yet firm, approach to a declaration of faith which he never seems to have made:

> It would be an ill-advised mysticism which would shroud things in romantic obscurity at a point where rational cognition is still practicable. Anyone who wants to drag in the irrational where the lucidity and acuity of reason still must rule by right merely shows that he is afraid to face the mystery at its legitimate source.

The ultimate "mystery" which Mannheim thus cautiously admitted as potentially impenetrable to reason had nothing to do with religious dogma, which he sternly refused to call to his aid. It resides in the belief, which is necessary if we are to legitimize our acceptance of truth as the handmaid of reality, in a principle of reason and rational progress discernible in the ordering of human affairs—the last dim reflection of Hegel's rational reality. This belief Mannheim, perhaps in part unconsciously and therefore the more tenaciously, held. He tore to pieces the gaudy and long tattered garments of the Enlightenment. But out of them he extracted this almost invisible thread; and on it his fertile and powerful system of thought is suspended. There is after all a supra-temporal Reason lurking somewhere, well out of sight and not to be invoked except as a last resort, in the background of human affairs.

Manheim's importance lay in an immense talent for synthesis—which less indulgent critics sometimes call by the less flattering names of "eclecticism" or "compromise". It was undoubtedly this gift which gave him his peculiar place among thinkers in Great Britain, where the climate is notoriously unpropitious to the unshaded outlines and starkly logical consistencies of some European systems of thought. Mannheim inspired many who did not share his views precisely because he seemed, from the other shore, to point the way to a middle ground. In his last years he even established points of contact with some Christian thinkers, though without in any way departing from the rigours of his own rationalist belief; and he was also much preoccupied with the reconciliation, in theory and in practice, of two conceptions falsely regarded as antithetical: freedom and planning. This was an excellent example of the way in which his thought, however abstract in form, was always attracted to concrete and topical problems. First and foremost, however, Mannheim was a teacher. It is on his dual contribution to scholarship, in extending and developing the scope of sociological studies in Germany, and in helping to plant the new tradition in Great Britain, that his reputation ultimately rests.

23 Lewis Namier

Lewis Namier was on all counts an outstanding personality, and has earned an outstanding biography.[1] Julia Namier was his wife for thirteen years, and had known him for five years longer. Every biographer, however consciously and deliberately self-effacing, enters side by side with his subject into the biography which he writes. This is an intimate and moving book. Unquestionably, Lady Namier's influence on her husband's last years, though never in the remotest degree self-assertive, was very great, and she gave his life a sheet-anchor which had hitherto been lacking. The whole book is in some sense suffused by this rich experience, and by the meeting of these so different, yet congruent, personalities.

Another element in its composition will quickly become apparent to the reader. Namier throughout his life was prone to searching, and sometimes painful, self-examination. The assured authority of his pronouncements, his arrogance in controversy, covered an inner core of tormenting doubt. In his last years he poured out his soul, and laid bare the experiences of his past life, his frustrations and his predicaments, in a way he had never done before. Namier was always an expansive and exhaustive talker on any topic near his heart. Towards the end he talked, as Lady Namier records, in the hope and intention that she would be his biographer. Characteristically, he wanted to get the facts right. Large sections of the book, for which no other witness exists, are pure autobiography, told in the words of an understanding and deeply sympathetic listener.

Another source, less widely and fruitfully exploited here, might have been provided by the recollections of the very numerous men and women, of varied occupations and interests, with whom he came into contact at different periods of his life. Some, perhaps most, of these are no longer alive; some, including those with whom he clashed most sharply on controversial issues, may be reluctant to

[1] Julia Namier, *Lewis Namier* (London: Oxford University Press).

write. Almost the only reminiscences to appear so far in print were in a volume of *Acquaintances* by Arnold Toynbee (1967): these, though not very substantial, add a few agreeable touches. Lady Namier quotes a few letters from an apparently extensive archive, and some tributes from former students and others. But this is, by and large, the story of Namier and of his views and reactions, not a study of the issues in which he became involved.

For most readers, the central theme of Namier's life and of his biography will be the sharp impact of this exotic figure on the traditional English scene, and the eddies and two-way reactions which it set up. From this point of view, the early and obviously autobiographical chapters deserve the generous space allocated to them, though they still leave out much that we should like to know. Born in Russian Poland, the homes of his childhood were two successive estates at the eastern extremity of Austrian Galicia, not far from the Russian frontier. His father was a medium-sized landowner, a polonized Jew, no longer a Jew and yet not quite a Pole; by profession a liberal and a reader of John Stuart Mill, in habit a martinet and a compulsive gambler.

When, in 1908, at the age of twenty, after a year at Lausanne University and a year at the London School of Economics, Namier (still under the name of Bernstein) came to Oxford and entered Balliol College, he was already in search—unwittingly—of a new life and a new identity. He was "socially omnivorous"; as Lady Namier puts it, "belonging to no group, he was uniquely acceptable throughout Balliol". Toynbee's account of his arrival shows how he polarized the society into firm friends and sceptics or mockers. It was a foretaste, at a crude and simple level, of many later experiences. The citadel of English prejudice was breached only slowly, and never completely. The story was one of the irresistible force meeting the immovable mass.

Balliol was the starting-point of a career; "they taught me to think", was Namier's later generous tribute to that unique institution. During the next few years, he was gradually shaking off, on vacation visits, the ties of allegiance that bound him to family and to central Europe. He changed his name by deed-poll—twice: first to Naymier, then, being dissatisfied with the un-English spelling, to Namier; and he acquired British nationality. By 1912, after a flirtation with the seventeenth-century Puritans (whose attraction did not last long), he had succumbed to the lure of the British Empire. Before 1914 he was already preparing for a book on

"The Imperial Problem during the American Revolution".

Compared with the beginnings, the remainder of Namier's career seems relatively plain sailing, and is well known. A short period of military service in 1914–15 was followed by employment in one of the political intelligence departments, which badly needed his specialized knowledge of central Europe, and then in the Foreign Office. An interlude of teaching at Oxford; and then three years of business and journalism in Vienna and Prague, with the avowed intention of making enough money to finance further historical research—a period of which he rarely spoke in detail, though he was known to boast mildly of a financial expertise beyond the scope of most academics and intellectuals.

The return to England in 1925 opened the period of his greatest financial stringency, when he had to live on his own resources and on limited grants; but this was also the period of his greatest historical creativity, which produced *The Structure of Politics* and *England in the Age of the American Revolution*, published in 1929 and 1930. It was also at this time, in 1929, that he first became associated with the Jewish Agency in London, as its political secretary. Finally, in 1931, his appointment as Professor of Modern History in Manchester brought him for the first time academic recognition and financial security.

The development of Namier's opinions makes an interesting sociological as well as psychological study. Like nearly all the intelligent young in central and Eastern Europe, he was drawn to "socialism", without any very clear definition of the term. The seeds were sown in boyhood by an intelligent tutor, also a polonized Jew, who achieved some distinction in political journalism, and by early hero-worship of Pilsudski, the implications of whose brand of national socialism had not yet been revealed. But the socialism imbibed by the adolescent Namier had a peculiar stamp. As Lady Namier records,

> The general political and economic assumptions were Marxist, but the urgent concern was with agrarian reform—the righting of the dispossessed native Ruthenian peasantry's wrongs.

The cause of the Ruthenian (or Ukrainian) peasant majority of East Galicia, and the attempt to save them from the fate—which befell them—of annexation by Poland, which was the chief preoccupation of Namier's period of service in the Foreign Office and at the Peace

Conference, earned him the undying hostility of the Polish nationalists, and helped to complete his breach with his family.

It is significant that the first oppressed people with whom the young Namier identified himself were not the Jews but the Ruthenians. It is more significant—for this bias remained with him for life—that they were peasants, not urban dwellers. Namier's mature political thinking, as he more than once proclaimed, revolved around the holding of land: political struggles were struggles for the possession of land.

But this feeling went deeper still. When Namier entered L.S.E., in 1907, he duly enrolled in the Fabian Society, and met the now famous leading Fabians of the day. But this was not his milieu. As he walked the sordid streets of central London, he was overpowered by "perplexing culinary stenches, spiced with coal dust", and saw "the bleary faces and misshapen bodies of nondescript women". The miseries of starved and land-hungry peasants he could understand and pity. The misery of urban poverty was a horror that passed his understanding, eluded his sympathy, and excited only revulsion.

The years in Oxford transformed him, in more than legal status, into a loyal British subject. It does not need to be stressed how much he still remained a foreigner, in outward aspect and manner, in his knowledge of Europe, in many of his habits of thought. But, with the zeal and thoroughness of the newcomer, he set out to assimilate and to make his own the fundamental assumptions and attitudes of the society to which he had given his allegiance. With the approach of war, hatred of the Germans, endemic—not without reason—among the Slavs of central and Eastern Europe, came to reinforce and stimulate his British patriotism. By 1914, in so far as this could be achieved by conviction and deliberate choice, he was a devoted member of the British establishment of that still imperial epoch.

It fitted into this picture that he should have immersed himself in English history, and have taken as his chosen field the great period of the unchallenged pre-eminence in English society and government of the land-holding aristocracy. This choice also influenced the sectors of contemporary English society to which he most naturally and eagerly sought access. Some rather unfair fun has been poked at Namier's addiction to the British landowning classes. He met some of them when he sought access to the hitherto untapped resources of their family archives. Mrs. Dugdale, A. J. Balfour's niece, whom he met during the First World War and with whom he worked at the Foreign Office, became a firm friend, and helped to ease his way into the society of the English countryside. Incidentally, she, earlier than he, became a fervent Zionist.

Though any label attached to so many-sided and complex a figure is liable to mislead, it seems proper to call Namier a conservative historian. In his two major works, he was the chronicler and analyst of a ruling class. He was not one to gloss over its defects or abuses; but he admired its effectiveness; he admired any system which, however oddly and paradoxically, worked, and preserved order and civilization. He took little account of the turbulence bubbling beneath the surface of life in the cities, which was to erupt just at the end of his period. Richard Cobb recalls a student who told Namier that he thought of doing research on the *sans culottes*, and was met by the question: "Why are you interested in those bandits?" One catches an echo of the old disgust at the sight of urban squalor. Still, relating to the group which sparked off so mighty an historical conflagration, it was an odd reaction.

It was perhaps the tiredness and disillusionment of old age which led him to a more and more outspokenly élitist view of history. The rudeness of students who harshly attacked a paper he had read at a seminar in Oxford in the 1950s, combined with the rudeness of a British Railways ticket inspector, provoked bitter reflections on the "new vulgarians" and the destruction of urbane living. Some years earlier he had written:

> Nazism, from the very outset so far as the Jews are concerned, starts with the worst characteristic of what is usually described as Bolshevism—disregard of the rights of persons and property, and the joy of humiliating people of higher standing and education than their tormentors.

One shrinks a little from the comment when one reflects that the vast majority of the Jews who went to the gas-chambers—or of the Russians who went to Stalin's camps—were not people of "standing and education" in Namier's sense.

The famous charge that Namier "took the mind out of history" is true only in one strictly limited sense. For Namier, common sense and enlightened self-interest were, and should be, the motive forces of history. He had the traditional conservative mistrust of abstract ideals; the invocation of abstractions like "democracy", "socialism", or "self-determination" seemed to him empty and dangerous. His major excursion into European history—the others were brilliant occasional essays on limited topics—was a slim volume on the revolutions of 1848, which started life as a British Academy lecture in 1944. Though much expanded from the lecture, it remained in essence an incomplete fragment, without summing-up and without conclusions. Tribute was paid to peasant discontent and to the forces of nationalism. But only scorn was reserved for the ideologues in Paris or Frankfurt, who dreamt of toppling thrones and reviving the principles of the French Revolution. The very title, *The Revolution of the Intellectuals*, indicated the character of the fiasco. The moral, implicit here, more explicitly expressed elsewhere, was clear: the pursuit of political ideals spelt the end, not the beginning, of political wisdom.

It is nevertheless tempting to believe that Namier's youthful idealism, driven underground in the pursuit of his historical studies, surfaced again in his mature years in his devotion to Jewry and to the creation of Israel as a national unit in a world of nations. Namier's Zionism was for many years his central and overriding preoccupation. Yet its course was neither smooth nor simple. Namier's first association with the Zionist organization in 1929 was short-lived, and ended in a quarrel which has never been documented on either side; though, when he referred to the Executive as "an absurd group", he was evidently condemning its methods and perhaps some of its policies, not its aims or ideals. The crisis of Jewry in the 1930s brought him back, and both then and throughout the Jewish agony of the Second World War he identified himself wholly and unreservedly with the Jewish people, and gave himself unsparingly to the cause of Israel.

After the war, he was uneasy at some of the methods by which the Israeli state established itself (twenty years earlier he had indulged the dream of Israel as a British Dominion); and when, in 1947, his closest friend and supporter among the Zionist leaders, Chaim Weizmann, expressed shocked and uncompromising disapproval of his Christian baptism and marriage, the breach was difficult to heal. Eleven years later, Namier and his wife visited Israel for the first and only time. He was profoundly moved by his reception. He was now an aged and ailing man; and any ambiguity in his divided loyalties to Christianity and Jewry melted away in the mood of warmth and reconciliation. It was a deeply-felt leavetaking of a central episode in his career.

Lady Namier fairly enough disclaims any call to assess Namier's work as an historian. But in the world of scholarship in which he chiefly moved the question has to be raised. The devil's advocate may have some searching points to make. Namier's two major works on English history have revised our view, probably for good, of certain aspects of the political scene in a span of the eighteenth century. But what the volumes contain is a series of essays. However bright and penetrating the illumination they provide on chosen topics, they do not add up to a history of England in the period; nor do they place the limited period to which they relate in the perspective of what went before and what came after. The analysis is static. The sense of the unending flow of history is missing. Namier is a great historian—so much cannot be gainsaid. But is he, like Acton, a great historian who has written no history?

Much nonsense has been talked about Namier's "method"; he has, it is said, "namierized history". His originality consisted in the systematic thoroughness with which he investigated the affiliations and backgrounds of a group of individuals. The method justified itself by the illumination it enabled him to provide on a single instituion, whose workings were governed by, or reflected in, the attitudes of these individuals. It was not a key to the study of history. It was useful in a limited sphere, and had its limitations and also its dangers. Namier devoted his last years to one enterprise—a vast encyclopedia of Members of Parliament of all periods—whose value has yet to be demonstrated. Bricks are important. But a pile of bricks is not a house. And should the master-builder spend his time in a brick-field? Perhaps nemesis awaits the historian who seeks to expunge ideas from the historical process.

These doubts, which only posterity can resolve, in no way excuse the melancholy fact that British scholars kept Namier at arm's length and, throughout his working life, refused him admittance to the inner sanctum of scholarship. When he stood for a fellowship of All Souls' in 1912, a majority of the fellows , as Pollard recorded in an unpublished letter, "shied at his race", and two other historians were elected. Revulsion against the unconventional and un-English, rather than anti-Semitism in particular, was probably the culprit; a well-integrated British Jew, even in 1912, would not have incurred this discrimination. That was a long time ago. It is less excusable that, in the later 1920s, when he was working on his masterpiece in straitened financial conditions, no Oxford college was willing to open its doors to him. It is almost inconceivable that after the Second World War, at the height of his powers and his fame, he should have been twice passed over in Oxford for chairs of Modern History and of International Relations. A conscience-stricken university did indeed confer on him more than one honour and distinction. But these were honours commonly awarded to outsiders.

Namier was an angular personality, relentless and sometimes over bearing in argument. Gifted by nature with acute powers of perception, he nevertheless became, when mounted on his hobby-horse of the moment, impervious to the reactions of the listener; and he never learnt that constant reiteration can be counter-productive. Yet all this did not weigh, or should not have weighed, in the balance against the magnitude and quality of his attainments. He towered above his contemporaries. His writings are an imperfect tribute to his intellectual stature. His widow's biography attests his stature as a human being.

24 Stanley Morison

The biography of Stanley Morison[1] offers an exacting challenge to the biographer and to the biographer's reviewer. To start with the platitudes, Morison was a man of many parts and many careers. He enjoyed, thanks partly to this, an exceptionally wide variety of friendships, which he tended to keep in watertight compartments, presenting to each acquaintance a large area of genial warmth and an area of impenetrable reserve. He was in essence a lonely man, leading a solitary life. How can one tie up all this in one bundle? How can one writer encompass the diversity of the theme?

The variety of careers is the most obvious, though not the most formidable, difficulty. Morison was, first and foremost, a typographer. This was the function which he exercised at the Monotype Corporation, at the Cambridge University Press, and—initially— at *The Times*. His scholarly researches, originally directed to the improvement of the prevailing state of printing, and never wholly divorced from that pragmatic aim, broadened out into the history of the subject from its beginnings, and into the kindred topic of calligraphy, so that the field of his professional interest embraced every form of the presentation of the written word to the reader. Throughout this field Morison became a master, and in many parts of it the unique master.

Such was the foundation of the immense reputation which Morison acquired with astonishing rapidity. It was appropriate that his biographer should be an expert in the field; indeed the blurb describes Nicolas Barker's work as not only "the definitive life of Stanley Morison" but also "the authoritative account of typography in the twentieth century". Morison came on the scene at the crucial moment of a vast expansion of the printed word, and of a reaction in every sphere of art against what were now felt as the narrow and constricting conventions of Victorian society. He was at the centre of a great explosion. There is no reason to doubt that his

[1] Nicolas Barker, *Stanley Morison* (London: Macmillan).

fame, specialized but secure, will endure as a great typographical reformer and innovator. Innovation, particularly in this country, likes to masquerade as the restoration of an ancient tradition. Here too Morison was in good company.

Mr Barker does full justice, not unmixed with the touch of adulation permissible in an official biography, to these achievements. He occasionally travels a little too briskly for the layman, throwing out names and technical details in bewildering profusion. But the untutored reader cannot really complain; the total picture is not blurred. On the other hand, a reviewer in the journal which Morison once edited, under the shadow of the parent newspaper to which he devoted a major part of his thought and activity over a period of thirty years, may be conscious of a certain perfunctoriness in the treatment of these years and of some lacunae which, perhaps necessarily, remain unfilled. But once again, the essentials are there. Mr Barker quotes an entirely private and personal letter in which Morison describes "the change from Dawson to Barrington-Ward" in the editorial chair of *The Times* as "a worthwhile contribution to the war effort", and speaks frankly of himself as "invested with much 'occult influence' so that little is done without prior knowledge".

A word should be said here of Morison's *History of The Times*, the four volumes of which absorbed him off and on—and rather more "on" than "off"—for upwards of fifteen years. They constitute the most solid, though probably not the most impressive, product of his meticulous scholarship, and are, like all his work, a phenomenal achievement by one who had no formal education after the age of fourteen. Some of the chapters were originally drafted for him by others—further research would reveal more about the processes of composition—but it is doubtful how much of these tentative drafts survived in the final version, almost every line of which bore the imprint of Morison's dominant personality.

The main personal assessments in the history—the elevation of Barnes, the demotion of Delane, the total eclipse of Buckle, the fascination and tragedy of Northcliffe—seem likely to survive. A few hobby-horses are ridden rather hard. A somewhat capricious selectivity is sometimes at work. The last volume sometimes threatens to diverge into an excursus on European diplomacy or British foreign policy; and there is some special pleading motivated by Morison's personal loyalty and devotion to R. M. Barrington-Ward. But no future historian will ignore it. Mr Barker goes to the root of the matter when he says that for Morison "history was the art, not of recording, but of exploring, the past". Morison understood more about history than some of our currently practising professionals.

The real problems of Morison's biographer are, however, the paradoxes of his opinions and of his personal life—both, no doubt, connected and intertwined. Barrington-Ward, in the early days of their acquaintance, described him as having "a good mind, which is yet an odd jumble of beliefs and prejudices continually in contradiction", and found the contradiction in a clash between traditionalism in religion and radicalism in everything else. This was a superficial diagnosis. Morison's radicalism preceded his Catholicism, and his Marxism followed close on its heels. Religion for Morison was a movement of revolt, and meant no acceptance of any establishment. A reference to the Catholic hierarchy as "this bunch of macaroni-merchants" could certainly be paralleled in utterances about the high priests of Marxist orthodoxy. Neither would imply any uncertainty about what he regarded as the fundamental doctrines of Christianity or of Marxism. The puzzling contradictions were not between the two but within both of them.

Mr Barker pays more attention to Morison's Catholicism than to his Marxism, partly perhaps from personal inclination, but mainly because he knew Morison only in the last years, when old age had tamed the rebellious vigour of his youth and maturity, and reconciled him to things he no longer had the strength to anathematize. But he very fairly provides the evidence to redress the balance. Exactly when Morison first heard of Marx is not clear; Mr Barker names the British Socialist Party, a sect of the extreme left, as a channel, but quotes no evidence. What is certain is that, when in prison as a conscientious objector in the First World War, he met Palme Dutt, Page Arnot, and other future founders and leaders of the British Communist Party. In 1923 he applied unsuccessfully for party membership; and in 1929 he addressed his friend Graham Pollard, a party member, as "Dear Comrade", apologizing in jest for the fact that he was "not technically a comrade".

Barrington-Ward in the verdict just quoted noticed Morison's "insistence on class". Contemptuous reference to "the boss class", or more briefly to "the narks", often decorated his conversation. What changed after 1931 was his assumption that the Labour Party was an effective spearhead of the campaign against capitalism. He now perceived that "the capitalist system is still strong, too strong for the idealists who have been for so long the support of the socialist"; the Labour Party was dead for thirty years, and the Liberal Party would revive. But the basis of his opinions did not change. In the last decade of his life he continued to denounce "many rich people in the West End and some pettifogging investors in Surbiton, all profiting by things of which they knew nothing", and he thought that the word profit "should stink in the nostrils of any decent man".

But here too there were contradictions. Morison did not spurn the amenities, and even some of the luxuries, of West End club life. If profit stank in his nostrils, he none the less worked hard to earn profits for *The Times* and rejoiced at the results. He said sometimes that, having been placed through no choice of his own in this repulsive society, he felt free to play the game by its rules so long as it lasted. He bargained sturdily with the Monotype Corporation and *The Times* for pensions sufficient to provide the comforts of old age. The *Encyclopaedia Britanaca*, to which he came too late to render much service, contributed substantially to the affluence of his last years. Morison had no capital; but he did better for himself, as the phrase goes, than many capitalists.

Paradoxes of character and behaviour go deeper than paradoxical opinions. "I was born a rationalist", declared Morison on a solemn occasion, "and a rationalist born is a rationalist for life; I see what I see and have seen less by the eye of faith than by the eye of reason". One hesitates whether to call this a classic example of self-misunderstanding or an unconscious cover-up for things he could not bear to contemplate. In 1908, at the age of nineteen, brought up as an agnostic, he was received into the Catholic Church, which he never left. On 10 September 1912, he lighted on the Printing Supplement published that day by *The Times*. It kindled a flame of excitement and enthusiasm which determined his vocation and the whole course of his career, and which burnt on, unextinguished and undimmed, till his dying day.

In 1916, still untried and inexperienced, in the throes of the struggle to assert his faith as a conscientious objector in the war, he married a wife more than sixteen years his senior; the unfortunate woman apparently understated her age by ten years. In 1924 the marriage was on the rocks; its history can probably never be written, but Mrs Morrison seems to have been sensitive to what was in store. The same year saw the beginning of an intimate friendship between Morison and a young American woman named Beatrice Warde, who shared his interests in typography and whose husband, after two years of strain and stress, left her on his account; this passionate, though platonic, relation endured for the rest of his days. None of these landmarks in Morison's career bore notable witness to a rational way of life.

The same thing may be said of the mounting enthusiasm which caused Morison to give long years of devoted service to that ancient monument of the British traditional establishment, *The Times*, and of the infatuation—the word is scarcely too strong—for Beaverbrook which overtook him in 1948. None of these events can be explained, or could have been predicted, in rational terms. Had his actions been so governed, Morison's achievement and Morison's personality would probably have been far less impressive. What drove him forward was a succession of violent eruptions of powerful and powerfully controlled emotion, which imparted a unique force and vividness to everything that he did.

Morison's letters and reported speech offer problems of interpretation. His utterances, written and spoken, were often tricked out in a dazzling Shavian display of wit, panache, and self-dramatization. A generation of excavators has failed to unearth from the records of Shaw's life much of that genial warmth that radiated from Morison over the circle of his friends. But for both men the sparkling epigram, the odd mixture of self-mockery and ostentatious self-assurance, the outrageous paradox, served as a façade for a hidden hollowness and emptiness at the core.

Morison himself has left clues. Two categories of his letters stand out as wholly free from this extraneous ornament, and entirely simple and sincere: those dealing with questions of professional scholarship, and those addressed to Beatrice Warde. In an odd little disquisition written for Beatrice in the early days of their association, Morison toyed, with the word "reality":

> Unless human relationships were founded upon reality, there could not be any permanence in them. And, when reality exists, a certain fire bursts forth spontaneous combustion if you like. . . . There is a specific real nature . . . and that is real which helps that nature to ascend from the implicit to the explicit.

Morison at that time could not define further—even to himself. But more than thirty years later, in a spoken tribute to Eric Gill after his death, he reverted to the word:

He believed in certain things—what? The fundamental basic things. The man, the woman, the child, the family, all of which he bore out. It is a very different thing for me. No wife, no child, no family, my golly, I mean I can see at once, without any further argument, I mean, how remote I am from the realities he faced and did. There's no doubt about it. I've felt it continually—continually.

Morison was by destiny, not by choice, a solitary.

The paradox of personal relations was the ultimate paradox in Morison's life. His present biographer has opened up much that he chose and strove to conceal; at a time when none of those closely concerned is still alive, this was legitimate and inevitable. He writes of Morison's "distinct if courteous misogyny, due to shyness and the fear of the strength of his own emotions". To call Morison a misogynist would be misleading to the point of perversity. His early relations with his mother can presumably never be documented. But she was a strong and able woman with a feckless and drunken husband who eventually deserted her; and everything points to the strong influences under which her only son (he had two sisters) grew up. The limited selections printed in the book from Morison's correspondence with Beatrice Warde testify to the unique role of that intimate and frustrated relationship in his later life.

Morison liked to say when moralizing about himself—often in contexts with a specifically sexual application—that he would have been a very wicked man if he had not submitted to the discipline of the church; and he commonly spoke of his religion not as a thing of joy but as a "hairshirt". It was psychologically an important resource for him to externalize his deep-seated inhibitions by debiting them to the injunctions of the church. The assertion of his own potential wickedness is as significant as it is unconvincing. It is tempting to trace in this hidden and tragic conflict between powerful passions and the powerful inhibitions which held them in check the dynamic force which filled his towering personality, with its inexhaustible intellectual fervour embracing both the broadest syntheses and the minutiae of scholarship.

One compensation found by Morison is particularly relevant to his service for *The Times*—his preoccupation with what he once called in another context "the reality of power". Morison had none of the gifts of the politician; his political judgments were frequently wrong. But his qualities were peculiarly suited to the role of *éminence grise*, the exercise of known but publicly unavowed power. Mr Barker does not exaggerate when he describes his role at *The Times* as "the unofficial adviser to successive editors"; indeed on some points he seems to underrate the extent of his influence. What, however, can hardly be overstated are the benefits which *The Times* derived from that influence at a crucial period of history. The reorganization of the *Times Literary Supplement* after the war falls into place as a supplementary benefit.

Mr Barker does however perhaps give less than due weight to the other side of the picture. He rightly dissents from Donald McLachlan's estimate of Morison in his recent biography of Barrington-Ward. But McLachlan reflects the view of those members of the editorial staff who resented Morison's intrusion and the position which he acquired; and one cannot feel that this reaction was surprising or wholly unreasonable. Morison was capable of a certain ruthlessness and asperity towards those whom he did not suffer gladly. When Sir William Haley acceded to the chair, Morison's reign was over. He was deeply hurt by the chillier climate of a changed Printing House Square, especially as he had promoted the new editor's candidature. But that was not a reason; and his hopes that things would go on as before were hardly realistic.

Morison's place in the history of the printed word is secure. But how much will remain of the impact which he produced beyond this technical sphere, on a far wider circle of his contemporaries, and which made so many of them feel that they were dealing not merely with an expert typographer or a meticulous scholar but with a great man? Much of the record must rest on oral tradition, which is already fading; and perhaps the opportunity for a great biography which would have recaptured the fire and drive of his personality in his most creative years is already past.

Meanwhile we shall remain lastingly grateful to Mr Barker for a book which does full and expert justice to his technical achievements, and assembles every scrap of information available about him in the printed or written record. Occasionally, indeed, one may feel that he tried too hard—does one care about the exact address of the tobacconist's shop kept at one time by Mrs Morison in Holloway? But the whole work has been done with affectionate care and masterly precision. In a volume of nearly 600 pages the present reviewer has spotted only two tiny specimens of what Morison once gleefully called "the flotsam and jetsam of illiteracy": Melk is not in

Czechoslovakia; and the indexer has conferred on Schramm, an obscure German librarian of the early 1920s, the initials of an historian of the same name who flourished in the Nazi epoch.

Part IV Socialism and Communism

25 Early Socialist Thinkers

Political movements generally arise out of a reaction against their opposites; but, since every political achievement stands on the shoulders of its predecessor, it is also true that political movements continue and complete the opposites against which they have reacted. Socialism is both the enemy and destroyer of liberalism, and the successor of liberalism. Socialism takes over and carries forward the basic liberal conception of the rights of man. It reacts against the liberal conception of the natural harmony of interests, against its one-sided emphasis on civil and political rights, against its belief that the social and economic order can be left to take care of itself. Both in its positive and its negative aspects, socialism can scarcely be defined except by reference to liberalism.

These reflections are suggested by the difficulties which Professor Cole feels in his latest book about the definition of socialism.[1] The word was coined—exactly by whom seems never to have been established—about 1830, and almost certainly in France. It was formed in conscious contrast to "individualism". All socialist theories rest, as Professor Cole puts it, "on a belief in the virtues of collaboration as against competition, or of planning as against what their opponents call 'free enterprise' ". This is the guiding thread on which Professor Cole hangs his rather miscellaneous collection of thinkers, ranging from Saint-Simon to Proudhon and from Fichte and Mazzini—both somewhat dubious candidates for admission—to Owen and Marx. What is not quite clear is how the anarchists fit into the definition. But William Godwin is here, and Bakunin is promised for a second volume.

The period of socialist thought covered by Professor Cole's present volume begins with the conspiracy of Babeuf and ends with the *Communist Manifesto*. It is worth noting that neither Babeuf nor (at

---

[1] G. D. H. Cole, *Socialist Thought: The Forerunners, 1789–1850*. Volume I: *A History of Socialist Thought* (London: Macmillan).

this period) Marx called himself a socialist. Babeuf professed himself a democrat of the school of Robespierre. Marx and Engels described themselves as "democratic communists"; and Marx was a vice-president of the Brussels Democratic Union. The famous manifesto was called "communist", not "socialist", because the latter word was too strongly tarred with the "utopian" brush. But the fact is that at this period it was "democracy" rather than "socialism" or even "communism" which carried with it the connotation of revolution and class-war. The Chartist movement with its "six points" was in essence democratic, not socialist, and soon came to be distrusted by socialists of the Owenite brand as being too extremist and revolutionary.

Throughout this period, therefore, socialism was a label which suggested somewhat airy speculation about a better organization of society, and in particular of its economic arrangements, rather than an active—still less, a revolutionary—political programme. It is natural that these speculations ranged widely and are difficult to classify. The first major figure to claim our attention is perhaps the strangest of them all, the Comte de Saint-Simon. It is arguable whether he should be called the first socialist, the first technocrat, or the first sociologist: he could make out some claim to any of the three titles. He was deeply imbued with the spirit of the industrial revolution and of progress through invention and technical development. This was for him the real essence of politics: "Politics is the science of production." On the other hand, he realized with astonishing prescience that the industrial revolution had brought into the centre of the political stage the new class of industrial workers—"la classe la plus nombreuse et la plus pauvre". In detail Saint-Simon's prescriptions for the future ordering of society were often puerile. But many of his ideas were pregnant. It was he who first spoke of the need to overcome "the anarchy of production" by "the organization of production", and first distinguished between "the government of men", which would disappear in an advanced socialist order, and "the administration of things"—a technical process which would continue even in the epoch of freedom. These were only two of several points on which Marx and Engels were directly in his debt.

Saint-Simon was distinguished from the "utopian socialists", properly so called, by a certain hard-headed realism about what was going on in the world around him. But it was their greater simplicity and their moral fervour which gave them a wider contemporary appeal. It is difficult to-day to read with admiration, or even with patience, Fourier's lucubrations about his ideal society organized in "phalansteries", with prescriptions for the division of labour, for diet and a hundred-and-one other absurdities, or to regard him as anything but a faddist and a crank. Yet his influence in progressive circles all over Europe, not excluding Russia, was immense; and Fourierist colonies ("at least twenty-nine of them", according to Professor Cole) were established in the United States in the 1840s. It was across the Atlantic, too, that Cabet travelled to found his "Icaria" somewhere in Illinois. It is said to have lasted in some form or other for 50 years.

Beside Fourier and Cabet, Louis Blanc was a practical man. Like Saint-Simon, he understood the cardinal significance of the industrial revolution and of the rise of the industrial working class; and, unlike Saint-Simon, Fourier and Cabet, he was prepared to be a revolutionary in action. But his most lasting contribution to socialist thought was the doctrine of the right to work; the short-lived Ateliers Nationaux of the 1848 Revolution, which were entirely due to his inspiration, were the first instance in history of public works for the relief of unemployment. Blanc was also an excellent as well as a prolific writer. His *Organisation du Travail*, written in 1839 to popularize the idea of workers' cooperatives, was a best-seller of its day; and some of his historical writings, notably the *Histoire de Dix Ans*, are still valuable.

Two important figures in the early record of French socialism—Blanqui and Proudhon—do not fit easily into the main stream. Blanqui was a revolutionary agitator and activist, a specialist in the organization of what has come to be known in our time as the *putsch*—the isolated revolutionary insurrection which is relied on to set the torch to a wider conflagration. He anticipated Marx in two respects—in preferring to call himself a "communist" rather than a "socialist", and in making "the proletariat" a term of revolutionary propaganda: it is, indeed, possible that he was the originator of the phrase "the dictatorship of the proletariat".

Proudhon defies all classification. He was more of an anarchist than a socialist; and, whatever else he was, he was an impenitent individualist. In recent years he has been both acclaimed and denounced as the enemy of socialism. He was as devoid as Fourier of any historical sense. A peasant by origin, he detested industry and regarded the proletariat with contempt. But the fertility of his ideas, and the eloquence and catholicity of his denunciation of the abuses of society, gave him an outstanding position in the French socialist movement which usually puzzles commentators of a later day— Professor Cole among them. His was the socialism, if that is its right label, of the small, independent artisan, who hated and feared all large-scale centralized organization, the large estate, the large factory, the massed proletariat, popular democracy; and, since the independent artisan continued longer in France than elsewhere to keep up the unequal struggle against the mass production of modern industry, Proudhon retained his fame and his influence. Even to-day individualism has stood out more stubbornly in France than elsewhere against the advance of mass civilization—with good results and bad.

In turning to the early British socialists Professor Cole is on the ground which he knows best of all; and here he also has the support of a very distinguished piece of earlier research, Max Beer's *History of British Socialism*. Early British socialist thought makes, however, a poor showing, both in quantity and in quality, in comparison with French thought of the same period. In France the intellectual ferment of the great revolution left behind it a trail of theoretical speculation, which went far beyond the practical framework of the French politics or French economic development of the day, and thus flowed over into utopian channels. In England the far more highly developed industrial revolution was presenting its practical social problems which urgently demanded solution and left little time or attention for theoretical speculation. The "socialist" theorists of the 1820s who first began to find chinks in the armour of capitalist economics—Hodgskin, Bray, and the rest—are now remembered only by specialists who are concerned to ferret out the intellectual antecedents of Marxism. The only great name in British socialism of this period is Robert Owen; and he is more remarkable for his role as the father of the cooperative movement, and for the impetus which he gave to certain aspects of a nascent trade unionism, than for the utopian speculations which he shared with the French socialists or for the model communities which he founded. The so-called "Christian socialists"—Maurice, Kingsley, and Ludlow—were ardent social reformers, but not really champions of socialist doctrine. Whatever there was of socialism in their ideas came—as Professor Cole convincingly and rather unexpectedly shows—straight from French sources through Ludlow, who was partly brought up in France and retained his connexions with that country. The British contribution, both direct and indirect, to the development of a workers' movement at this time was immense. But the direct British contribution to socialist theory was almost negligible.

In his last chapters Professor Cole turns from French and British to German socialism and thus foreshadows the great change which was to come over the European scene after the middle of the century. The failure of the revolution of 1848 in France, the swift reaction which followed it, and the descent into the Second Empire, marked the effective end of revolutionary democracy and the end of French revolutionary leadership in Europe: the Paris commune of 1871 was a last despairing convulsion born of military defeat and shame rather than of a still living revolutionary faith. As the centre of gravity on the Continent shifted to a Germany now in rapid process of industrialization, the character of the European revolutionary movement also underwent a fundamental change; and a new revolutionary socialism, very unlike the socialism of the days before 1848, took the place of the old revolutionary democracy.

In this volume, however, we are concerned only with what may be called the pre-history of the German movement. Bruno Bauer, Moses Hess and Karl Grün are to-day little more than the names of men whom Marx unmercifully attacked, but from whom none the less he borrowed something. It was the role of the Germans to transpose socialism to a philosophical plane: it remained for Marx to bring it to earth by linking it with the cause of the rising proletariat. But the roots of Marxism in Hegel and Feuerbach have never been contested or concealed. Marxism is a philosophy as well as a social and political doctrine.

One consequence of the failure of 1848 for the future of socialism was to destroy the belief, which lay behind the projects of the utopian socialists, that the old ruling classes might, by preaching and persuasion, be induced to abandon the existing State structures and to sponsor these new prescriptions for universal harmony. Henceforth it came to be everywhere assumed that socialism could triumph only through the overthrow of the existing order, though opinions still differed as to whether this act of dispossession could be achieved through the agency of the ballot-box or only through violent revolution. The view that socialism might ultimately vote itself into power gained ground, in spite of the discouraging experiences of the use of universal suffrage in France under Napoleon III; and it ultimately became the dominant belief of the socialist parties of western Europe. But though this element of "utopianism" remained, the socialism or social-democracy which flourished on the Continent of Europe in the latter part of the nineteenth century was a very different affair from the idealistic non-proletarian socialism which is the main theme of Professor Cole's present volume.

Professor Cole is a fluent and engaging writer with a natural sense of style, and avoids like the plague anything that smacks of obscurity or pseudo-profundity. His conversational manner, which probably owes something to the lecture-room, makes him always easy to read, though it is also responsible for a certain looseness of texture which sometimes seems more appropriate to the spoken than to the written word. Any impression, however, that Professor Cole is only skimming the surface of his subject may be corrected by consulting the very thorough and systematic bibliography at the end of the volume. This is a work of encyclopaedic learning, however lightly the learning may be worn. Few people to-day have browsed so widely and so far afield as Professor Cole among these lesser known French and British progenitors of socialist ideas.

A more serious criticism may be made of the restriction of subject which Professor Cole has imposed on himself. He carefully explains that he is writing here of socialist thought, not of the socialist movement; and still less does he treat of the economic and social background of the period. It may seem a sufficient alibi that he has devoted himself to these subjects elsewhere—in a series of important works, documentary and analytical, on the history of the British working-class movement and on the economic history of the industrial revolution. But it is precisely because Professor Cole was so well qualified to give a rounded picture that we may feel some regret at his deliberate limitation of his perspective. The present book earns the epithet "encyclopaedic", not only by the wealth of detailed information which it contains, but also for the less flattering reason that it contains too little of the essential analysis required for the digestion of this information. It remains too much of an anatomical structure which ignores the connecting tissues. We are told most adequately what individual thinkers thought, but not nearly enough about the social, economic or national backgrounds which explain the origins and divergences of their thinking. It always seems an ungrateful kind of criticism to ask for what an author has not professed or attempted to provide. But there are two or three volumes still to come in this series of studies of socialist thought; and, for all the modern claims of specialization, one must venture the hope that so outstanding an authority as Professor Cole will not give too many hostages to the view that social and economic thought is an entity which can be successfully studied in isolation from social and economic history and social and economic action.

26 Socialism and Marxism

The rise of socialism in Europe in the latter half of the nineteenth century once seemed a phenomenon peripheral to the main course of history. The events of the twentieth century, and in particular the Russian revolution, have turned it into one of the cardinal themes of modern history; and it is not surprising to find two books on the subject by Oxford scholars—though neither a professed historian— published almost simultaneously. Professor Cole's volume, which bears the title *Marxism and Anarchism, 1850–1890*, is the second instalment in his series on the history of socialist thought.[1] Mr. Plamenatz[2] limits his scope to Marxism, and to German Marxism at that (though this is a part which almost stands for the whole), but extends his survey to Russian Communism as the offspring, legitimate or illegitimate, of German Marxism; his work, far more than Professor Cole's, is written specifically and avowedly with one eye on the present ideological conflict between Communism and western democracy.

The merits of Professor Cole's survey will be familiar to readers of his earlier volume, and indeed of the whole corpus of his works on the Labour movement. He is factual, thorough, and in a slightly chilly and detached way, sympathetic. Perhaps he is sometimes a little too detached: in writing of figures like Herzen and Lassalle, he is frankly impatient of the intrusion of their private lives into their political thought. His chapters on the First International and on the Paris Commune are among the best in the book, his chapter on the ideas of Marx and Engels the weakest. There is no book in English which covers this particular ground so completely; and the minor movements, Belgian, American and British, get their due with the rest. This comes near to being a picture of how it looked at the time, before posterity had had the chance to simplify and systematize it in

---

[1] G. D. H. Cole, *Socialist Thought: Marxism and Anarchism, 1850–1890* (London: Macmillan).
[2] John Plamenatz, *German Marxism and Russian Communism* (London: Longmans).

the light of superior hindsight. Professor Cole is remarkably successful in appearing as a straightforward recorder with no axes to grind. He also provides an admirable bibliography of works in English and French. It betrays a weakness to which he frankly confesses: he has little German and no Russian.

Mr. Plamenatz has no prejudices at all against grinding axes and has, perhaps for this reason, produced a livelier book. He begins with an epigram from Montesquieu: "On peut poser pour maxime générale que toute révolution prévue n'arrivera jamais"; and he pronounces a no less epigrammatic verdict of his own on the failure of the German, and the success of the Russian, revolution:

> It was precisely because the conditions that Marx thought necessary for a successful proletarian revolution did exist in Germany that there was no desire to make it; and it was also because they did not exist in Russia that Lenin was able to seize power in the name of Marx and the proletariat.

Apart from the epigrams Mr. Plamenatz makes many good points. It is nowadays worth while pointing out that Marx "remained all his life in principle a believer in extreme democracy" and "denounced what the Liberals called democracy only because he believed it to be a sham". The debt which Marx owed to French thought is also suitably emphasized in the statement, only slightly exaggerated, that

> the greater part of what belongs to the properly social and political side of Marx's doctrine can be found in the writings of Frenchmen or Englishmen who died before the world had heard of Marx.

In the book's much less satisfactory section on Russian Communism, Mr. Plamenatz is right to remark that "there is nothing specifically undemocratic" about the opinions expressed in Lenin's *What is to be Done?* The undemocratic practice resulted from Russian conditions. He notes that the dissolution of the Constituent Assembly did not damage Bolshevik prestige, since the Bolshevik merely "destroyed an unvalued and alien thing whose uses were not known to the great majority of the peasants". He comes to the defence of the utopianism of Lenin's *State and Revolution* (which he elsewhere describes as "the most simple-minded and improbable of all famous political pamphlets") by an implied comparison with the Sermon on the Mount:

> We, too, are brought up in the same way. When we are young we are taught to admire the saying: "Sell all that thou hast and give to the poor." When we first hear it, it can do us no harm, for we are children with nothing to sell and nothing to give. And when we grow up we quickly discover that the advice is impracticable. This process of inoculation against the impossible virtues, which we ought to admire but not to practice, is a usual part of nearly all education.

It must, nevertheless, be confessed that, for a writer on the topics he has chosen, Mr. Plamenatz is sometimes disturbingly insular. One need not be a Hegelian (though reputable British philosophers have been in the past), or doubt the pernicious influence of some of Hegel's doctrines, or of the interpretations placed on them by some of his disciples. But Hegel remains a colossal figure in the history of thought; and to write that "we no longer admire Hegel", and that "it does not matter what Hegel meant, if indeed he meant anything, by such expressions as 'general will', 'world spirit', 'manifest' and 'objective' ", is surely to be separated by the Channel—if not by the Atlantic—not merely from the Continent of Europe but from the whole climate of European nineteenth-century philosophy. A comment on the "poverty" of German philosophy in the 1840s seems equally perilous. Difficulties of translation are partly to blame. "Relations of production" is not, in English, a very elegant phrase; and one may quarrel with the argument which Marx built around it. But there is really no point in guying it as incomprehensible and meaningless.

The development of Marxism from the form in which it was evolved by Marx himself, before 1848 in Germany and France and afterwards in England, through the glosses of Engels and through Lenin's reformulation of the doctrine in the early years of the present century, down to its apotheosis as the ideology of the victorious Russian revolution, first under Lenin, later under Stalin, is a fascinating study. Nowadays the impact of current emotions has unfortunately made it fashionable to tell the story in terms of betrayal. According to some, true Marxism was betrayed by Lenin when he proclaimed the socialist revolution in an economically backward, predominantly peasant, country. According to others, Lenin, the faithful disciple of Marx, had his legacy betrayed and distorted by Stalin. Only the stalwarts dare to pretend that there has been no "betrayal" at all.

Professor Cole has not yet reached the point in time at which he will have to balance very delicately if he is to remain detached from this controversy. Mr. Plamenatz fairly impartially distributes blame all round, and convicts everyone concerned of inconsistency, not perhaps without incurring the same charge here and there on his own account. But, propaganda apart, is the question of blame particularly fruitful or relevant? No political doctrine, especially when it inspires or explains political practice, is likely to remain unchanged over an eventful century—or half-century. Even if the same words are repeated, they come to mean different things. "Leninism is Marxism of the epoch of imperialism", "Stalinism is Leninism of to-day"—the claims made in the familiar phrases have an historical meaning, and can be fruitfully discussed. But a discussion of their literal truth, turning on the issue of orthodoxy or heresy, leads nowhere but to totalitarianism or to the witch-hunt.

Like other political and social thinkers, Marx could not altogether escape from the basic dilemma which confronts all such thought. If we can learn about the processes of change and dvelopment in human society by studying the past and present of that society, it follows that we must regard these processes as subject to some kind of laws or generalizations, and that the power of the individual to affect these processes by his actions is to that extent limited. If, on the other hand, we believe that we can and should affect and alter these processes, then the laws or generalizations which we discover in them are not absolute. It is undeniable that Marx sometimes wrote about "iron laws" governing the rise and the inevitable downfall of capitalism, and that Lenin attributed to Marx's teaching a power of "scientific prediction". But it is also undeniable that Marx—and still more conspicuously Lenin—passionately believed in the need for, and in the efficacy of, human action to set these "inevitable" processes in motion. This logical self-contradiction, if such it is, lies at the roots of Marxism. Marxism, like other kinds of social and political theory, is hortatory as well as factual, ethical as well as "scientific".

It is possible, by using certain quotations from Marx's writings and omitting others, to tidy up Marx and make him into an "economic determinist"; and this is what Mr. Plamenatz does. He refers in several places to the famous dictum that "no social order ever disappears before all the productive forces for which there is room in it have developed"—which, at any rate in some interpretations, apparently means that no revolution can ever occur until economic conditions have made it inevitable. But he makes only one passing mention of the *Theses on Feuerbach*, and does not quote their trenchant conclusion: "Philosophers have only interpreted the world differently; what matters is to change it." He says a great deal about the *Address to the Communist League*, in which Marx coins the slogan of "permanent revolution" (faintly foreshadowed, by the way, in a passage of the *Communist Manifesto*). But he treats this as a passing aberration which was, "for good Marxist reasons, advice improperly given", and regards it as overruled and cancelled by what he calls "the 'classic formulation' of historical materialism in the preface to *The Critique of Political Economy*" (the passage about "productive forces" already quoted). He quite accurately remarks that what Marx disliked about the Paris Commune was "its hostility to strong central government", but fails to observe that what he did like about it was its revolutionary violence.

This rather arbitrary selection of the evidence leads to the conclusion that Marxists are "not very interested" in dialectical materialism, and that "what really matters to them is 'historical materialism', the theory of society supposed to be derived from it". The trouble is that Marx and Engels, and generations of Marxists after them, have constantly insisted that the "historical materialism" which they preached was, in fact, dialectical materialism, and that they did not accept, or believe in, any form of materialism that was not dialectical. Mr. Plamenatz is entitled to reject dialectical materialism as nonsense and to treat it as *per se* negligible, but not surely to deny its importance as a component in Marxism, or to father on Marx and his disciples a form of historical materialism which they themselves always declared to be unacceptable. This error pursues him into the later section of his book on Russian Communism, where he observes that the Stalinist "calls himself, in honour of a doctrine he no longer understands, an economic determinist". Whatever the relations of Stalinism to Marxism, and whether Stalinists understand Marxism or not, it is certain that neither Marxists nor Stalinists call themselves economic determinists.

The dispute about the interpretation of Marx reaches down to the roots of the history of the German Social-Democratic Party. When Bismarck's ban on the party was at last removed in 1891 and it emerged into the light of legality, it drew up a programme, the famous Erfurt programme, which repeated the creed of orthodox Marxism as it had existed since 1848. Yet, while the ideas and the words were the same, the climate had somehow changed. As Professor Cole puts it:

> Let us say that the Erfurt programme, in emphasizing the need of action by the working class, left the long-run method of action undefined, but clearly contemplated in the short run the exclusive use of parliamentary methods, and that there was no hint of any sort of proletarian dictatorship as contemplated at any stage.

Four years later came the awkward incident of the expurgation by the party leaders of a passage of the introduction which Engels wrote, in the last year of his life, for a new edition of Marx's *Class Struggles in France,* in which he had discussed the role of street fighting in future revolutions. As Professor Cole says, it is difficult to believe that the reasons for the omission were purely tactical.

At this time, however, and above all in Germany, the tradition of revolutionary Marxism was too strong to allow the doctrine to be bowdlerized into one of "scientific" economic determinism, in which human action had to wait for the forces of evolution to perform their inevitable function. When in the later 1890s the "evolutionists" in the German Social-Democratic Party openly confronted the "revolutionaries", they called themselves "Revisionists" and admitted that they were adapting Marx to what they regarded as fundamentally changed conditions. It was only much later, under the influence of patriotism engendered by the First World War and of the Russian revolution, that Kautsky, who at the turn of the century had championed the defence of orthodox Marxism against the Revisionists, began to soften down his Marxism into an evolutionary "historical materialism" from which revolutionary activism had almost disappeared. But by this time the interest of the controversy had shifted to Russian soil.

The issue which arose in the Russian Social-Democratic Party between Bolsheviks and Mensheviks had superficial affinities with the German controversy between orthodoxy and revisionism, but rested in fact on quite different conditions. Marx had predicated his scheme of revolution on what had happened in France and England in the past and on what he expected to happen there. In both countries a revolution had brought to power a régime which could fairly be described as bourgeois, and a democratic form of government: it seemed to Marx a reasonable prediction that this would pave the way to a proletarian and socialist revolution. This scheme could, with a little stretching, be applied to Germany, but not to Russia, where no semblance of a bourgeois-democratic revolution had taken place or was in prospect. The abortive attempt of 1905 revealed what had long been evident to well-informed observers, the weakness of the Russian middle class, the lack of any close analogy between conditions in Russia and those in western Europe, and the improbability—to put it no higher—that anything like a democratic revolution on the western pattern could ever succeed in Russia. Trotsky, who had seen the events of 1905 at close quarters, was the first revolutionary to grapple with the theoretical difficulty which this situation presented to the faithful Marxist. Lenin grappled with it pragmatically in 1917. The two men differed on some theoretical details. But they agreed on the main point: that proletarian revolution could not be indefinitely delayed in Russia by the failure of the Russian middle class to make a democratic revolution. The proletariat must take the lead and somehow contrive to act as midwife to both revolutions.

But how did this fit into the classical Marxist scheme? Evidently, if Marxism were interpreted in terms of economic determinism, the Russian problem permitted of no answer—except that the revolutionaries must wait, hoping against hope for conditions to ripen in which the bourgeois-democratic revolution would become possible, and so provide the foundations on which the socialist revolution might ultimately be built. This was, broadly speaking, the answer of the Mensheviks, who, on the strength of their answer, could accuse Lenin and the Bolsheviks of betraying Marxism. The socialist revolution in Russia was impossible because no democratic revolution had yet taken place: you could not unite or telescope the two phases, which is what Lenin and Trotsky in their different ways were attempting.

It is easy to see that the Menshevik answer was unrealistic, in the sense that determined and impatient men, with the backing of revolutionary masses, are unlikely to be held back by theoretical arguments about the inappositeness of their action to some preconceived scheme or programme. But did Lenin act in a manner contrary to Marxist teaching? This also is not certain. The question how a great man would have reacted to conditions which never existed in his lifetime and which he could not have foreseen is rarely worth asking: the answer will be a literary exercise and little more. But texts in Marx that speak for unflagging revolutionary activity are as valid and as cogent as those conceived in terms of evolutionary laws; and the situation in which Marx commended "permanent revolution" to his German followers in 1850 was not so far removed from the situation which confronted the Russian revolutionaries after 1905. It seems that one should be cautious before preferring the charge that Lenin and the Bolsheviks betrayed the authentic Marxist teaching in 1917.

But behind this scholastic question, which to-day is of interest mainly to political propagandists, lies the real issue of the destinies of the Russian revolution. The early Bolshevik were sceptical of the ultimate success of a socialist revolution in a country politically and economically as backward as Russia: the course of the Russian revolution could run smoothly on Marxist lines only on the assumption that it served as a signal for the proletarian revolution in the advanced countries of Europe. When this failed to occur, the Bolsheviks were faced by a problem of the same character as the problem presented to the previous generation by the failure of the Russian democratic revolution. Once more, determined and impatient men could not wait indefinitely in the hope that conditions beyond their control would mature; and Stalin made haste to proclaim the doctrine and enforce the practice of socialism in one country, thus raising the same scholastic question whether Stalinism was a betrayal of Leninism and *a fortiori* of Marxism.

The historian, as distinct from the propagandist, may be content to withhold judgment on this point. He will note that the "socialism in one country" realized under the Stalinist régime was far removed from the visions of socialism nourished by western nineteenth-century writers. But this is not the only occasion in history on which realization has proved very different from expectation. He may diagnose among the causes of this difference the fact that the Russian revolution took place in a country which had had little experience of the form of capitalist development familiar in the west, and even less of the procedures and traditions of western democracy. But it is an historical commonplace that all revolutions, once the fury of the first onslaught is spent, begin to take on some of the colours and qualities of the *ancien régime* which they purport to have overthrown for ever; and it is not surprising that the Russian revolution, as it proceeded on its course, should have appeared to revert, in some of its manifestations, to an older Russian national tradition. How far these problems of the Russian revolution can be profitably discussed within a framework of Marxist doctrine is a moot point. This is history still in the making, and opens up horizons beyond the limits which Professor Cole and Mr. Plamenatz have set for their undertakings.

27 Socialist Twilight

When G. D. H. Cole died in January 1959, the last volume of *A History of Socialist Thought*, which was the *magnum opus* of his last years, had been completed, except for one or two missing chapters (nothing had been done on Asia except the chapter on China) and a final revision. The missing chapters will remain unwritten. But the revision has been undertaken by the author's widow and son, and the volume as published gives no impression of being unfinished.[1] The final chapter is a summing up, and Cole had already renounced the intention of carrying on the narrative in any systematic way beyond 1939. The later phases were in his view "not yet finished or ripe for the pen of the historian".

As Cole frankly said in the final chapter, his story leaves the socialist movement throughout the world in a state of great weakness and eclipse. In 1939 it had disappeared from central and eastern Europe. More significant still, "the upsurge of working-class consciousness connected with Roosevelt's New Deal had failed to take at all a socialist form" in the United States. The communist movement outside the Soviet Union had dissipated its initial energy, and degenerated into a series of chronic faction fights. If Cole had re-surveyed the situation twenty years later he would have had to record many changes—some superficial, some profound.

A revival of socialism in the countries of central Europe where it had been suppressed by Fascist or quasi-Fascist governments in the 1930s has proved unreal and abortive: none of the socialist or social-democratic parties has become a real force. In Great Britain and in France socialism has decayed not through repression but through internal weakness; and party leaders have tried to save the shell of their parties (this has happened in Germany as well as in France and

[1] G. D. H. Cole, *A History of Socialist Thought.* Volume V: *Socialism and Fascism. 1931–1939* (London: Macmillan).

Great Britain) by running away from socialism. In the United States socialism is no longer even an effective bogy.

The major development of these years from the point of view of the left has, of course, been the victory of national and revolutionary movements in Asia and Africa. In some countries, notably in India and Indonesia, the rivalry between socialism and communism which marked the period between the two wars in Europe has been resumed in a new setting. The struggle seems, however, somewhat unequal. The growing power of the Soviet Union and the prestige of a communism which has triumphed in China are powerful factors, both material and moral, on the communist side; and the weakness of socialism in Europe, as well as its inclination to compromise on "colonial" questions, easily makes it appear a milk-and-water doctrine to ardent young champions of national independence in Asia and Africa. The bankruptcy of western socialism is one of the gravest handicaps under which western policy in the "backward" countries labours today.

The story told in Cole's last volume is, therefore, gloomy in itself, and is also coloured by the knowledge of still less encouraging developments ahead. He is, as usual, at his best where his narrative is reinforced by personal knowledge and experience. Probably few people now remember the beginnings of the Socialist League or of its relations with the Labour Party in the Britain of the early 1930s. It never became in itself an effective body (Cole himself left it early); but its history is significant for the story of the Labour Party and for the role of the intellectuals in it. Cole traces to this episode Ernest Bevin's persistent feud with the party intellectuals. There may be something in this, though Bevin had moved over much earlier—not long after his election to the General Council of the T.U.C. in the middle 1920s—to the extreme right of the trade union movement.

In fact, in spite of much underground ferment, the 1930s were a depressing period for the British left. The splitting away of National Labour with Ramsay MacDonald, which should have left the rump of the party more united and stronger in its opinions, merely led to fresh dissensions—many of them centring in foreign policy. The Socialist League with Cripps, the Left Book Club with Laski and Strachey, and various pacifist groups, all stood well to the left of the new party leadership and of the trade unions, now increasingly dominated by Bevin's massive conservatism. The most effective opposition to the Hoare-Laval plan, and later to Munich, came from the Conservative benches and not from the Labour Opposition. Nor was the domestic policy of the Labour Party strikingly progressive. It was not till after the war that the Labour Party made a short-lived come-back with an extensive social programme. But this unfortunately falls outside the scope of Cole's book.

Other chapters deal with the confused story of French socialism in the 1930s, with the collapse of German Social-Democracy without a fight and of Austrian Social-Democracy after a fight, with the civil war in Spain and the New Deal in the United States, with events in the Soviet Union and in China. These chapters show Cole at his best as a teacher and popularizer rather than as a thinker. He attempts little fundamental analysis; and his accounts will not satisfy the specialist. But he has provided in orderly and accessible form the basic facts which the well-informed newspaper reader—or writer— will require. In this sense, as well as in its far-reaching comprehensiveness, *A History of Socialist Thought* may fairly be called encyclopaedic.

A survey of the whole work presents a striking picture of consistency both in its qualities and its limitations. Cole achieved, one feels, exactly what he set out to do. The title is indeed inappropriate. It was no doubt devised for the first volume, in which Cole was dealing with the early socialists—men of ideas who had as yet no opportunity of transforming them into action or even into concrete programmes. But Cole was never really interested in theory, he was too "English" for that; and, as the volumes proceeded, movements rather than ideas, what people did rather than what they thought, became the predominant theme. But even this had its limitations. Though Cole was not primarily a thinker, his approach was that of the intellectual, and he cared little for mass movements. Considering the enormous part played by the trade unions of many countries in the development of socialism, both in theory and in practice, they take a very modest place in Cole's history.

The publication of this posthumous volume—apparently destined to be the last in a varied and extensive *corpus* of writings— seems, however, to call for an assessment not merely of the present history but of Cole's achievement as a whole. A warm tribute by Dr. Julius Braunthal, until recently secretary of what was left of the Socialist International, forms the introduction to the volume. Dr.

Braunthal speaks of Cole as "a great figure of international Socialism no less than of British Socialism". Here some explanation may be required: Cole never took any part in the socialist movements of other countries; nor till the last years of his life was he particularly interested in them. He was neither a great traveller nor a great linguist. His influence in the international movement was due to his role as the interpreter and historian of the British movement. Dr. Braunthal is doubtless right in claiming that his *Short History of the British Working Class Movement* has been a university textbook in many countries, and in the dozen languages into which his writings have been translated.

Probably the most creative period in Cole's career, and the one which has exercised most influence on the socialist movement at large, was the period before and immediately after the First World War, when he was the leading figure—one might almost say the creator—of what was known as "Guild Socialism". The main concept of a socialism built on small groups of producers, free from the evils of bureaucracy and centralization, was one which appeared in many contexts at that time—among the French syndicalists and among Russian advocates of "workers' control" in industry. (*Self-Government in Industry* was the title of one of Cole's earliest books.) It had its utopian aspects, and was unlikely to be realized in a world moving towards ever larger and more complex forms of organization. But it continued to haunt socialist literature and to influence socialist ideals. According to Dr. Braunthal, Cole continued to trace affinities with his beliefs in the Histadruth and in the Kibbutzim settlements in Israel, and in the philosophy of Bhave and the Bhoodan movement in India.

But Cole the crusader for Guild Socialism was soon superseded, though never entirely eclipsed, by Cole the teacher. His fame and influence as a teacher—especially, on Dr. Braunthal's testimony, among students from overseas regions, including Asia—suggests an inevitable comparison with Laski, that other great left-wing university teacher of the period between the two wars.

The two men had much in common. Both were fluent, clear in speech and in writing, immensely well-informed and immensely productive, and capable of inspiring as well as instructing their audience in the lecture-room. Both sought to find an intellectual standpoint some way to the left of the official Labour Party position, which they mistrusted, but far short of the position of the communists, totally alien to their way of thought. Laski's initial pluralism, like Cole's initial Guild Socialism, was an attempt to establish such a standpoint. Realization that both were impracticable as answers to the problems of the contemporary world was the tragedy of both.

Yet behind these points of contact and similarity there were fundamental differences of temperament and approach. Laski, more versatile and more flexible, was intensely interested in pulling the strings of current politics. He loved to be near the seats of power, and to be on intimate terms with those who wielded it. And this arose partly from a vivid and untiring intellectual curiosity about the way in which things actually worked in political life—a quality which fascinated his students—and partly from a desire to influence them.

These characteristics Cole possessed only to a mediocre degree. He recoiled from the seamier side of politics, and never sought to influence them except on the abstract plane of intellectual persuasion. Hence his convictions could seem both more consistent and more profound than Laski's, since he never experienced that compelling necessity of adjustment and compromise which is inseparable from political practice. Cole was a man of outstanding sincerity and devotion to truth as he saw it. He wrote, as he spoke, without *arrière-pensée* and without calculation. His writings flowed, so to speak, directly out of his well-stocked and well-organized mind.

If one wishes, in conclusion, to find for Cole his precise place in the political spectrum, one must look back to that moment in the years just before the First World War when liberalism was gradually, under Fabian impulses, evolving towards socialism. Cole's essential type of thought was moulded at this turning-point. It would not be unfair to call his political creed liberal in form, socialist in content. He accepted without qualms or reservations the orthodox aims of socialism: they seemed to him the unquestionable ultimate goal of that progress through rational persuasion which was the essence of political liberalism. But they seemed in no way incompatible with a rather old-fashioned kind of individualism and with a strong infusion of economic laisser-faire only abandoned, and then only in part, after the great depression of the 1930s. This combination made it difficult for him to find a congenial home in any of the left parties.

The final testimony must be sought in the concluding words of the

History of Socialist Thought, which, if not the last words which Cole wrote, were presumably the last which he passed for the press:

> I am neither a Communist nor a Social Democrat because I regard both as creeds of centralization and bureaucracy, whereas I feel that a Socialist society that is to be true to its equalitarian principles of human brotherhood must rest on the widest possible diffusion of power and responsibility, so as to enlist the active participation of as many as possible of its citizens in the tasks of democratic self-government.

These are sound traditional liberal principles. But did Cole ever really come to terms with the age of mass-production, automation and the bomb?

28 Roots of Revolution

The story of the Russian revolutionaries of the nineteenth century, which has just been retold by Mr. Avrahm Yarmolinsky, till recently head of the Slavonic Division of the New York Public Library, in a noteworthy volume,[1] has become a popular and familiar theme in recent years. It can be read as a prelude to the Russian revolution of the twentieth century. As Mr. Yarmolinsky says in his introduction:

> It is doubtful if the doctrine of Leninism can be fully understood without taking account of the indigenous social revolutionary tradition as it developed in the second half of the nineteenth century.

Even in the Soviet Union the continuity of Russian history is not subject to the same sweeping and unconditional denial as in the earlier years of the régime. Chernyshevsky as well as Marx can be recognized as the ancestor of the revolution of 1917; and even Slavophils and *narodniks* are prophets not wholly without honour in their own country.

But another strand has also woven itself into recent studies of Russian nineteenth-century revolutionaries and is not absent from the work of Mr. Yarmolinsky, who writes that "the Soviet phenomenon . . . contrasts with all that the nineteenth-century radicalism dreamed or stood for". Has the Bolshevik revolution proved to be not so much a continuation as a betrayal of the ideals for which the nineteenth-century Russian revolutionaries fought and died? Those who like to pursue the might-have-beens of history are fond of pointing out that the Bolsheviks appeared, until the very eve of the revolution, to be one of the weakest of the revolutionary groups, and that their victory cannot be taken as a foregone

[1] Avrahm Yarmolinsky, *Road to Revolution* (London: Cassell).

conclusion. What if the victorious revolution had in fact been made by the Social-Revolutionaries?

Mr. Yarmolinsky indulges in no such idle speculations. But his discreetly veiled sympathies seem to be on the side of the Social-Revolutionaries—or of the *narodniks* from whom they sprang; and, however much he may insist on the influence of an "indigenous social-revolutionary tradition" in Bolshevism, he would be unlikely to recognize Bolshevism as the legitimate child and heir of the nineteenth-century revolutionaries. To recall that Marxism was a western doctrine which initially had no roots in Russia, and made its first impact on Russians in exile in western Europe, is to draw attention to an important aspect of the truth, though not to the whole truth. The revolution of 1917 was in one sense a sharp break in Russian history, and in another a long-awaited fulfilment of it.

This intermingling of the processes of change with the forces of continuity is a feature of the history of all revolutions—and indeed of all history, of which revolutions are only outstanding and culminating points. It is a strongly marked feature of Russian history in the nineteenth century, when the impact of western Europe struck sharply on a traditional and retarded indigenous civilization. It is in this sense that the whole previous century can be read as a prelude and preparation for 1917. Can we indeed any longer—for good or evil—read Russian nineteenth-century history except in the light of this denouement, since, whether we accept or reject it as a legitimate culmination, we cannot close our minds to it or pretend that it has not happened? Does the perspective of 1917 lend significance to what has gone before and enable us to understand the past more profoundly and study it with more sympathy? Or is it a distorting lens which prevents us from seeing the nineteenth century as it really was by importing anachronistic points of view and irrelevant prejudices derived from the experience of a later period? These questions are never far beneath the surface of Mr. Yarmolinsky's book. But he treads lightly and, while letting us know from time to time that he is not unconscious of these major issues, is content on the whole to leave them undisturbed.

Most writers on the nineteenth-century revolutionary movement in Russia begin with the Decembrist insurrection, or mutiny, of 1825. Mr. Yarmolinsky begins, quite as appropriately, with the publication in 1790 of Radishchev's *Journey from Petersburg to Moscow*. It was apparently written before the fall of the Bastille, though not before the American revolution. The precise date is of no great importance: it was plainly inspired by the rationalism and egalitarianism of the Enlightenment. In this sense Radishchev was a westernizer. But at this period the Russian autocracy itself was western in its orientation and thinking; Catherine the Great had patronized, and even read, the Encyclopedists. The difference was rather one between theory and practice. Radishchev might be described as the father of the Russian intelligentsia—the aristocrat turned intellectual. He was certainly the forerunner of the group of "conscience-stricken gentry" who played so fruitful a role in Russian nineteenth-century thought and literature. His most radical demand was for the emancipation of the serfs. But he can scarcely be said to have had a positive social or political programme. His was a lonely voice of protest against the backwardness, cruelty, and disorder of Russian life, an appeal to what may be vaguely called the principles of western liberalism.

The Decembrist leaders had not travelled far beyond Radishchev in the scope of their ideas. But they added action to thought, and thus became important —if only in the reaction which they provoked. It was after the Decembrist insurrection that the issue of revolution and reaction began to take the form of the issue of East and West. Against a revolution which ever more clearly and unequivocally took its cue from the West and from the principles of 1789, the autocracy of Nicholas I pitted the appeal to the national tradition— "Autocracy, Orthodoxy, Nationality". Thus was born one of the *leitmotifs* which runs through all Russian nineteenth-century literature about revolution. The revolution, the intelligentsia, nihilism, everything that is negative and destructive, comes from the West. What is distinctively Russian stands for order, religion, morality and the traditional values. Patriotism, decency, conservatism are welded together in the impregnable structure of the Tsarist autocracy.

But the revolutionaries themselves quickly became involved in this antithesis between East and West. The two great schools—or tendencies—which divided all Russian thinkers of whatever complexion in the nineteenth century, the westerners and the Slavophils, were born in the 1830s. The original Slavophils were romantics after the German pattern, and worshippers of the *narod* or *Volk*. But though in this sense they were patriots and traditionalists, they were not upholders of Nicholas I or of an autocracy which sought to level out all eccentricities, and standardize all thought, in the name of military or administrative efficiency. The Slavophils in their sentimental moments went back to a Muscovite Russia before Peter the Great and before the foundation of Petersburg, the alien capital. They were fond of pointing out that the dynasty itself was German, and that much of the bureaucracy was German. Even Herzen, who moved uneasily between westerners and Slavophils, poked a finger of scorn at Nicholas as a scion of the house of Holstein-Gottorp. The Slavophils were in their way intellectuals like the westerners and, whatever their original intentions, brought their quota of inspiration to the revolutionary movement.

Thus when, after the death of Nicholas I, his successor, Alexander II, set the floodgates ajar by decreeing the emancipation of the serfs, and the revolutionary movement began to assume the form—or forms—which it was to retain right down to 1917, it appeared that the revolutionary movement was also divided into western and indigenous camps. Since the 1840s the intelligentsia had swollen enormously and had overstepped the boundaries of class: the revolution was no longer an affair of the "conscience-stricken gentry". The children of the new professional classes, sons of priests, students of most varied social origins, provided a driving force of a kind unknown in the earlier, more aristocratic, more literary stages of the movement. What Mr. Yarmolinsky calls, in a slightly different context, the "children's crusade" had begun.

The body of revolutionaries who dominated the scene in the 1870s under the name of the *narodniks,* or "populists" (to use an unmeaning, but commonly accepted, translation), were an amorphous group, whose scope and purposes were difficult to define. But they represented for the first time an exclusively Russian revolutionary movement, drawing its inspiration and ways of thought and action from the native soil; there could have been no English or French or even German *narodniks.* The *narodniks* were the Slavophils of the revolutionary camp. The revolutionary intellectuals of the 1860s—Chernyshevsky, Dobrolyubov, Pisarev—were still outstanding westerners, students of Fourier and Feuerbach and John Stuart Mill. They marked the change from the humanist liberalism of the 1840s to the materialist radicalism of the 1860s. But the change followed an unbroken line—the line of western intellectual development. The change in revolutionary theory and practice introduced by the *narodniks* was a great deal more far-reaching. It was at one and the same time a change from the western to the national, from the "fourth estate" of western Europe to the Russian peasant, and from thought to action.

Mr. Yarmolinsky has rightly given much attention in his story to the *narodniks*. The movement was full of contradictions—it was both futile and practical, both self-sacrificing and unorganized, both generous and violent. It sprang from diverse sources. Alexander Herzen is often named as the father of the movement. As a westerner who, in the crucial and formative period of the early 1860s, made his peace with the Slavophils and began to build up—significantly, in exile—that idealization of the Russian peasant which was the one consistent centrepiece of *narodnik* doctrine, his claim is difficult to refute, though he would have been the last man to see himself as the founder of a school. But among the *narodniks* in Russia, in their days of hope and glory, the name to conjure with was that of Bakunin, and his influence ranked far above that of Herzen. The contradictions of Bakunin's enigmatic character—the combination of childish simplicity and undisciplined violence—are also the contradictions of the *narodnik* movement.

The story of the "going to the people"—the missionary effort to bring the glad tidings of revolution to the peasant and the factory worker, to make a bridge between the idealistic young intellectual and the "people" which was the hitherto remote and little understood object of his ideals—has often been told. The story of the other side of *narodnik* activity—the terror campaign with its bomb-throwings and assassinations—is equally familiar, but has never been told in English with such wealth of detail as in Mr. Yarmolinsky's pages: it is here that the rich resources of the New York Public Library have proved most valuable to his work. Both these spheres of action—though they seemed in part contradictory, and there were always groups in the movement which opposed the terror—were equally part of the *narodnik* tradition. The conception of peasant revolt, stemming from dim historical recollections of Stenka Razin—already a legendary figure—and Pugachev, formed the staple of the *narodnik* revolution. "Land and liberty", "The land for the peasant" were its typical slogans and defined all that it had in the way of positive goals.

The terrorist campaign, like the "going to the people", ended in failure, and in disaster for those who took part in it. What the *narodnik* movement left behind it was a living revolutionary tradition, a roll-call of revolutionary martyrs and a firm alliance between the revolution and the land-hunger of the Russian peasant. This was the rich heritage taken over, when the *narodniks* themselves had passed into history, by the Social-Revolutionary Party, founded at the beginning of the twentieth century. For a dozen years the Social-Revolutionaries seemed the most Russian, and therefore potentially most effective, of Russian revolutionary parties. The Russian peasant formed 80 per cent of the Russian population; and in so far as anyone could claim to speak for the Russian peasant, it was the Social-Revolutionary Party. Yet this, too, like the *narodnik* movement, ended in failure, leaving nothing but a name and a tradition behind it. How is the historian to explain what happened in what Mr. Yarmolinsky calls this "final stretch of the road to the revolution"?

Here we meet yet again, in a fresh guise, the antithesis between westerners and Slavophils, between a western European and an indigenous Russian tradition, round which the whole of Russian nineteenth-century history revolves. The final episode in the story of the Russian revolutionary movement before the revolution takes the form of a struggle between the Social-Revolutionaries, heirs of the *narodniks* and of the Slavophils, and the Social-Democrats, disciples of Marx and of western radicalism. In detail the issues which divided them seemed infinitely complex. In principle, the single issue was the one which had arisen in every major question of Russian policy for a hundred years. Was Russia to follow and imitate the course of development already familiar in the West? Or was Russia to develop along lines determined by national conditions, national traditions and national values? In terms of the revolutionary movement, was the Russian revolution to be a Marxist proletarian revolution or a *narodnik* peasant revolution? This was the controversy about which ink began to be split in quantity in the 1880s, and which continued down to the moment of the revolution—and after.

The situation was complicated by the fact that Marx himself, at the very end of his life, appeared to take a *narodnik* view of the prospects of the Russian revolution. Asked whether Russia must inevitably travel the western capitalist path—the sequence of bourgeois and socialist revolutions laid down in the *Communist Manifesto*—he had tentatively admitted that, given favourable conditions, the traditional Russian peasant commune might serve as the foundation for a future Russian socialism, thus enabling Russia to by-pass altogether the western capitalist stage. The admission was postulated on the achievement of a proletarian socialist revolution in the West; and, as Mr. Yarmolinsky says, Marx still believed in the early prospect of such an achievement. Marx was clearly influenced by the desire to conciliate his Russian correspondents, and his *obiter dicta* on the subject were perhaps not to be taken too seriously. After Marx's death Engels more or less withdrew the admission: in the 1890s Russia was already well launched on the capitalist path.

The events which rendered Marx's concession nugatory and decided the whole issue against the *narodniks* and in favour of the Marxists occurred in a field altogether outside the control of the revolutionaries of either camp. The vital decision was one of economic policy. The emancipation of the serfs, by liberating the peasant from the land, had created the condition of a free labour market; and by the 1880s the pressure of surplus population in the countryside was already becoming acute. By slow degrees the lure of cheap labour began to attract foreign capital. This was a great period of overseas expansion and investment for western Europe; and the exploitation of investment opportunities in Russia became a minor feature in the process. In the 1890s political factors intervened to accelerate and intensify it. The military threat from Germany created the Franco-Russian alliance. It became an urgent interest of the Tsarist Government to build up in Russia a modern heavy industry capable of meeting the needs of transport and of armaments manufacture, and a no less urgent interest of French capitalists to stimulate the process by generous and (it was hoped) profitable loans. Under those influences industrial development and the modernization of the economy made gigantic strides in Russia in the years between 1890 and 1914. Russia was once more wide open to the West.

The paradox of the situation was that the progress of westernization set in motion by the rising class of Russian industrialists was no less favourable to the westernizers among the revolutionaries, that is to say, to the Marxists. Up to a point Witte and Lenin were natural allies. The development of capitalism in Russia served the cause of both. The rise of Russian industry also meant the rise of a class-conscious proletariat and of a Social-Democratic Party which, though it professed a Marxist creed and had its origins and its spiritual home in the West, now struck indigenous roots in Russia. To judge the relative strength of the rival socialist and revolutionary parties in Russia—the Social-Revolutionaries with their peasant revolution and the Social Democrats with their Marxist creed—is scarcely possible, since no common standard of political measurement can really be applied to the numerically extensive but amorphous and backward peasant following of the Social-Revolutionaries and the much smaller but concentrated and organized proletarian group that rallied round the Social-Democrats. The experience of 1917 was to demonstrate the effectiveness of the one and the ineffectiveness of the other in the crude terms which alone are operative when revolutions are on foot. In terms of Russian history, it proved once more that it was the westerners who in the long run provided the agents and the driving force of revolutionary change.

It would be possible, and fair, to continue the argument by developing the theme, which could be amply illustrated in Russian history, that innovations introduced into Russia from the West and in imitation of western models quickly take on a Russian colour and become something quite different from what they appeared to be in their native environment. It could be pointed out that social-democracy, once planted in Russian soil, inevitably began to admit and to practise certain derogations or variations from the original Marxist scheme; that this issue was to some extent at the bottom of the split between Bolsheviks and Mensheviks, with the latter as the new westerners and the former as the adapters of the western corpus of Marxism to Russian national requirements; that the revolution, as the Bolsheviks made it in 1917, was based on a marriage of convenience between the proletarian socialism of the Marxists and the peasant socialism of the *narodniks* centring on the demand for the equal distribution of the land; and that, after the revolution, the victory of Stalin, flying the flag of socialism in one country, over Trotsky, faithful as a true westerner to the banner of international revolution, represented a further reaction of the Russian national tradition against the intrusion of the West. But it is more prudent to call a halt, with Mr. Yarmolinsky (perhaps some day he will give us a sequel), at the turn of the century, and not to plunge into problems to which contemporary history has not yet given an answer.

Two minor criticisms might be made of Mr. Yarmolinsky's book. It is "intended for the common reader as well as the student", and this may be held to excuse some poetic licence. But the aspect of the work is unimpeachably scholarly, and the facts quoted and statements made are most carefully documented. It seems a pity, therefore, that Mr. Yarmolinsky should be content from time to time to take up towards his sources a detached and uncritical attitude which does not bother to distinguish between probable fact and hero-making myth. Most of the stories of Nechaev in prison, for instance, surely belong to the second category. The other regret is that Mr. Yarmolinsky sticks too closely to his last that revolutionary ideas and movement appear in his pages to be born and to unfold themselves almost *in vacuo* without regard to anything else that is happening at the time. One does not expect the historian of ideas to be at the same time a political and an economic historian. But, if the ideas and actions of the Russian nineteenth-century revolutionaries, and the causes of their successes and failures are to be made comprehensible, the reader needs sometimes to remind himself of the political and, still more perhaps, of the economic background of the period. The fact that Mr. Yarmolinsky is writing for the common reader would have made a little more help in these matters all the more appropriate.

29 The Marxist Credo

Two different approaches—which can be broadly distinguished as the theological and the historical—can be made to problems of belief and creed. The theologian who discusses the Divinity of Christ or the doctrine of the procession of the Holy Ghost from the Son is concerned with the question of absolute truth or falsehood: he seeks to validate his belief by an appeal to authority, or in terms of its consistency with other accepted items of belief or of its own inherent rationality. The historian dealing with the Arian heresy or the Filioque clause is not, as an historian, interested in the truth or falsehood of the doctrines. He is interested in them as the ideologies of powerful movements, as the expression of social or political discontents, as instruments in a struggle for power between conflicting factions. Both approaches are—for different purposes and different terms of reference—equally valid.

It is perhaps significant of the scant attention paid in the West to problems of belief in the Soviet Union that the approach by Western writers to Soviet Marxism has hitherto been almost exclusively "theological". They begin by tracing the origins of Marxism in Hegel. They go on to expound Marx's teaching and the differences—of emphasis, if no more—between Marx and Engels: they discuss the modifications or additions imported into Marxism by Lenin, and into Leninism by Stalin, and analyse the doctrinal discussions which have taken place in the Soviet Union over the past forty years. The questions which they ask and answer revolve round the criteria of truth and consistency. Is dialectical materialism a true or a tenable creed? Did Marx produce a body of doctrine consistent with itself and defensible in philosophical terms? Was Lenin an orthodox Marxist? Was Stalin an orthodox Leninist? Can the current Marxist orthodoxy in the Soviet Union be validated in terms either of its fidelity to the original doctrines of Marx or of its own inherent consistency?

Among works of this character scholars have, during the past few years, generally agreed to assign preeminence to the comprehensive work of Father Wetter, *Dialectical Materialism*, which appeared some ten years ago in Italian, then in an enlarged version in German, and is now available—in a further amended form—in what appears to be a first-rate English translation.[1] The first half of the book is devoted to an account of the development of Marxist philosophy through Plekhanov to Lenin, and thence—with a side-glance at Bukharin and Trotsky and at the philosophical controversies which centred in the 1930s on the name of Deborin—to Stalin. The second half contains critical discussions of the principal doctrines of Soviet Marxism. Much of the criticism is pointed, and by no means all of it is hostile. Father Wetter correctly notes that the Marxist conception of matter often seems to approach more closely to realism than to orthodox materialism, since the notion of "an immutable substance of things" is specifically rejected, and emphasis is laid on the property of matter as an objective reality existing outside the mind; a passage is quoted in which Lenin referred to this as "the sole property" of matter which was essential to Marxist philosophy.

In a curious and interesting last chapter Father Wetter invokes some interesting parallels between the Marxism of Lenin and certain trends of religious thought. In so far as he discovers these parallels with Marxism in the religious orthodoxy of the Slavophils, it is perhaps sufficient to point to the debt which all the Slavophils, consciously or unconsciously, owed to Hegel. The "points of contact" between the philosophical doctrine of Lenin and that of the Catholic Church turn out to be mainly of a "formal" character, and Father Wetter draws a consoling moral:

> That of all the historical forms of Christianity it should prove to be Catholicism which exhibits the largest number of formal similarities with Bolshevism, albeit with the signs reversed, is perhaps an indication that, on the other side, the opposition between Bolshevism and the Catholic church is also the most radical of all.

Yet at one point Father Wetter seems to move on dangerous ground.

[1] Gustav A. Wetter, *Dialectical Materialism*. Translated by Peter Health (London: Routledge & Kegan Paul).

Can Catholicism—or indeed any form of Christianity—safely argue that it begins by establishing the truth of the basic Christian doctrines "by purely scientific and historical methods of enquiry", whereas for Marxist philosophers the appeal to "the authority of the 'classics' of Marxism" admits of no argument? For the impartial critic, the claim on the one side may seem as dangerous and unsubstantial as the similar claim on the other side.

As will be seen, Father Wetter's approach to Soviet Marxism is primarily "theological" in character. He does indeed note the "conservative tendency" of Stalin's last public deliverances, and thinks that they may have been inspired by a reaction against assertions of the omnipotence of the party. But in general he is interested in the truth or falsehood of the doctrines which he discusses, not in their historical significance. He records, for example, that "the law of the negative of the negative" as a constituent of the dialectic fell out of favour for many years "about 1938" and was resuscitated only after Stalin's death. But he does recognize the probable explanation of the phenomenon—the association of the doctrine with Bukharin, who had used it in his conservative period as a philosophical justification of a policy of the reconciliation of opposites. The rise and fall of philosophical doctrines in the Soviet Union can rarely be detached from the economic and political interpretations which lie behind them.

It is for this reason that the "theological" approach to Soviet Marxism, and indeed to any form of Marxism, proves in the long run unsatisfactory. Marx himself wrote in the second of his well-known *Theses on Feuerbach*:

> The question whether objective truth can be attributed to human thinking is not a question of theory, but a *practical* question. Man must prove in practice the truth, that is to say, the reality and efficacy, the this-sidedness of his thinking.

It is the great merit of Professor Marcuse's new book on *Soviet Marxism*[2] that the author, though not himself a Marxist, has approached his subject from the angle of its own presuppositions, and not—like almost all other Western writers—from the angle of presuppositions alien to it. His book is slighter and less detailed than

[2] Herbert Marcuse, *Soviet Marxism* (London: Routledge & Kegan Paul).

Father Wetter's, but it is also fresher and more original. It is in its way a pioneer work.

Professor Marcuse starts from the assumption that Soviet Marxism "is not merely an ideology promulgated by the Kremlin in order to rationalize and justify its policies, but expresses in various forms the realities of Soviet developments." From this point of view, as Professor Marcuse says, "the extreme poverty and even dishonesty of Soviet theory" would not vitiate its importance, and their mere exposure in the light of Western beliefs and assumptions becomes irrelevant and meaningless: these theoretical shortcomings are themselves an index of other factors. Hence Professor Marcuse proceeds by the method of what he calls an "immanent critique", examining the evolution of Marxist theory from the standpoint not of some external standard but of its own historical development, and seeking to show how theory has reflected current realities, and has at the same time affected, and been designed to affect, these realities.

> Marxian theory [writes Professor Marcuse] purports to be an essentially new philosophy, substantially different from the main tradition of Western philosophy. Marxism claims to fulfil this tradition by passing from ideology to reality, from philosophical interpretation to political action. . . . A critique which merely applies the traditional criteria of philosophical truth to Soviet Marxism does not, in a strict sense, reach its objective.

This quality in Marxism has been misunderstood and obscured in most Western criticism, which has tended to over-emphasize the determinist elements in Marx. Such elements exist in Marxism, as they must exist in any rational view of the universe; and Marx himself, especially in his later writings, sometimes placed excessive weight on them. But Marx never denied the conscious activity of men in moulding their destiny. That action is not merely a method of verifying theory but an integral part of it is an essential ingredient of Marxist doctrine. This, as Professor Marcuse points out, goes back to Hegel: "For Hegel freedom is not merely 'insight' into necessity, but 'comprehended' necessity, which implies a change in the actual conditions." For Marx, as for Hegel, the reconciliation of freedom and necessity is conceivable only as part of a revolutionary process.

The emphasis on consciousness in Marxist doctrine, and on the necessity of leadership to create consciousness, appropriately reached its highest point in Lenin at the critical moment of the revolution. Passages could be quoted from the later Engels, if not from Marx, which seemed to treat class-consciousness as a spontaneous growth:

> Until the oppressed class—in this case the proletariat—has become ripe for its own self-liberation, it will in its majority recognize the existing social order as the only possible one, and will march politically at the tail of the capitalist class, and constitute its extreme Left wing. In proportion as it grows ripe for its own liberation, it forms itself into its own party and elects its own representatives, and not those of the capitalists.

For Lenin ripeness was necessary, but ripeness was not all. The implanting of consciousness in the proletariat "from without" was a necessary function of revolutionary theory, of a devoted organization of revolutionary intellectuals. Nor was this view, as has sometimes been said, a product of the unexpected turn of history which made the backward Russian proletariat the spearhead of the proletarian revolution. This was a doctrine which Lenin inherited from Kautsky, the mentor of German Social-Democracy. It was rooted in the essential Marxist doctrine of the unity of theory and practice.

It would be easy to show how this emphasis on the role of consciousness in a necessary historical process, conceived by Hegel under the influence of the French revolution, was given practical shape by Marx in the revolutionary period of the 1840s, once more obscured in the non-revolutionary latter half of the nineteenth century, and resuscitated primarily by Lenin in the first revolutionary years of the twentieth century. Professor Marcuse tries to determine what has happened to the doctrine in Soviet Marxism with the ebb of the revolution, and concludes that freedom has once more been reduced to the concept of "recognized necessity". Theory is no longer a call for action. This does not perhaps do full justice to the tension in current Soviet Marxism between what may be called the needs of the home market and the requirements of export. If it is true, with some qualifications, that the revolutionary impulse has slackened in the Soviet Union, and doctrine has been modified accordingly, Marxism is still a revolutionary doctrine, and a revolutionary doctrine emanating from the Soviet Union, throughout Asia and Africa. With much of the world in ferment,

and Marxism still serving as the main standard-bearer of revolution, a theoretical revision of Marxism in a determinist and
non-revolutionary sense seems an unlikely contingency.

On the other hand, Professor Marcuse is certainly right in regarding
the distinction introduced into Soviet Marxism by Stalin between
dialectical and historical materialism—a distinction accepted
without question by Father Wetter—as a derogation from the
Marxism of Marx (who used neither term) and indeed of Lenin.
The Marxist conception of the dialectic applied to nature in so far as
nature is an historical process; but Engels's attempt to elaborate a
"dialectics of nature" was not conspicuously successful. Engels's
development plays, however, an essential part in the recent Soviet
conception of dialectical materialism as a philosophical system or
Weltanschauung, in which historical materialism is only one of the
constituent parts. The dialectic thus becomes a super-historical
process with objective laws not themselves subject to historical
change and removed from the sphere of consciousness—a move
towards determinism which Professor Marcuse rightly diagnoses as
a "conservative" revision in Soviet Marxism.

A point which commonly puzzles Western critics of Marxism is its
attitude to relativism. Though recent Soviet ethical philosophy
recognizes elementary principles of human morality independent of
class content, passages can certainly be cited from Marx and Lenin
which appear to contradict this view. Historically, for the Marxist,
everything is relative. Yet Marxism certainly postulates an absolute
truth—and in two senses. In the first place, there is the ultimate goal
of the classless, stateless, and powerless society—the "one far-off
divine event," or Second Advent, the *deus ex machina* which stands
behind the ultimate unfolding of the Marxist drama. But, in a
second sense and more practically, the process itself, the progress
towards the ultimate fulfilment, becomes the Absolute, an Absolute
constantly changing and creating itself. In Marxism the relative is
transformed into the Absolute.

This explains the character of the ethical teachings of Soviet
Marxism, to which Professor Marcuse devotes the final, and not the
least illuminating, section of his book. The traditional Western
system of values is based on the assumption of a fundamental
identity of interests between individual and individual and between
individual and society. Both freedom and the full development of
the individual imply the subordination of society as a whole to the

individual, the autonomous *ego cogitans* who is the source of all initiative and the repository of ultimate value. Marxism purports to show that these concepts, though they served a progressive purpose at a certain stage of history, have now been falsified and rendered meaningless by the conditions of an advanced capitalist society, and that freedom and the development of the individual can re-acquire meaning and reality only if they are re-interpreted in Marxist terms as a function of society. This is what Professor Marcuse calls the "externalization" or the "politicalization" of ethics. He points out incidentally the analogies between the Platonic and the Soviet conceptions of the ethical function of the *res publica*.

But the Soviet system of values is not only "political". It is also creative in the sense that it postulates not an existing ideal but action to create an ideal. It is the function of society to mould the individual and to create for him the conditions of freedom and development which he can no longer create for himself within the old social framework. This is responsible for the common, and on Western hypotheses justifiable, charge that Soviet ethics is instrumentalist in character, and subordinates means to ends. The realization of freedom requires the transformation of society, and the transformation of society brings with it in turn the transformation of the individual—the creation of "Soviet man". This conception is implicitly used to solve the theoretical problem of the victory of the proletarian revolution in a country where the proletariat was weak and backward. The proletariat in whose name the revolution was made, and in whose name the dictatorship is exercised, is not so much the existing proletariat, but the idealized proletariat of the future, the proletariat in course of creation. Thus, as Professor Marcuse points out, Soviet morality, like Christian morality, ultimately rests on "the image of a future which will compensate the individuals for their present sufferings and frustrations", the difference being that the image is supposedly "not a matter of faith, but a matter of scientific analysis and reason—of necessity".

The fate of Professor Marcuse's book can be foreseen. It will annoy those out-and-out Marxists who will object to the application of historical methods of criticism to the Marxist text. It will equally annoy those out-and-out Westerners who still think it proper to judge Marxism by the allegedly absolute standards of the West, and who will treat any attempt to discuss Marxism on the basis of its own assumptions as a compounding with evil. But to those whose aim is understanding rather than polemics Professor Marcuse's study may be warmly commended, and should provide much food for thought, if not always for agreement. Both these books suggest in their different ways that the divergences between the ways of thought and belief of East and West are not always as fundamental as they appear at first sight, or that, if they are fundamental, they can often be traced back to non-ideological causes.

30 Lukács and Class-consciousness

What exactly did Marx mean by a "class"? It is an old crux on which much ink has been spilt. But it cannot be dismissed with the assurance that anyone knows a class when he sees one—which is manifestly untrue. Marx was a precise thinker who was never content with empirical approximations. While he failed to produce a formal definition of class—owing, it is presumed, to the unfinished state in which his major work reached the world—it is plain that he defined class in the objective terms of its relation to the instruments of production. Class-consciousness was for Marx a vital element in the class struggle. But class was not a voluntary agglomeration of individuals. Its essence was not determined simply by the conscious will and purpose of its individual members.

The issue is especially acute in the English-speaking world, where the word "class" is in common use in the quite different sense of a social group. A social group may contain members of more than one Marxist class, or, conversely, a Marxist class may be broken up into different social groups. The whole basis of the conception is different. An individual generally, no doubt, remains in the "class" (in the English sense) in which he is born. But he may legitimately have the ambition to move into another class ("social mobility"); whether he succeeds will depend partly on his own ability, resources, and strength of purpose, partly on the readiness of members of the other "class" to recognize him as one of themselves. All this is far away from the Marxist conception of class. This terminological misunderstanding may be one of the reasons (others will be discussed later) why so many British and American intellectuals have failed, or perhaps not seriously tried, to understand what Marx was saying.

It may therefore be opportune that a classic commentary on Marx's theory of class has just appeared for the first time in English translation.[1] *History and Class Consciousness* is a collection of essays written between 1919 and 1924 by the famous critic and philosopher Georg Lukács, who died at the age of eighty-six. Lukács, Hungarian by birth, German by intellectual formation, started as a Hegelian, became a good communist after 1917, and was a minor minister in Béla Kun's revolutionary government in Budapest in 1919. But, partly as a sequel to infighting between Hungarian émigrés in Moscow, the book was quickly attacked as heretical, though in the relatively tolerant atmosphere of the 1920s not formally banned.

Lukács, never by nature a fighter, retired into the role of a Marxist literary critic, in which he achieved international distinction. *History and Class Consciousness* had a sort of twilight existence for several decades, known to the *cognoscenti* of many countries, but caviar to the general, until in 1967 it was at length republished with a preface in which Lukács confessed, in somewhat obscure language, the "errors" in the work resulting from the attempt to "overrule the priority of economics", and to treat the problems of society and revolution in purely philosophical terms. The translation has been made from this edition.

The translator, Rodney Livingstone, has done all, and more than all, that could have been expected. He has rendered Lukács's dense style into English, not jargon, and has broken up some of Lukács's more unmanageable sentences without, so far as can be judged, distorting his meaning. But it would be idle to pretend that this is an easy book to read. Critiques of Marx, like Marx's own writings, are almost necessarily couched in a Hegelian idiom which, while it seems to present no terrors to Russian, French, or Italian scholars, has been mastered and assimilated by few in the English-speaking world. Lukács, even more than Marx, was a Hegelian through and through, and could express himself in no other terms. This has to be faced.

Lukács's approach to class was through the concept of "class-consciousness", which is what distinguishes—to use Hegelian and Marxist language—the "class-for-itself" from the mere "class-in-itself". But what is the nature of class-consciousness and how does it arise? This is the theme of the key essay in this volume, with the title "Class-Consciousness", and it was Lukács's searching and

[1] Georg Lukács, *History and Class Consciousness. Studies in Marxist Dialectics.* Translated by Rodney Livingstone (London: Merlin Press).

distinctive answer to this question which got him into trouble. Since class is defined in terms of objective situation in the historical process, class-consciousness cannot be understood as a subjective phenomenon, a state of mind. The concrete cannot be "located in the empirical individual of history . . . and in his empirically given (and hence psychological or mass-psychological) consciousness". Lukács pursued the argument to its logical conclusion:

> Class consciousness consists in fact of the appropriate and rational reactions "imputed" to a particular typical position in the process of production. This consciousness is, therefore, neither the sum nor the average of what is though and felt by the single individuals who make up the class. And yet the historically significant actions of the class as a whole are determined in the last resort by this consciousness and not by the thought of the individual, and these actions can be understood only by reference to this consciousness.

It does not need to be said that this conception is rooted in the Marxist—and Hegelian—view of the historical process as the ultimate reality. Becoming, as Hegel puts it, is the truth of Being, so that the process constitutes a deeper level of reality than the empirical fact. Man, in Lukács's words, comprehends the present by seeing in it "the tendencies out of whose dialectical opposition he can *make* the future". This precludes the notion of "natural laws" of society which lie outside history and to which history has to conform. Marx made the point that natural law was a bourgeois conception which was at first invoked against feudal society and was to this extent progressive, and was then transformed into a conservative concept designed to defend the rule of the bourgeoisie. This view also rules out the notion of relativity, which can have no meaning in a system which postulates no other absolute than change.

Hegel has always been reproached with unfaithfulness to his own vision when he invoked World-Spirit as the *deus ex machina* to bring the historical drama to a close, and saw the end of history in the consummation of his own philosophy and in the concrete form of a purified Prussian state. But Marx, too, needed the prophetic vision of a climax to the historical process, and, protesting against the "mystification" perpetrated by Hegel, found it in the proletariat. It has been convincingly shown that Marx, in his intellectual development, arrived at his vision of the proletariat as the consummation of history through the study of Hegel and his critics, before he had embarked on those economic studies and speculations which produced his final analysis of the economic role of the proletariat in history. To this extent Lukács's determination to treat Marx's proletariat as a philosophical rather than an empirical entity may be historically justified.

This is, however, where Lukács eventually comes to grief. He fully accepts, and continually emphasizes, the Marxist principle of the unity of theory and practice. Theoretical truth, divorced from practice, is an empty abstraction. The point of philosophy is not merely to understand the world but to change it—indeed, the two processes are indistinguishable. "The present", says Lukács, "is a problem of history, a problem that refuses to be ignored." But this involved him in an approach to current politics. In the Europe of 1920—and after the experience of the abortive Hungarian re-volution of the previous year—the proletariat had somehow to be brought to earth, and theory attuned to practical experience. In this desperate period, revolutionary idealism was still a living force. Lukács could still hail the Soviets, in the concluding passage of his essay, as the form of organization through which the proletariat (not, of course, exclusively or primarily the Russian proletariat) would attain class-consciousness, and so liberate itself and society as a whole from the rule of the bourgeoisie and the capitalist system.

Two or three years later, with the decay of the Russian Soviets and a succession of revolutionary defeats in Western Europe, and especially in Germany, the vision had begun to fade. In 1922, in an article on the problem of organization, Lukács devoted some embarrassing paragraphs to the role of the Communist Party, which had not appeared at all in his earlier essay. "The pre-eminently practical character of the communist party", he explained, "the fact that it is a fighting party, presupposes its possession of a correct theory." Proletarian class-consciousness must necessarily be "re-flected in the organized form of that class consciousness, in the communist party". It is not difficult, by using a little hindsight, to imagine where these arguments would lead, and Lukács never appears to have returned to them in so explicit a form.

When at the end of 1922 Lukács collected his essays of the past three years for republication in a volume, he did two things. In the essay of 1920 on class-consciousness he toned down, without removing, the reference to Soviets, and introduced rather unobtrusively a brief passage once more describing the Communist Party as "the organized form" of "the correct class consciousness of the proletariat"; and he wrote a further essay on "Reification and the Consciousness of the Proletariat", the longest and the one entirely new item in the volume. The first section is devoted to an analysis of the Marxist theory of "fetichism" ("reification"); the second is a brilliant exposure of reification in capitalist economics; in the third, entitled "The Standpoint of the Proletariat", he retreats on to the ground of pure abstraction, and fails to touch at all on the current situation or to discuss the role of the party, contenting himself with the concluding cryptic remark that "any transformation can come about only as the product of the—free—action of the proletariat itself". This seemed to betray a shrinking on the part of Lukács from his own conclusions, and a refusal to deal with the current situation at all.

The work of Lukács is important, not because he solves but because he poses in its sharpest and most acute form the fundamental dilemma of the Marxist conception of class and of the proletariat, the dilemma of the gap between the proletariat as an empirical entity and the role assigned by history to the proletariat as a class— the gap which Marx revealed, but did not explore, when he invented the dismissive category of the "Lumpenproletariat". Lenin in his early essay *What is to be Done?* was the first to face this issue as a practical problem of the creation of a revolutionary party. As is well known, Lenin argued that the proletariat left to itself would develop spontaneously, out of its experience of the day-to-day struggle between workers and employers, only a "trade-union" consciousness; this struggle would never become a genuine class struggle until true class-consciousness was implanted in the proletariat "from without" by an organized revolutionary party.

Lenin admitted that he had propounded this doctrine in *What is to be Done?* in a one-sided form; and the experience of the Soviets in 1905 led him to take a more optimistic view of mass action. But the dilemma remained. It is noteworthy that Lukács, in his preface to the 1967 edition of *History and Class Consciousness*, compared his analysis of proletarian class-consciousness with the view taken by Lenin in *What is to be Done?* and, though he dutifully explained that Lenin was, of course, right where he had been wrong, the distinction is not altogether obvious. In the 1920s Lukács's views found some echoes in the thought of Karl Korsch, expelled from the German party as a heretic, and later of Gramsci (Lukács and Gramsci both opposed Stalin's "turn to the Left" in the Comintern in 1928, though Lukács immediately recanted). In the days when the pundits in Moscow worked hard to play down the Hegelian pedigree of Marxism, all these were freely accused of importing Hegelian glosses into the pure corpus of Marxist-Leninist doctrine.

Lukács's analysis of proletarian class-consciousness and of the party as its "organized form" has been exposed, and can be exposed, to some fairly devastating criticism. He dissects skilfully and profoundly the process of "reification" in capitalist society, whereby what are essentially human relations are transformed into entities apparently possessing an independent existence of their own (commodities, exchange-value, laws of the market). This process not only stands in the way of any true understanding of reality, except at its most superficial empirical level, but protects and perpetuates exploitation, since both exploiters and exploited see themselves as subject to the rigid compulsion of external realities, though these are in fact merely the relations which bourgeois society has itself created.

The trouble begins when the scene changes with the overthrow of the bourgeoisie by the proletariat. Marx and Engels attribute to the bourgeoisie, misled by the "fetichism" or "reification" inherent in capitalist thinking, only a "false consciousness" which they called "ideology". The proletariat, triumphing over the bourgeoisie, would attain true consciousness, and ideology would disappear. Lenin, on the other hand, used the term "ideology" neutrally, applying it both to the (false) consciousness of the bourgeoisie and to the (hypothetically true) consciousness of the proletariat. The innovation may have been significant. Certainly when Lukács effects his divorce between an abstract proletarian class-consciousness, whose concrete embodiment is the authority of the Communist Party, and the empirically observed thoughts and feelings of proletarians submitted to that authority, he opens the door wide for a return to a regime of "reified" laws and institutions, in the form of the party and its discipline, imposing a false consciousness or ideology on the mass of workers.

The numerous recantations and changes of front which marked Lukács's later career bear witness to his eagerness to disclaim these consequences of his argument and to deny that anything of this kind really happened. But, leaving this question aside, how far is Lukács's interpretation of Marx valid? Or can we rescue Marx from a false gloss put on him by these Hegelian critics? The defence may follow two quite different lines.

It would be foolish to deny that the initial impetus to Marx's approach to the problems of society and class came from Hegel, and that he continued throughout life, though in a diminishing degree, to think and write in a Hegelian idiom. His own tributes to the master, and his contempt for those who purported to treat Hegel as a "dead dog", are on record. But it is equally true, and more important, that Marx did not remain within the world of abstractions. Marx's thought was a constant struggle to unify the empirically observed and the abstract theory. If his theory of the class struggle and of the liberating role of the proletariat owed much to Hegelian inspiration, and had characteristically Hegelian undertones, it was also based on profound study of the concrete problems of contemporary society. *The Eighteenth Brumaire*, which Lukács nowhere mentions, is full of acute empirical observations on the class situation.

The same concrete approach to economic problems is inseparable from all the work of Marx's maturity. Lukács was right in confessing that his own attempt "to deduce the revolutionary implications of Marxism" was "deprived of a genuinely economic foundation". The analysis of capitalist economy and capitalist society which absorbed the last three decades of Marx's life, the identification of the proletariat as the producer of surplus value, as at once the essential cog in the economic machine and its predestined victim and destroyer—all this, the foundation of his fame and lasting influence, was the result of unremitting and penetrating study of a concrete situation. The proletariat of Marx, whatever its initial inspiration, and whatever utopian elements may have crept into his final designation of its role, was an army of actual factory-workers, not Lukács's quasi-metaphysical abstraction. The Marxist class, though not defined by the same criterion as the class of most Western sociologists, is a collection of real workers, not a party or trade union or other authority acting in its name.

This is not to say that Marx could have reached his conclusions on the basis of empirical study and observation alone, and without the framework of theory dating in the main from his earlier years, though this underwent modification in the course of his later work. The relation between thought and action, between theory and practice, between reflection and observation, between the abstract and the concrete, between the general and the particular, is the fundamental problem of all sociology, economics, politics, and history. The immense power of Marx's thought resides in his continuous awareness of this problem and in his response to it. The Marxist theory of class and the class-struggle is both a general theory seen in its particular application to nineteenth-century capitalist society and a programme of action designed to change that society.

This brings us to the second line along which the relevance of Marxism can be vindicated in the contemporary world. Lukács, in one of the earlier essays in this volume, entitled "What is Orthodox Marxism?", put the point with exaggerated emphasis:

> Let us assume for the sake of argument that recent research had disproved once for all every one of Marx's individual theses. Even if this were to be proved, every serious "orthodox" Marxist would still be able to accept all such modern findings without re-servation and hence dismiss all of Marx's theses *in toto*, without having to renounce his orthodoxy for a single moment. Orthodox Marxism therefore does not imply uncritical acceptance of the results of Marx's investigations. It is not the "belief" in this or that thesis, nor the exegesis of a "sacred" book. On the contrary, orthodoxy refers exclusively to method.

This involves, among other things, the duty to apply orthodox Marxist "method" to the criticism of some of Marx's conclusions.

It is not, of course, by and large true that Marx's main theses and predictions have been discredited or become obsolete. In the Russia of 1920 Bukharin noted that, with the dissolution of capitalism, the "fetichistic" economic categories exposed by Marx had disap-peared and had been replaced by the forms of a natural economy. In this country, fifty years later, we are beginning to understand that our economic problems cannot be solved, or profitably discussed, in the "fetichistic" terms of exchange-value and laws of the market, and that we are driven back to such "natural" categories as social value and productivity. It *is* true that Marx uncovered the canker at the root of nineteenth-century capitalism, and, whatever details in his analysis may require correction, unerringly diagnosed the source from which the trouble would come.

But it is also true that the Marxist theory of the class struggle, though it has illuminated many dark places not only of the contemporary world but of a remoter past (ancient history has in recent years been transformed by it), calls for a good many reservations and corrections before it can be applied to periods and events before the French Revolution, by which it was mainly inspired. It is true that in our own age the former "colonial" world has impinged on the Marxist analysis in ways which Lenin and Rosa Luxemburg were among the first to investigate, and which are still wreathed in uncertainty. It is also true that some Marxist theories have been affected, in ways yet to be investigated, by the advance in modern technology and by the defences put up by Western capitalism to the first serious assaults on its citadel.

But none of this touches on the question of method. It is this, far more than any specific doctrine, which has so fatally separated Marx from the thinkers of the English-speaking world, and has accounted for a thinness and lack of depth in so much recent English political and historical writing. The tradition of the English-speaking world is profoundly empirical. Facts speak for themselves. A particular issue is debated "on its merits". Themes, episodes, periods are isolated for historical study in the light of some undeclared, and probably unconscious, standard of relevance. At worst, history becomes a succession of happenings whose causal connexions we are in principle not qualified to discover. All this would have been anathema to Marx. Marx was no empiricist. To study the part without reference to the whole, the fact without reference to its significance, the event without reference to cause or consequence, the particular crisis without reference to the general situation, would have seemed to Marx a barren exercise.

The difference has its historical roots. Not for nothing has the English-speaking world remained so obstinately empirical. In a firmly established social order, whose credentials nobody wishes to question, empiricism serves to effect running repairs—those minor corrections and adjustments which are needed to keep the machine ticking over. Of such a world nineteenth-century Britain provided the perfect model. But in a time when every foundation is challenged, and we flounder from crisis to crisis in the absence of any guide-line, empiricism is not enough. We need to cut deeper. Whatever the relevance of particular Marxist doctrines, Marx has revolutionized ways of thinking about society and about history. We cannot begin to understand, much less to refute Marx, with our old blunt tools.

Our present needs should surely drive us to a re-examination of

Marx's method of inquiry, and put an end to a situation in which so many historians, philosophers and sociologists of the English-speaking world (the economists, impressed by the economic foundations of Marxism, have done rather better) by-pass Marx altogether or treat him as of barely peripheral interest to their concerns. Lukács's extreme anti-empiricism may be an exemplar of the opposite vice. But this should not excuse our myopia. It is rather as if a modern mathematician did not take the trouble to master Einstein, and went on with his studies as if Einstein had never existed.

31 Turning to the Right

It is not surprising that "the Right" is nowadays all the go among western intellectuals. For twenty years the political pendulum in the West has been swinging towards the Right. The political rift between the West and Soviet Russia after the war—the usual dispute between the victorious allies over the disposal of the spoils and the treatment of the defeated—quickly took on ideological forms. After the Fulton speech, fear and detestation of communism, never quite silent even during the war, found free and increasingly vociferous expression, and combined with fear of Soviet military power to provide the cement of the Atlantic Alliance. The adoption of anti-communism as a quasi-official ideology discredited a Left which had dabbled largely in fellow-travelling, and played into the hands of the Right. In some countries this process was reinforced by the association of wartime restrictions with the economic policies of the Left. In Great Britain Stafford Cripps became the favourite bogyman of Conservative propaganda, designed to fasten on the Left a perpetual policy of tightening the belt and to depict the Right as the champion of economic freedom and a return to better days. Nationally and internationally, "liberation" became a slogan of the Right.

It was inevitable that western intellectuals should sooner or later be harnessed to this movement of opinion. In our mass society intellectual eccentricity, like other kinds of eccentricity, is at a discount. The notion so recently prevalent of a natural and inescapable affinity between the intellectuals and the Left is stone dead. Conservative clubs flourish at the universities. The Bow Group sets up as the brains trust of the Conservative Party; and the corridors of the London School of Economics are alive with busy young Tories. For the first time since Disraeli "young Tory" is not a term of derision. The days are forgotten, or remembered with shame, when the typical young intellectual made his pilgrimage to Moscow, or rooted for the united front and for an ideological synthesis between Marxism and western radicalism, or idealized Franklin Roosevelt and the New Deal, or crowded Laski's lectures. The repentant intellectual sons of today are consciously or unconsciously doing penance for the sins of the intellectual fathers of the 1930s.

Nothing is indeed more characteristic of the present ideological predominance of the Right than the extent to which the radicalism of thirty years ago has become an historical phenomenon. The C.N.D. is interesting and significant as a pale reflection, an indication of past attitudes still surviving to lead a ghostlike underground existence, rather than as a serious force in current politics. In the United States, since McCarthyism, no intellectual movement of the Left has been able to get off the ground. It remains to be seen whether the movement against the war in Vietnam will break through this barrier, or whether it has any deeper ideological content than dislike of a particularly repulsive and apparently pointless war. Journals like the *New Republic* and the *Nation* are historical relics. In this country, where historical momuments are treated with greater respect, the *New Statesman* has retained more of its prestige and circulation. But its historical record is more interesting, and more often discussed, than its influence in the political world of today. Twinges of a vestigial Leftist conscience are still felt in unexpected places. Journals like *Dissent* and *The Reporter* in the United States, or *Encounter* in this country, camouflage an essentially Right outlook with splashes of protective colouring from the Left.

But the new intellectual climate has engulfed more than the politicians and the journalists. Historians also bask in the comfortable warmth of conservative respectability—including some who might be shocked if they were fully conscious of their new affiliations. Gone are the days when the English were proud of having executed one king and expelled another in defence of their liberties. Of contemporary historians, only Mr. Christopher Hill still seems on nodding terms with the seventeenth-century English revolution. Mr. Laurence Stone, also an Oxford historian though now an American professor, in one of the most brilliant manifestos of the current historical Right, talks of *The Crisis of the Aristocracy*. The notorious Whig interpretation of history is dead, buried and damned. Some ten years ago an American historian of England, Professor Hexter, invited us to ask the question, How did the aristocracy do it? as a framework for English History from the eleventh to the eighteenth century". The time seems ripe for a Conservative interpretation of English history which will carry the rule of aristocracy down to the 1860s and 1870s, when Disraeli so neatly prepared the transition from Tory aristocracy to Tory democracy.

In economic history the ascendancy of the Right is still more complete, since fear of being thought to agree with Marx has become a powerful emotion among most English economic historians. Marx described the rise of capitalism, dripping with blood and sweat, from seas of human misery; Dickens added some highlights to the picture; and the Hammonds in more prosaic style recounted the sufferings and barbarities which accompanied the English industrial revolution. Now we have changed all that. We know that Marx was a propagandist, Dickens an artist, and the Hammonds biased and inaccurate. In the 1920s Clapham avoided the word "revolution" and began to tone down the more garish hues in the traditional picture. In 1948 Professor Ashton launched a vigorous campaign in refutation of the charge that industrialization had inflicted intolerable hardships on the worker and lowered his standard of living, and has since found a large company of disciples and imitators.

It might be suggested that this change of heart could be partly explained by an increased sensitiveness to the national reputation and reluctance to wash dirty national linen in public, due to consciousness of a reduced status in the world. But the same thing has happened in the United States, where the "muck-rakers" of the early years of the century are quite out of fashion, and the rehabilitation of the founders of American big business is well under way. Imperialism, too, has ceased to be a dirty word. Richard Koebner, the author of the most recent full-scale study of the subject, went a long way to dissociate it from the motives of economic aggrandisement formerly assigned to it; and the latest British contribution to the theme, Messrs. Robinson and Gallagher's *Africa and the Victorians*, goes further still. Indeed, the authors would probably not care to admit how many hostages, in their anxiety not to be confused with Hobson and Lenin, they have given to the good old doctrine of the fit of absence of mind. The revival of Kipling is not an exclusively literary phenomenon.

The trouble, then, about the triumph of the Right in the western world is not its lack of appeal to the intellectuals, who may be said, without much exaggeration, to have gone over *en masse* with no more than a token resistance, but in its lack of the ideological foundations which intellectuals—and nowadays even some politicians—demand. In the past the Right has often been under-pinned by ecclesiastical doctrine and authority. But this did not prove very successful, and has never been popular in the English-speaking countries. Variations on a theme by Burke provide a well-tried melody. But it cannot be repeated *ad infinitum*; and there is not much else. What in fact do we mean when we apply this vague, if indispensable, label "the Right"? What does it stand for? And whither will it lead us if we give it our allegiance?

In recent years much attention has been devoted to the Right—significantly more in the United States than in this country. The latest offering is a volume entitled *The European Right* edited by two professors of the University of California, and originally published last year by the University Press.[1] Though better organized and more substantial than many examples of that tiresome literary species, the symposium, it does suffer from the multiplicity of authorship. Ten contributors discuss the Right in ten different European countries; the ten include the two editors Dr. Weber and Dr. Rogger, who also write respectively an introduction and "afterthoughts". The Right in all the major countries is dealt with. The choice of the other countries may owe something to chance. Rumania is there, but not Yugoslavia or Greece; Spain, but not Portugal; Finland, but not (Quisling notwithstanding) Norway.

More baffling is the lack of any uniformity in the chronological setting. The story of the Right begins in Germany and Spain in the 1780s, in Italy and Austria after 1870, in Hungary and Finland after the First World War. The Russian Right understandably comes to an end in 1913 (or should it not have been 1917?), though Right or Fascist organizations of Russian émigrés abroad have existed since the 1930s, and still claim to smuggle in literature to sympathizers in the Soviet Union. Some account of these is given in an article in the new *Journal of Contemporary History*, whose first issue is devoted, perhaps significantly, to "International Fascism, 1920–1945".[2] The

---

[1] *The European Right. A Historical Profile.* Edited by Hans Rogger and Eugen Weber (London: Weidenfeld & Nicolson).
[2] *Journal of Contemporary History*, Vol. 1, Number 1, 1966. International Fascism, 1920–1945 (London: Weidenfeld and Nicolson).

European Right remains at best a nebulous conception. Its obscurity is thrown into relief by the failure of the contributors to agree among themselves about its meaning and its chronological limits; and a volume with this title is, perhaps inevitably, a book without a single clearly defined subject.

To discuss politics at all in terms of Right and Left is to some extent, no doubt, to juggle with words. But we cannot proceed far in argument without omnibus generalizations which are necessarily vague and imprecise; and, as the editor claims in his introduction, "the Left-Right dichotomy" offers a meaningful framework. It also makes sense to distinguish between the pre-democratic Right and the post-democratic (or post-liberal or post-industrial) Right, the modern Right, and to confine our attentions to the latter. But the issue which haunts us throughout these pages, and which is never really solved, is the relation of this modern Right to Fascism. Is Fascism the essence of the modern Right? or a subsidiary part of it? or a deviation from it and a distortion of its purposes and character?

The author of the chapter on England, Mr. J. R. Jones, is the only British contributor to the volume, and also the only one who is able to make a complete divorce between Fascism and the traditional Right. It is difficult to remember how recently "the Right" was thought of as an unEnglish phenomenon proper to lesser Continental breeds. The relevant volume of the *Oxford English Dictionary*, published in 1933, in an entry of six and a half columns devoted to the noun Right, curtly dismissed its political meaning as "In continental legislative chambers the party or parties of conservative principles". Mr. Jones nowadays regards the term as applicable "largely to groups within the Tory party". It was the Right in this sense, headed by Churchill and Beaverbrook, which, in his diagnosis, led the party to defeat in 1945; since that time the control of the party has passed into the hands of "the orthodox, the liberal Tories and the professionals". Mr. Jones has no difficulty in exculpating the traditional British Right from any association with Oswald Mosley's Fascist party and other similar factions. But he might have been harder put to it to absolve some of its leaders from warm expressions of sympathy with Continental Fascism; and he does not mention the Vigilante groups, some of them with Fascist labels, which came into being in this country at the time of the General Strike.

None of the contributors dealing with other countries has sought to deny or conceal complicity between the historical Right and Fascism. It was not merely that, in words quoted from Lord Hayter, "the non-Fascist Right in England and Germany"—the aphorism need not have been restricted to them—"thought that Fascism would do their dirty work for them". Paradoxically, the Right in Germany, though slavishly subservient to Hitler once it discovered that it could not dominate and use him, contrived to maintain to the end a greater measure of aloofness than in any other Continental country. This was partly because the Right was historically at its strongest in Germany—far stronger, for example, than in France— and partly because Nazism in its early days, more than any other Fascist movement, made a parade of radical and socialist elements in its creed which it failed to implement, but which alienated and frightened the Right. But everywhere else—Hungary is perhaps another partial exception, due to the strength of the Right—the coalescence between the historical Right and the new Fascist Right was virtually complete. In France particularly, where some have seen in Napoleon III the primeval ancestor of Fascism, the Right had exhibited, from Boulanger onwards, traits that could later be identified as Fascist.

Fascism, like other modern movements of the Right, was weak in positive aims and ideals. What it had were borrowed from the historical Right, and accentuated the affiliation between them. Courage, hierarchy, discipline—these were the animating ideas of the military caste which sustained the monarchy, and were the dominant values, in the France of Louis XIV and the Prussia of Frederick the Great. Since then, though never entirely extinguished where aristocracy survived as an effective force, they had rarely been held in honour. They were revived by Fascism. Militarism, rather than nationalism in its nineteenth-century meaning, provided its hard core; and it is significant that a revival of the military virtues was most successfully preached in countries smarting from military defeat—in France by Maurras at the turn of the century, and by Mussolini and Hitler after the First World War. In all Fascist thinking war was a good thing. It was a clarion call to reinstate cardinal virtues which had rotted away under the regime of bourgeois pacifism and materialism.

The other traditional value of the Right to which Fascism made a more cautious and tentative appeal was religion. The appeal to faith against reason was a recurrent *leitmotif* of its propaganda.

Mussolini called Fascism "a religious conception"; and a credo of the Fascist youth organization is quoted as invoking "our Holy Father, Fascism". Codreanu, the Rumanian leader, called his Fascist thugs "the legion of Saint Michael"; and Finnish Fascists believed in "one great God and one Greater Finland". Nor was the urge purely ideological. Mussolini hastened to stabilize his authority by a concordat with the Vatican. Hitler, more megalomaniac than Mussolini, would have liked to recreate a primitive German national religion. Yet, when it came to the point, he never openly broke with the Christian churches, nor they with him.

These positive aspects of Fascist doctrine were, however, at all times less convincing and less influential than its character as a doctrine of denial or rejection of the beliefs or policies of other groups. Since the French Revolution, we have been familiar with the picture of a Left seething with revolutionary theories and programmes of action and of a Right opposing them in the name of traditional values or national interest or empirical common sense. Fascism has on the whole fitted into this conception of a Right on the defensive. The Russian Revolution of 1917 was the most dramatic upset of an established order of society since 1789; and, since the soil out of which Fascism grew was the challenge to bourgeois society, it might have seemed logical that the rising forces of Fascism should join hands with those of Bolshevism. Georges Sorel, who might be claimed as the most serious theorist of Fascism, and was cited by Mussolini as one of his teachers, hailed the Bolshevik revolution with enthusiasm and eulogized Lenin. But Sorel died a few weeks before the "march on Rome", and history took a different course. Fascism developed not only an anti-bourgeois but also a fanatically anti-Marxist ideology, and posed as the principal bulwark of western society against Bolshevism.

This development has been the guiding thread in the ambiguous and complex relation between Fascism and the European Right. Ever since 1919 hostility to communism has been the most firmly and consistently held tenet of the Right wing in conservative parties everywhere in Europe—a trend interrupted, but not fundamentally altered, by the Second World War, and resumed with still greater intensity after it. And in this cause the Right, though with increasing embarrassment, has been forced to accept Fascism as its ally and even as its spearhead (the theory of getting the Fascists to do "the dirty work"). Dr. Weber, in his introduction to the volume under review, quotes a British military attaché in Berlin as saying in the early 1930s that "most decent Britons, were they Germans of today, would be Stahlhelmers", supporting "a sane patriotism with the idea of consolidating the orderly elements of society against Bolshevik ideas"; and a few years later Halifax told Hitler that he and his colleagues

> were fully aware that the Führer had not only achieved a great deal inside Germany herself, but that, by destroying communism in his country, he had barred the road to Western Europe and that Germany therefore could rightly be regarded as a bulwark of the West against Bolshevism.

The view that resistance to communism covers and redeems a multitude of sins is by no means dead today.

The dilemma of the contemporary Right is that, in default of any positive ideology, it has become entangled in an obsessional opposition to a revolution now fifty years old which, though of immense historical significance, no longer actively threatens any-body or anything in western society. Some responsibility here must be placed on the shoulders of American policies and American opinion. In the United States—this is no longer true of Europe—it is still widely believed that Russian or Chinese communism con-stitutes a threat to American free enterprise and the American way of life—a belief so far removed from realities as to be possible only in a country still suffering from a large overdose of ideological isolationism. Direct American attempts to intervene in the European political constellation were never officially countenan-ced, and have long been abandoned. But the weight of American diplomacy and of American propaganda against communism lies heavily on the political and intellectual life of western Europe.

Perhaps, however, the main cause of the ideological bankruptcy of the European Right must be sought in the bankruptcy of the European Left. This would be logical enough, since the historical function of the modern Right has been to oppose the Left. On this hypothesis, the root evil of our western society in the past fifty years has been the failure of the Left to produce any constructive ideals, any agenda for progress, which could move public opinion and evoke new loyalties. Much has been written of the disillusionment of the younger generation. But disillusionment is not enough. Waiting for Godot is hardly a programme of action; and when angry young men rage furiously together, it is not always clear what, apart from their own ineffectiveness, they are being angry about. But the cynical assurance that we have never had it so good is not in the long run a satisfying answer.

It could indeed be argued that the same obsession which stultifies the Right has also done much to corrode the Left. The Left, unlike the Right, has been exposed by the Russian Revolution and its consequences to alternate bouts of attraction and repulsion; but, like the Right, it has never been able to face it dispassionately, or to escape from its orbit. The influence of Moscow has, though in a rather different way, been as stultifying for the Left as that of Washington for the Right. Communism has become as dirty a word for the Left as for the Right. It is invidious to express an opinion which might be attributed to Marx, or to advocate a reform which might have been preached by the communists. Much of the shadow-boxing characteristic of the struggle between Right and Left in western countries in recent years stems from this common obsession with communism.

It was more than fifty years after the event before the French Revolution could be discussed with sanity and detachment, and the fears and resentments aroused by it ceased to affect current politics. But the world moves quickly nowadays. In Africa, a whole new range of experience is dawning on our consciousness. The line-up of communist and anti-communist powers is a nuisance and an anachronism, which confuses every issue and clearly makes no sense to the newly emergent nations. In Asia, the sharp rift between the two major communist powers makes the slogan of anti-communism still more irrelevant and bewildering; and common dislike of western intervention appears to be the only link which holds together a number of potentially dissident forces. If we need a new Right and a new Left capable of coping in relevant terms with the contemporary world, we have first to rid ourselves of this tiresome obsession. It is too late to turn our back on the significance of Marxism or the legacy of the Russian Revolution. They have to be studied and digested. But it is no longer a touchstone of political wisdom or of intellectual integrity to refute Marx or to exorcize the Red Menace.

32 The Left Today: An Interview

You have now completed 'A History of Soviet Russia', which covers the years from 1917 to 1929 in fourteen volumes, and commands the whole field of studies of the early experience of the USSR. In the widest historical retrospect, how do you judge the significance of the October Revolution today—for Russia, and for the rest of the world?

Let us begin with its significance for Russia itself. One need hardly dwell today on the negative consequences of the Revolution. For several years, and especially in the last few months, they have been an obsessive topic in published books, newspapers, radio and television. The danger is not that we shall draw a veil over the enormous blots on the record of the Revolution, over its cost in human suffering, over the crimes committed in its name. The danger is that we shall be tempted to forget altogether, and to pass over in silence, its immense achievements. I am thinking in part of the determination, the dedication, the organization, the sheer hard work which in the last sixty years have transformed Russia into a major industrial country and one of the super-powers. Who before 1917 could have predicted or imagined this? But, far more than this, I am thinking of the transformation since 1917 in the lives of ordinary people: the transformation of Russia from a country more than eighty per cent of whose population consisted of illiterate or semi-literate peasants into a country with a population more than sixty per cent urban, which is totally literate and is rapidly acquiring the elements of urban culture. Most of the members of this new society are grand-children of peasants; some of them are great-grand-children of serfs. They cannot help being conscious of what the Revolution has done for them. And these things have been brought about by rejecting the main criteria of capitalist production—profits and the laws of the market—and substituting a comprehensive economic plan aimed at promoting the common welfare. However much performance may have lagged behind promise, what has been done in the USSR in the past sixty years, in spite of fearful interruptions from without, is a striking advance towards the realization of the economic programme of socialism. Of course, I know that anyone who speaks of the achievements of the Revolution will at once be branded as a Stalinist. But I am not prepared to submit to this kind of moral blackmail. After all, an English historian can praise the achievements of the reign of Henry VIII without being supposed to condone the beheading of wives.

Your 'History' covers the period in which Stalin established his autocratic power within the Bolshevik Party, defeating and eliminating successive oppositions to him, and laying the foundations for what was later to be called Stalinism as a political system. How far do you think that his victory was inevitable within the CPSU? What were the margins of choice during the twenties?

I tend to fight shy of the crux of inevitability in history, which very quickly leads into a blind alley. The historian asks the question 'Why?', including the question why, of several courses apparently available at any given moment, one particular one was followed. If different antecedents had been at work, the results would have been different. I have no great faith in what is called 'counter-factual history'. I am reminded of the Russian proverb which Alec Nove is fond of quoting: 'If grandma had a beard, grandma would be grandpa'. To re-arrange the past to suit one's own predilections and one's own point of view is a very pleasant occupation. But I am not sure that it is otherwise very profitable.

If, however, you ask me to speculate, I will say this. Lenin, if he had lived through the twenties and thirties in the full possession of his faculties, would have faced exactly the same problems. He knew perfectly well that large-scale mechanized agriculture was the first condition of any economic advance. I do not think he would have been satisfied with Bukharin's 'snail's pace industrialization'. I do not think he would have made too many concessions to the market (remember his insistence on maintaining the monopoly of foreign trade). He knew that you could get nowhere without some effective control and direction of labour (remember his remarks on 'one-man management' in industry, and even about 'Taylorism'). But Lenin was not only reared in a humane tradition, he enjoyed enormous prestige, great moral authority and powers of persuasion; and these qualities, shared by none of the other leaders, would have prompted and enabled him to minimize and mitigate the element of coercion. Stalin had no moral authority whatever (later he tried to build it up in the crudest ways). He understood nothing but coercion, and from the first employed this openly and brutally. Under Lenin the passage might not have been altogether smooth, but it would have been nothing like what happened. Lenin would not have tolerated the falsification of the record in which Stalin constantly indulged. If failures occurred in Party policy or practice, he would have openly recognized and admitted them as such; he would not, like Stalin, have acclaimed desperate expedients as brilliant victories. The USSR under Lenin would never have become, in Ciliga's phrase, 'the land of the big lie'. These are my speculations. If they serve no other purpose, they may reveal something of my beliefs and of my standpoint.

Your 'History' ends on the threshold of the thirties, with the launching of the First Five-Year Plan. Collectivization and the purges lie ahead. You wrote in the preface to your first volume that Soviet sources so dwindled for the thirties that pursuit of your research into them on the same scale was impossible. Is the situation still the same today, or have more documents been published in selected areas in recent years? Does the paucity of archives prevent you from continuing beyond 1929?

More has been published since I wrote that preface in 1950, but there are still dark places. R. W. Davies, who collaborated with me in my last economic volume, is working on the economic history of the early nineteen thirties, and will I think produce convincing results. I have lately been interesting myself in the external affairs of the period and the run-up to the popular front; here, too, I find no shortage of materials. But political history in the narrower sense is more or less a closed book. Big controversies obviously occurred. But between whom? Who were the winners, who the defeated, what compromises were reached? We have no documents comparable to the relatively free debates at Party congresses in the twenties or the platforms of oppositions. A dense fog of mystery still envelops such episodes as the Kirov murder, the purge of the generals, or the secret contracts between Soviet and German emissaries which many people believe to have occurred in the later thirties. I could not have continued my *History* beyond 1929 with the same confidence that I had some clue to what really happened.

The thirties are often presented as a decisive watershed, or break, in the history of the USSR. The scale of repression unleashed in the countryside with collectivization, and throughout the Party and State apparatuses themselves with the great terror—it is argued—qualitatively altered the nature of the Soviet régime. The political rationale of the purges and camps—not repeated on the same scale in any subsequent socialist revolution—remains obscure to this day. What is your view of them? Do you regard the notion of a political rupture, especially after the 17th Party Congress, which is widely held within the Soviet Union itself, as valid?

This introduces the famous question of 'periodization'. An event like the Revolution of 1917 is so dramatic and so sweeping in its consequences that it imposes itself on every historian as a turning-point in history, the end or beginning of a period. Broadly speaking, however, the historian has to define his periods and, in the process of organizing his material, to choose his 'turning-points' or 'watersheds'; and this choice reflects—often, no doubt, unconsciously—his own standpoint, his own view of the sequence of events. Historians of the Russian Revolution from 1917 to, say, 1940 face a dilemma. The revolutionary régime which began as a liberating force was associated, long before the end of that period, with repression of the most ruthless kind. Should the historian treat this as a single period with a continuous process of development—and degeneration? Or should he split it into separate periods of liberation and repression, divided by some significant watershed?

Serious historians who take the first view (I exclude cold-war writers who merely want to blacken Lenin with the sins of Stalin) will point out that both Marx and Lenin (the latter with great emphasis) assert the essentially repressive character of the State; that from the moment when the Russian Soviet Republic proclaimed itself as a state it became by its nature an instrument of repression; and that this element was monstrously inflated, but not in principle changed, by the pressures and vicissitudes to which it was later subjected. The historian who takes the two-period line seems to have a more plausible case, till he has to locate his watershed. Should one place the transition to policies of mass repression at the time of the Kronstadt revolt of March 1921—or perhaps of the peasant risings in central Russia in the previous winter? Or should one identify it with Stalin's conquest of the Party and State machine in the middle twenties, with the campaigns against Trotsky and Zinoviev, and with the expulsion and exile of scores of leading oppositionists in 1928? Or with the first large-scale public trials, at which defendants pleaded guilty to bizarre charges of sabotage and treason, in 1930 and 1931? Concentration camps and forced labour existed well before 1930. I am not much impressed with a solution which defers the watershed till the middle thirties. As I said, the choice of periods reflects the standpoint of the historian. I cannot help feeling that this bit of periodization is rather neatly tailored to explain and condone the long blindness of left intellectuals in the West to the repressive character of the régime. Yet even this will not quite do. Even while the great purges and trials were in progress, an unprecedented number of left intellectuals were flocking into western Communist parties.

Well, this brings us to the second part of our original question—the significance of the Russian Revolution for the capitalist world.

Let me try to sum up very briefly. Initially, the Revolution polarized Left and Right in the capitalist world. In central Europe, revolution loomed on the horizon. Even in this country there were extremes: the communists who hoisted the red flag in Glasgow, and Churchill who wanted to use the British army to destroy the revolution in Russia. A sizeable number, though nowhere a majority, of workers entered Communist parties in Germany, France, Italy and Czechoslovakia. But by the middle of the nineteen twenties the ebb had set in—especially among the organized workers. The Red Trade Union International never succeeded in shaking the authority of the social-democratic Amsterdam International, which became more and more bitterly anti-communist. The TUC under Citrine and Bevin followed suit. The workers in western countries were no longer revolutionary; they fought to improve their position within the capitalist system, not to destroy it. The 'popular front' of the nineteen thirties (at any rate in this country) was predominantly an affair of liberals and intellectuals. After 1945, the intellectuals— like the workers twenty years earlier—also turned away from the Revolution. Orwell and Camus are typical names. Since then, the process has continued at an increasing rate. The polarization of Left and Right in 1917 has been replaced by a polarization of East and West. Revulsion against Stalinism has produced—nowhere more conspicuously than in this country—a united front of Right and Left against the USSR.

But, before going further, I should like to hazard two generalizations. First, the astounding swings of opinion about the Russian Revolution in the western countries since 1917 are to be explained by what was happening in those countries quite as much as by anything happening in the USSR. Secondly, where these swings have been prompted by Soviet activities, they have related to the international policies of the USSR, and not to its domestic affairs. It is difficult to reconstruct the state of British opinion of the Russian Revolution during its first year: we had so much else to think about. But, of one thing I am sure from my own recollections. The vast majority of people who disapproved of the Revolution were moved to indignation, not by stories of community of goods or community of women, but by the hard fact that the Bolsheviks had taken Russia out of the war, and deserted her allies at the most critical moment of their fortunes.

Once the Germans were beaten everything changed. War-weariness set in, intervention in Russia was widely condemned, and the climate in Britain became sympathetic to the Bolsheviks, who were vaguely 'left', democratic and peace-loving. But there was very little ideology about this: capitalism versus socialism was really not an issue. After the Pyrrhic victory of the first Labour Government, the tide ebbed. The anti-Soviet wave of 1924–9 was fostered partly by party-political considerations (the Zinoviev letter had been a great vote-winner), partly by the not unfounded belief that the Russians were helping to undermine British prestige and prosperity in China. This was the time when Austen Chamberlain thought that Stalin was a good thing, because he was concerned to build socialism in his own country and not, like the more noxious Trotsky and Zinoviev, to foment international revolution.

All this was blotted out by the great economic crisis of 1930–33 which preoccupied the whole western world. For the first time, widespread disillusionment with capitalism created a movement of sympathy for the USSR. The British public knew nothing of what was going on there. But it had heard of the five-year plan, and had a general impression that the grass over there was greener. Litvinov's disarmament campaign at Geneva made a powerful impact on the prevailing pacifist mood. But one reservation must be made. The trade unions successfully beat off all attempts at infiltration, and the workers were not much involved. The story of the nineteen thirties is a stampede of liberal and left intellectuals into the Soviet camp. The one Stalinist purge which had a serious effect in Britain was the purge of generals. This discouraged the anti-German wing of the

Conservative Party, which had given some support to the pro-Soviet campaign, by convincing them that the Red Army would be useless as an instrument against Hitler. These doubts were increased by Soviet hesitation at the time of Munich. The event which finally destroyed the whole edifice of British-Soviet friendship was the Nazi-Soviet pact. Even the British Party, which had sailed comfortably through the purges, was rocked to its foundations by the pact. It was a blow from which Soviet prestige in Britain, in spite of the episode of wartime enthusiasm, has never really recovered.

I need not go on after the war. A Soviet threat to Europe was soon detected and publicized. Churchill's Fulton speech brought down the iron curtain. The first Sputnik heralded the emergence of a new super-power, challenging the former monopoly of the United States. Since then, the growth of Soviet military and economic power, and its expanding influence in other continents, have elevated the USSR to the role of Public Enemy No. 1 and have made it the target of a propaganda barrage which now exceeds in intensity the 'cold wars' of the twenties and fifties. That, in barest outline, is the murky and tangled story of the reactions of the West to the Russian Revolution.

How would you assess the political evolution of the Soviet State system? How does cultural and intellectual life in the USSR today compare with, say, that of the fifties, and of the twenties? In the West, the phenomenon of dissent virtually monopolizes the attention of the Left today. Do you regard it as an appropriate prism through which to view the political situation in contemporary Russia?

To review economic, social, political and cultural conditions in the USSR today is far beyond the scope of this interview, and I must really stick to this question of East-West relations. The current prominence of the dissidents in these relations is, of course, a symptom, not a causal factor. But it presents a very complex and embarrassing problem for the Left in western countries. Historically, the Left, not the Right, has been the champion of victims of oppressive régimes. The dissidents in Soviet Russia and eastern Europe are in this category, and can rightly count on organized sympathy and protest from the Left. The trouble is that their cause has been taken up in a big way by the Right, and that what began as a humanitarian movement has been transformed into a great political campaign, inspired by quite different motives, serving different purposes and conducted in a different style; and, since the Right possesses most of the wealth and resources, has the most powerful organization, and to a large extent controls the media, it determines the strategy and dominates the campaign. The Left finds itself in the position of a camp-follower, struggling vainly to maintain its independence, serving purposes not its own, and smeared with the fundamental dishonesty of the campaign.

Two points need to be made here. The first is that human rights are universal, something belonging to human beings as such, not to members of a particular nation. A big campaign for human rights is vitiated if it confines itself to one corner of the world. Iran is the seat of a notoriously repressive régime. Yet President Carter, in the full flush of his campaign for human rights in Russia, received the Shah with full honours in the White House, and both Carter and Callaghan have sent good wishes to him for success in dealing with his dissidents. Evidently Iranian dissidents have no human rights. In China the Gang of Four, and the hundreds or perhaps thousands of their supporters in Shanghai and other Chinese cities, have simply disappeared. No trials have been held, no charges preferred against them. What has become of them—if they are still alive? Nobody either knows or cares. We prefer not to know. The human rights of Chinese dissidents are a matter of indifference. All this is comprehensible enough in a campaign conducted by politicians who are primarily interested not in protecting human rights, but in exciting popular indignation and hostility against Soviet Russia. But is the moral integrity of the Left compatible with involvement in a campaign which exploits the sincerely and deeply felt emotions of decent, but politically naïve people for purposes totally foreign to its professed object?

The other point concerns the style and character of the campaign. A few days ago I came across a quotation from Macaulay: 'There is no spectacle so ridiculous as the British public in one of its periodic fits of morality.' I am afraid I find the present fit not so much ridiculous as sinister and frightening. You cannot open a newspaper without coming up against this obsessive hatred and fear of Russia. The persecution of the dissidents, Russian military and naval armaments, Russian spies, Marxism as a current term of abuse in party political controversy—all these contribute to the build-up. An outburst of national hysteria on this scale is surely the symptom of a sick society—one of those societies which seek to unload the sense of their own predicament, their own helplessness, their own guilt, by making a scapegoat of some external group—

Russians, Blacks, Jews or whatever. I find the question where all this can lead truly alarming. It is consoling to reflect that popular hysteria has infected no other European country in quite the same degree, and that even in the United States a reaction seems to have started against Carter's pulpit diplomacy; but I am sorry that so much of our Left has been engulfed in the flood.

One of the most striking developments of the seventies has been the detachment of the West European Communist Parties from their traditional loyalty towards the USSR. In the name of Eurocommunism, the Spanish Party now speaks of the USA and USSR as equivalent threats to a socialist Europe, and the Italian Party refers benevolently to NATO as a shield against Soviet incursions. Such positions would have been unthinkable a decade ago. What is your view of the trend they represent? Does the search for a model of socialist society distinct from the USSR, adapted to the more advanced West, justify the current anti-Soviet tonality of Eurocommunism?

Eurocommunism is surely a still-born movement, a desperate attempt to escape from reality. If you want to return to Kautsky and denounce the renegade Lenin, fair enough. But why muddy the waters by labelling yourselves communist? In the hitherto accepted terminology you are right-wing social-democrats. The one solid plank of Eurocommunism is independence of, and opposition to, the Russian Party; it jumps eagerly on to the anti-Soviet band-wagon. The rest of the platform is entirely amorphous, the kind of thing which we in this country used to call 'Lib-Lab'. Its excursions into practical politics betray its hollowness. The Italian Euro-communists stand somewhat to the right of the socialists. The French Eurocommunists stand in several different places at once. The Spanish Eurocommunists stand nowhere at all. The British Eurocommunists are barely visible. One could have done without this sad demonstration of the bankruptcy of western Communist parties.

Marx envisaged socialism as a society of incomparably greater liberty and productivity than capitalism—a harmonious, advanced association of free producers without economic exploitation or political duress. The transition to such a society in the Soviet Union, although it has proceeded beyond capitalism, remains far from the goals of Marx or Lenin. In the much richer countries of the West, capitalism has yet to be overthrown, partly because of the disappointment within the working class at the progress so far registered in the

USSR. In a situation that may seem at times like a dual deadlock, do you think that the possibilities of a political breakthrough, an acceleration, towards the classical goals of revolutionary socialism are greater in the East or in the West today? You ended your book 'What is History?' with Galileo's words, E pur si muove—*'yet it moves'. Where is the main locus of historical movement towards the close of the twentieth century?*

This question has so many facets that I shall have to break it up and answer rather discursively. First, a short digression on the place of Marx and Marxism in our thinking. Adam Smith had insights of genius; and the *Wealth of Nations* became for a whole century, and for more than one country, the bible of emergent capitalism. Today the changed economic scene has invalidated some of his postulates, and altered our view of some of his predictions and injunctions. Karl Marx had even profounder insights of genius; he not only foresaw and analysed the impending decline of capitalism, but provided us with fresh tools of thought to uncover the sources of social behaviour. But much has happened since he wrote: and recent developments, while they have confirmed his analysis, have thrown some doubts on his prognosis. To admit such doubts, and to investigate them, is not to dishonour Marx. What seem to be incompatible with the spirit of Marxism are scholastically ingenious attempts—such as I have occasionally seen in articles in the NLR— to fit Marxist texts to conditions and problems of which he took no account and which he could not have foreseen. What I should like to see from Marxist intellectuals is less abstract analysis of Marxist texts, and more application of Marxist methods to the examination of social and economic conditions which differentiate our age from his.

You ask about the prospects of a breakthrough to a socialist or Marxist society in the USSR and in the West. These are two very different problems. The Russian Revolution overthrew the old order, and hoisted the Marxist flag. But the Marxist premises were not present, and realization of the Marxist perspectives could not therefore have been expected. The tiny Russian proletariat, almost without education, was quite unlike the proletariat envisaged by Marx as the standard-bearer of revolution, and was unequal to the role imposed on it in the Marxist scheme of things. Lenin in one of his last essays deplored the shortage of 'genuine proletarians', and remarked sadly that Marx was writing 'not about Russia, but about capitalism in general'. The dictatorship of the proletariat, however one interpreted the phrase, was a pipe-dream. What Trotsky called 'substitutism', the substitution of the Party for the proletariat, was inevitable, resulting by slow stages in the rise of a privileged bureaucracy, the divorce of the leadership from the masses, the dragooning of workers and peasants, and the concentration camps. On the other hand, something was done which has not been done in the West. Capitalism has been dismantled and replaced by planned production and distribution; and, if socialism has not been realized, some of the conditions for its realization have, however imperfectly, been created. The proletariat has enormously increased in numbers; its standard of living, its health, its education have improved remarkably. If one wanted to indulge in flights of fancy, one might imagine that this new proletariat will one day take up the burden which its weak forebears could not carry sixty years ago, and move forward to socialism. Personally I am not much addicted to such speculations. History rarely produces theoretically tidy solutions. Soviet society is still advancing. But to what end, and whether the rest of the world will allow it to pursue its advance undisturbed — these are questions which I shall not attempt to answer.

The problem of Marxism in the West is more complicated. Here the Marxist premises exist, but have not led —so far—to the Marxist dénouement. Marx formulated his theories in the light of conditions in Western Europe, and especially in England. His insight and his foresight have been brilliantly vindicated—up to a point. The capitalist system has declined under the gathering weight of its internal contradictions. It has been severely shaken by two world wars and by recurrent economic crises. It shows itself impotent in face of rising unemployment. The organized workers have gained enormously in strength, and have not hesitated to use that strength for their own ends. Yet the one thing that has not happened is the proletarian revolution. Wherever in the capitalist world revolution has momentarily loomed on the horizon—in Germany in 1919, in Britain in 1926, in France in 1968—the workers hastened to turn their backs on it. Whatever they wanted it was not revolution. I find it difficult to reject the evidence that, in spite of all the chinks that have developed in the armour of capitalism, the mood of the workers is less, not more, revolutionary today than it was sixty years ago. In the West today, the proletariat—meaning, as Marx meant by the term, the organized workers in industry—is not a revolutionary, perhaps even a counter-revolutionary, force.

Why does the worker in the West today—for I think we must

accept the fact—not want revolution? The first answer is 'Fear', stimulated in part by the example of 1917. The Russian Revolution, whatever good ultimately came out of it, caused endless misery and devastation. To overthrow the ruling class in the capitalist world today would be a still more desperate enterprise, its costs even higher. The Russian worker in 1917 may have had nothing to lose but his chains. The western worker has far more than that to lose, and does not want to lose it. When this question is raised, I sometimes resort to an analogy. The doctor tells the patient that he has an incurable disease, which will get worse at an unpredictable rate, but that he may hope to carry on somehow for a few years longer. The disease can be cured by an operation, but there is quite a chance that the operation will kill the patient. The patient decides to carry on. Rosa Luxemburg said that the decay of capitalism would end either in socialism or in barbarism. I suspect that most workers today prefer to face the slow decay of capitalism, hoping that it will last out their time, rather than face the surgical knife of revolution, which may or may not produce socialism. It is a tenable point of view.

But I want to go deeper than that. I do not know who invented the phrase 'consumer sovereignty'. But the idea is implicit in Adam Smith and the whole of classical economics. Marx rightly put the producer in the centre of the economic process. But he took it for granted that the producer produced for the market, and therefore had to produce what the consumer wanted to buy; and this is probably a fair description of what happened till about the end of the last century—several years after Marx's death. Since then the tables have been turned and the power of the producer has increased at a frantic rate. The entrepreneur, now more and more often a big corporation, controlled and standardized prices. Mass production made it imperative to create a uniform market. Advertising grew by leaps and bounds in extent and in ingenuity. For the first time the producer was able to mould consumer taste, and to persuade the consumer to want what the producer found it most convenient and profitable to produce. We had arrived at the age of producer sovereignty.

The point is, however, that, as the proletariat increased in numbers and in sophistication, it could more and more effectively assert its claim to share in the rising profits of the new age. Engels discovered the corruption by the capitalists of what he called a workers' aristocracy. Lenin applied the same concept to the working class of capitalist countries *vis-à-vis* the colonial world. But even Lenin did not foresee a partnership of producers, i.e. of employers and workers, to exploit the consumer throughout the home market. It requires no great acumen to see what is happening. 'Job protection' for the producer has become a decisive factor in economic policy. Over-manning in management and on the shop floor is condoned; increased prices will take care of the cost. Technological improvements which would cut costs and prices are resisted because they would involve loss of jobs; the consumer can pay. Some serious body the other day proposed to slaughter a quarter of a million laying hens in order to reduce the supply of eggs and prevent a disastrous slump in prices. The odd performances of the EEC with butter, wine and beef are familiar. So crazy an economy cannot in the long run survive. But the run can be long — longer than those who now profit by it need envisage. I have not mentioned such a minor matter as the investment of the very large pension funds of the unions in industrial and commercial equities. If capitalist profits collapse, so does the provision for the old age of the workers. 'Where your treasure is, there shall your heart be also.' The workers now have in many ways a large stake in the survival of capitalism. In present conditions, the nationalization of industries, and the placing of workers on boards of directors (in which, incidentally, British workers have shown no great interest), represent not a take-over of industry by the workers, but further steps in the integration of the workers into the capitalist system. Lord Robens is quite as good a capitalist as Lord Robbins.

It is from this standpoint that we must diagnose the sickness of the Left, which is a conspicuous part of the sickness of our whole society. The Left has lost the core of its creed, and goes on repeating formulas which have lost their credibility. For a hundred years or more, the hopes of the Left had been pinned on the workers as the revolutionary class of the future. Capitalist democracy would be overthrown and replaced by the dictatorship of the proletariat. It is possible to hold that this vision will yet be realized. Large transformations of society have in the past been spread over many decades and centuries; perhaps we are merely being too impatient. But I confess that, with so many signals pointing in another direction, this prospect puts a severe strain on my capacities for optimism. I am not reassured when I look at the present disarray of the Left, divided into a galaxy of minute warring sects, united only by their failure to attract more than an insignificant fringe of the

workers' movement, and by the brave illusion that their prescriptions for revolution represent the interests and ambitions of the
workers. I recall that Trotsky, in an article written shortly after the
outbreak of war in September 1939, admitted, hesitantly and with
many reservations, that if the war did not provoke a revolution one
would be forced to seek the reason for the failure 'not in the
backwardness of the country, and not in the imperialist environment, but in the congenital incapacity of the proletariat to become a
ruling class'. One should not perhaps make too much of an
admission wrung from him in a dark hour of despair. I jib at the
word 'congenital'; the article was published in English, and I do not
know what Russian word Trotsky may have written. But, had he
survived to witness the contemporary scene, I do not think he would
have found much occasion to retract his verdict.

How then does one analyse the situation and see the future? First,
employers and workers still fight in the traditional way over the
division of the profits of capitalist enterprise, though occasions have
occurred recently where employers and workers came to an
agreement, and the agreement was resisted by the government on
the ground of public interest. Secondly, a silent, but very powerful,
consensus has been established between employers and workers on
the need to maintain profits. The parties may still quarrel about the
division of the spoils, but are united in the desire to maximise them.
It is still open to ask which of these two factors will ultimately come
out on top. A case could be made out for the argument that, when
the physical limits of exploitation of the consumer market are
reached, and when the opportunities of the reinforcement of
capitalism from without are exhausted in any given country, the
clash between the interests of employer and worker will once more
become predominant, and that the way will be clear for the long
delayed proletarian revolution on a Marxist model. But I must
confess myself sceptical about this prospect. I am impressed by the
fact that the only considerable revolutions achieved since 1917 have
been in China and in Cuba, and that revolutionary movements are
alive today only in countries where the proletariat is weak or non-
existent.

You challenge me by quoting the last words of my *What is History?*
Yes, I believe that the world is moving forward. I have not altered
my view of 1917 as one of the turning-points of history. I will still say
that it, together with the war of 1914–18, marked the beginning of
the end of the capitalist system. But the world does not move all the

time or in all places at once. I should now feel tempted to say that the Bolsheviks won their victory in 1917, not in spite of the backwardness of the Russian economy and society, but because of it. I think we have to consider seriously the hypothesis that the world revolution of which it was the first stage, and which will complete the downfall of capitalism, will prove to be the revolt of the colonial peoples against capitalism in the guise of imperialism rather than a revolt of the proletariat of the advanced capitalist countries.

What conclusions can one draw for our own Left in its present plight? Not very encouraging ones, I fear, since this is a profoundly counter-revolutionary period in the West, and the Left has no solid revolutionary base. It seems to me that there are two alternatives open to serious members of the Left today. The first is to remain communists, and to remain an educational and propagandist group divorced from political action. The functions of such a group would be to analyse the social and economic transformation now taking place in the capitalist world; to study the revolutionary movements occurring in other parts of the world—their achievements, their defects and their potentialities; and to try to draw some more or less realistic picture of what socialism should and could mean in the contemporary world. The second alternative for the Left is to go into current politics, become social-democrats, frankly recognize and accept the capitalist system, pursue those limited ends which can be achieved within the system, and work for those compromises between employers and workers which serve to maintain it.

One cannot be both a communist and a social-democrat. The social-democrat criticizes capitalism, but in the last resort defends it. The communist rejects it, and believes that in the end it will destroy itself. But the communist in western countries at the present time is conscious of the strength of the forces which still uphold it, and of the lack of any revolutionary force powerful enough to overthrow it.

Index